THE COMPLETE LETTERWRITER'S ALMANAC

A Handbook of Model Letters for Business, Social and Personal Occasions

Dianna Booher

PRENTICE HALL
Englewood Cliffs, New Jersey 07632

Prentice-Hall International (UK) Limited, London
Prentice-Hall of Australia Pty. Limited, Sydney
Prentice-Hall of Canada, Inc., Toronto
Prentice-Hall Hispanoamericana, S.A., Mexico
Prentice-Hall of India Private Limited, New Delhi
Prentice-Hall of Japan, Inc., Tokyo
Simon & Schuster Asia Pte. Ltd., Singapore
Editora Prentice-Hall do Brasil, Ltda., Rio de Janeiro

© 1992 by

Dianna Booher

10 9 8 7 6 5 4 3 2 1

Library of Congress Cataloging-in-Publication Data

Booher, Dianna Daniels.
    The complete letterwriter's almanac: a handbook of model letters
for business, social, and personal occasions / by Dianna Booher.
        p.   cm.
    Includes index.
    ISBN 0-13-155904-4
    1. Letter-writing. I. Title. II. Title: Complete letter writer's
almanac.
PE1483.B66   1991
808.6—dc20
                                                        91-23491
                                                        CIP

ISBN 0-13-155904-4

PRENTICE HALL
Business Information & Publishing Division
Englewood Cliffs, NJ 07632
Simon & Schuster, A Paramount Communications Company

Printed in the United States of America

ACKNOWLEDGMENTS

I'd like to express my appreciation to client organizations for their contribution to my work: effective letters from their own companies and positive reactions to well-written ones they have received.

Also, I want to thank Janet Houston-Spore for her capable assistance with the manuscript preparation.

INTRODUCTION

General Motors, IBM, and Exxon employees don't stare at their computer screens or note pads, waiting for inspiration to pen that perfect letter. Or do they? Surprisingly, many of those employees hear the same muse. Those standard letters of policies, apologies, requests for proposals, dismissals, and credit have a familiar ring. Somebody "up there" has the boilerplates that make the lives of their employees much easier. Why shouldn't you?

You needn't hire a lawyer, an accountant, or a PR specialist to outline the letters that help your own company function efficiently and that keep your career on target. Simply look up your topic in the Table of Contents and select the models and alternative phrases here to customize letters that will

- lend authority to your plans
- motivate your colleagues and customers
- close a deal
- create goodwill
- sell your product, your service, your ideas, and yourself

As the best models based on those from an array of Fortune 500 companies, these letters come from CEOs as well as technical professionals—engineers, lawyers, accountants. From those who know the ins and outs of what you can and can't put in writing.

You'll also note the "General Guidelines and Alternative Phrases" section under each subject category. The true lasting value of the book will be these sentences that generate your own ideas and phrasing for customizing letter after letter. In other words, you won't "use up" these letters after you send them to one client or one employee. You can continue to use the guidelines and phrases for an infinite number of variations.

One more thing: You don't have to leave this handbook on your office credenza when you head for home. The remainder of the collection offers personal and social models that will make your friends and loved ones sigh, "I wish I'd said that." What to write in that special note to a couple on their first or fiftieth wedding anniversary? How do you persuade neighbors to come to a community gathering to hear your candidate's plans for the mayoral office? Or how do you express the lump in your throat when that best of all friends flies 500 miles to your hospital bed the night before surgery? What apt phrase can you use in your own invitations to special events? The answers are yours for simply turning the pages.

Whether it's a formal retirement dinner or two lines that your lover will cherish and lock away in a dresser drawer for decades, this collection can help. THE LETTERWRITER'S ALMANAC will show you how to turn a thought into a phrase that will keep your marriage, your social circle, and your business and career center stage.

Dianna Booher

P.S. Do you have a favorite business, social, or personal letter that you've been saving for years—just to show someone who cares? We'd love to hear from you and have a copy of your samples; perhaps they'll find their way into our next book. Here's to making letter writing once again an art—as well as a means of communication!

CONTENTS

Introduction

PART I: GENERAL BUSINESS LETTERS

Anniversaries   1

    Of employee service to your firm   1
    Of your own firm   4

Announcements   7

    Acquisition, merger or restructuring   7
    New hours/location/name/logo   10
    New policy/procedure   13
    New service/product   19
    New rates/prices/terms   24

Appointments   **28**

    Requesting   28
    Postponing or canceling   31
    Declining   33

Bids   **37**

    Soliciting   37
    Accepting   41
    Rejecting   43

Commendations   **46**

    To speaker   46
    To your own staff   49
    To others for outstanding service   53
    Response to a commendation   56

Complaints   **59**

    About poor service/delivery/performance/product/
      advertising/communication   59
    Responding to a complaint when admitting fault   64
    Responding to a complaint without admitting fault 69

Condolences   **75**

    To business associate upon death of a loved one   75
    To family upon death of a business associate   78

Congratulations   **82**

    Award/honor/distinction   82
    Birth   84
    Birthday   86
    Civic achievement   89
    Engagement/wedding   90
    New job/promotion   93
    Opening new business   96
    Publication   98
    Retirement   100
    Service award   102
    Response to a congratulatory note   105

Cover Letters   **107**

    For invoices/explanation of fees   107
    For proposals/price quotes   110
    For reports   113
    For résumés   116

Credit and Collections   **119**

    Billing discrepancies/errors   119
    Verifying credit records   122
    Offering credit   125
    Refusing credit   128
    Canceling credit   130
    Series of collection letters   132
    Responding to collection letters   143

Declining to Do Business   **146**

    Declining to Do Business   146

Employment   **150**

    Acknowledging receipt of resumes   150
    Announcing promotions/transfers   151
    Employment offers   153
    Nonselection of applicants—no opening   155
    Nonselection of applicants—salary requirements   156
    Nonselection of applicants—otherwise unsuitable   161
    Policy and benefit statements/explanations   163
    Recruitment letters   165
    Reprimand   167
    Request for raise/promotion/transfer   169

Offer of raise/promotion/transfer   172
Disapproval of raise/promotion/transfer   173
Thank you for the interview   176

Farewell   **179**

From employee leaving   179
To employee leaving   181

Holiday Greetings   **185**

Holiday Greetings   185

Invitations   **189**

Open house   189
Special company event   191

Meetings   **194**

Announcing agenda   194
Confirming attendance   198
Declining attendance   199
Canceling/postponing   201
Inviting speaker   202
Confirming speaker   206
Soliciting details about the audience   208
Thank you for the opportunity to speak   209
Thank you to speaker   212

Public Relations/Issues   **213**

Response to crisis   213
Letter to the editor   216
Letter to legislators   218
Suggestion for interview   220
Thank you for interview   222
Permission to use quote or copyrighted materials   223

References   **226**

Requesting from supervisor/colleague   226
Supplying for suitable employee   229
Supplying for unsuitable employee   231

Referrals   **233**

Requesting   233
Offering   235

Resignations   **237**

   Offering   237
   Accepting   241

Solicitations   **244**

   Seeking   244
   —research help   246
   —funding for charitable/civic projects   247
   —volunteer time   249
   —honorary use of name   250
   Negative response   251
   Positive response   253
   Thank you for successful campaign   255

Terminations   **258**

   Layoffs   258
   Unsuitable employee   261

Thank Yous (Business)   **263**

   For arranging beneficial meeting/conference   263
   For award or bonus   265
   For donation   267
   For gift   269
   For hospitality at conference/meeting/visit   270
   For buying   272
   For service to community   274
   For speaking   276
   For referral/reference   280

Welcomes   **283**

   To new staff   283
   To potential customers/clients new in the community   286

PART II: PERSONAL AND SOCIAL LETTERS   **289**

Charitable Contributions   **291**

College   **293**

   Making application   293
   Requesting references   294
   Supplying references   295

Complaints/Requests for Adjustments   **298**

Billing error   298
Car   299
Defective product   300
Home repair   300
Misleading ad   301
Personal service   302
Rent issues   303
Restaurant/food service   303
Governmental agency   304
Better Business Bureau   305

Condolences   **306**

Accident   307
Death of a child   308
Death of a parent   308
Death of a spouse   309
Death of another relative   310
Illness   310
Loss of business/home   311

Congratulations   **312**

Anniversary   312
Birth   313
Birthday   315
Engagement/Wedding   316
Graduation   317

Credit   **319**

Changes in account responsibility/arrangements   319
Request for extended credit   320
Response for special repayment arrangements   320
Response to collection letter   322

Friendship Notes/Greetings   **324**

Inquiries   **331**

Information on event   332
Information on product/service   332

Issues   **334**

Letter to the editor   335
Letter to legislators   336
Letter to meet political candidate   337

Love Notes/Greetings   **338**

Thank Yous (Personal)   **348**

    Comforting note   348
    Dinner   349
    Hospitality   349
    Personal favor   350

Index   **351**

PART I

GENERAL
BUSINESS LETTERS

ANNIVERSARIES

Anniversaries should never be routine—especially for the loyal employee who has contributed much to the organization. As a manager, you can use service anniversaries to add that personal touch to the business relationship. Taking the trouble to word a letter especially for an individual means much to an employee's sense of belonging and creates the team or family atmosphere at work.

For some employees, such letters should commend the individual for the routine day-to-day activities completed with efficiency, integrity, and commitment. For other employees, such letters should include comments on outstanding achievements that deserve special recognition. Don't let such milestones in the lives of your employees go by without acknowledgement in this small way.

Likewise, use the anniversary date of your own organization to reflect on accomplishments and plans. In today's competitive environment, simply staying in business implies success. These anniversary announcements let your customers celebrate with you and feel as though they are part of your success.

OF EMPLOYEE SERVICE TO YOUR FIRM

Guidelines and Alternate Phrasing

Commend the employee on the occasion.

⇨ Thank you, Harvey, for the past ten years of your life. From what I've observed, you've probably been as committed to us here at Universal as you have to your own personal goals.

⇨ For the past twenty years, we've profited from your expertise; the time's past due for us to say a big, special thank you.

⇨ You have a special occasion on the horizon. As of July 6, you will have been part of the Universal family for ten years—a productive part, I'll be quick to add.

⇨ You've been a real asset to our company since you joined us ten years ago. In those ten years, you've contributed skill, time, ideas, energy, and loyalty. We've noticed and appreciated all these contributions on our behalf.

Mention what you plan to do, if anything, to commemorate the occasion such as a luncheon, reception, or gift.

⇨ We're planning a departmental reception in your honor on May 2 at 4:00 P.M. Would you please invite your family and any special friends to join us all in Conference C, where we plan to put our sentiments into words.

⇨ Shortly, you will be receiving a plaque commemorating the twenty-five years of loyal service you've given to Universal. Display it or put it away with your keepsakes—either way, please accept it as a small gift that represents a big thank-you for your skill and dedication to the company.

⇨ The enclosed tickets are our way of expressing a heartfelt thank-you for the kind of time and commitment to excellence that can't be bought with a paycheck. You're the kind of employee who gives 100 percent to whatever the project at hand; we want to be the kind of employer that shows gratitude for your contribution. Enjoy your trip and the time off.

Make the letter personal by mentioning specific contributions to the company or department, accomplishments and awards, or even personal attributes or attitudes exhibited during the employee's tenure.

⇨ Your knowledge of the financial world and investment opportunities has contributed most directly to our profitability during the past five years.

⇨ On several occasions your supervisor has commented that he wished he had a dozen employees just like you—conscientious, dedicated, punctual, skilled. You're the kind of employee who keeps us in business year after year. We try not to forget that.

⇨ Your ability to identify the root cause and your determination to follow a problem through to resolution is exactly what we've needed around here. That insight and conscientiousness provide the framework for everything we do.

⇨ We really appreciate the long hours, the persistence, the attention to detail, and your usual cooperative attitude about anything we've assigned you in these past years. You've shown commitment to whatever the goal set in front of you.

⇨ Your cheerful smile, your focused attention, and your uncanny way in dealing with difficult customers have contributed most directly to all our efforts in the department.

⇨ Despite what the diplomas from your two universities said about your abilities, we put you to our own tests around here. We're happy to report that our efforts have verified what both universities said long ago—you're a brilliant and talented engineer. We thank for proving that to us over and over again.

⇨ Kevin, we can't mention your name around the department without the Headstrum project coming to mind. In all the years you've worked so diligently around here, that specific contribution has been the cornerstone of our new customer base. We value that contribution as one of the most noteworthy of our company's history.

Imply that you are expecting many more years together in the organization.

⇨ We are looking forward to having you with us for years to come.

⇨ We will continue to count on seeing your smiling face every morning.

⇨ Best wishes for many more years in the job you enjoy and we appreciate.

⇨ Please be assured that we value your expertise.

⇨ Let us know how we can help you continue to do the fine job you're performing for this company.

⇨ Here's to many more work anniversaries to come.

⇨ Thank you for such dedication and loyalty. We will be depending on you as we move into the next decade.

⇨ Your work will continue to be of even more value to us as we make plans to increase market share.

⇨ We are thinking of you especially today and focusing on your excellent work—what we've come to expect from you and will be counting on for many years to come.

⇨ We value your work; you're the kind of employee we aim to please.

⇨ We hope you'll be with us for many years to come; we have much to gain from your expertise and dedication.

⇨ Our future looks bright with you in it. Thank you for your commitment.

❖ ❖ ❖

Dear Beverly:

My calendar has a big red mark around August 1, and I'd say it's been a red-letter year since you joined us. I'll have reservations for us in the Sierra

Room of the Fayette Inn at 11:30 A.M. on Tuesday, August 2. Can you join me?

Let me take this opportunity to say how much I've appreciated your excellent coordination of this year's meetings. The two meetings in Baltimore and in Orlando come to mind as being the most eventful in terms of weather problems and potential hotel disasters you averted. Thanks to your efforts on those meetings, as well as the many others, our staff and prospective clients both arrived and left in a pleasant frame of mind.

Although I can't say I'm looking forward to more crises in the years to come, I can assure you that my mind is at ease knowing you're so capably willing to handle whatever crops up. Thank you for your continuing efforts at making us at headquarters look so good.

Sincerely,

❖   ❖   ❖

OF YOUR OWN FIRM

Guidelines and Alternate Phrasing

Announce the occasion.

⇨ This year marks our tenth anniversary in the Harrisburg community of friends.

⇨ Ten years of hard work, sincere referrals, and repeat customers—we're celebrating our anniversary this month.

⇨ I think you'll agree that the last ten years in this economic climate have not been the brightest for business. That's why we're thrilled that our customers have been able to depend on us for their ____ needs over the past decade. This is our tenth anniversary year!

⇨ We've been serving the Harrisburg community for the past ten years, and we've learned a lot about your ____ needs. Our anniversary is a celebration of the past and a promise for the future.

Thank your customers, clients, suppliers, and other colleagues for their part in your successful business operations.

⇨ We appreciate your contribution to our success—your loyalty and your own dedication to service.

⇨ Thank you so much for your part in our success—your purchases, your confidence, and your referrals.

⇨ Without your confidence in our products and services through the years, our story would not have been so successful.

⇨ You've bought our products, shared your concerns and your needs with us, and passed our name on to your friends and colleagues. Because they respect you and your opinions, they bought from us. And for that, we owe you a great deal of appreciation.

⇨ Thank you for trusting us to give you the kind of service you've needed through the years.

⇨ You've been patient with the new employees through the years as they learned your names and your needs; you've been loyal to keep buying from us; and you've been talkative in passing on our name to colleagues. How could we ask for more? Thank you so much for contributing to our success.

Mention any special promotional efforts that you're linking to the anniversary, such as a special discount or momento.

⇨ As a new business, we tried to impress you with our fast service and knowledge of the merchandise. And as a "mature" business of ten years, we're still trying to impress you. That's why we want to offer you . . .

⇨ As our way of thanking you, we're enclosing here a certificate good for . . . .

⇨ To celebrate, we're offering a 10 percent discount on any workshops booked within this month.

State your plans for future growth.

⇨ Thanks to your business and partnerships, we plan to live happily ever after—serving you.

⇨ We don't want to change a thing in our way of doing business. We plan to keep the prices competitive and the service efficient.

⇨ We pledge to you our continued efforts to improve our service to you.

⇨ During the coming months, we plan to open two new stores in the ____ areas of the city. We'll keep you posted on where you can find us for the next ten years!

⇨ We plan to continue our efforts to listen to what our customers have to say and to educate ourselves on the changing needs of our world.

⇨ Our continued growth depends on our attention to customer needs and wants. So, you as customers will remain center stage in our upcoming months of production!

⇨ Thanks to you, we plan to keep on growing.

⇨ We have a challenging decade ahead. With our customers as partners, we can change the way the industry does business.

⇨ We're excited about the challenging decade ahead.

⇨ We plan to listen more, hire smart, sell low, and serve right.

⇨ Our game plan for the coming years? To continue to do what we do right even better.

❖ ❖ ❖

Dear Mr. Greyson:

We're celebrating here—October 11 marks ten years in the Harrisburg community. Thank you for being one of those customers who've continued to depend on us for their office supply needs. Your confidence in our products, our low prices, and our fast service has been vital to our growth, and we want to express our appreciation with a little more fanfare than this letter.

For the entire month of October, we are offering a **ten percent discount on any purchase in any of our stores.** Simply bring this letter with you and present it to the cashier when you make your selections.

Thank you again for depending on us "to be there" with all the usual—and the unusual—supplies you need to help your office operate efficiently. We're celebrating our business partnership; *our* business is to keep *you* in business.

Sincerely,

❖ ❖ ❖

ANNOUNCEMENTS

Any growing business must communicate change to its customers, suppliers, and prospects. Some announcements practically write themselves because they present an opportunity to say to the audience "look how we're prospering." In such situations, we are eager to make others aware of new products, more prestigious addresses, or expanded services and hours of operation.

On the other hand, new businesses must also announce those less-than-positive messages such as more restrictive terms or policies, more complex procedures, and even plans and decisions such as acquisitions, layoffs and mergers.

With positive messages, the challenge is to generate an excitement in the minds of customers, suppliers, and the general public. With less-than-positive announcements, the challenge is to calm fears, create trust about the company's decisions and integrity, and highlight any not-so-obvious benefits to the reader. Both challenges require extra attention to content as well as tone.

ACQUISITION, MERGER, OR RESTRUCTURING

Guidelines and Alternate Phrasing

Give an overview of the acquisition, merger, or restructuring plan.

⇨ We have learned today that an agreement has been reached for Farmington investors to acquire the stock of Bledson International. Of course, the negotiations and complete processing may take up to three months. In the interim period, we anticipate operating as we do currently; no changes in management have been discussed or approved.

⇨ We are expanding. Yes, effective March 1, Universal will merge its operations with Dupco United to become the world's largest supplier of _____.

⇨ Today Universal and Harrington Uptown have reached an agreement to merge and restructure their organizations so that both can devote time, resources, and expertise to what they know best in the _____ industry.This week Fullerton, Inc. will begin a major restructuring effort to decentralize our operations and push decision-making lower in the organization. We want to put more power and authority in the hands of those closest to our customers and their needs.

⇨ Bozell, Inc., has charted a new course through the murky economic waters of the industry downturn. Effective October 1, we will begin to put in place a restructuring plan that will help us eliminate duplication of efforts in our field operations while preserving the autonomy of individual regions.

Address immediate questions employees will have in their mind, such as those about layoffs or new openings, benefits, share values, or market position.

⇨ I'm sure the question in most minds is that of layoffs. Let me assure you that we have no plans to lay off any employees or offer any early retirement incentives. In fact, our plans as they now stand call for immediate growth and the resultant creation of approximately 400 new jobs in the community.

⇨ Your benefits such as medical and life insurance and our stock owner-ship plans will remain intact. We anticipate no changes in coverage or costs as a result of this agreement.

⇨ We are pleased to say that the immediate effect of this announcement on your share holdings has been positive.

⇨ Although this merger will not immediately increase our market share in the _____ arena, our plans for growth should position us to challenge the industry leaders within the next three to five years. We are pleased to say that we now have a goal, and we have a plan.

⇨ Your medical benefits and your hospitalization coverage will remain in force through the end of the year. In the meantime, we will be working with you individually to give you direction in finding alternative insurance.

⇨ We anticipate very little, if any, disruption in our normal day-to-day operations. You will report to the division directors, who will report to the same regional directors. The only visible change evident immediately will be . . .

Let readers know where they can direct other questions about changes.

⇨ We are making every effort to answer all your questions with speed and accuracy. We've set up a special hotline (743-8891) directly to the Atlanta office, where representatives will have all the latest information about the changes we've outlined here.

⇨ If you have questions not answered in the attached press release, you may direct questions to your immediate supervisors.

⇨ We can answer few other questions at this time because all decisions regarding ____ are still pending. Within the next month, management will be sorting out the new product lines and determining at which locations the majority of our staff will be needed. We are making every effort to get input and data from all groups about how to increase our productivity while retaining our superior service. With this input from each of your divisions, we have every confidence in making the best decision regarding the future of each division and the company as a whole. Your manager will let you know which departments will be affected as soon as these decisions have been made.

⇨ We will continue to update you with details of this decision as soon as we ourselves learn of further plans.

Convey a positive, upbeat tone.

⇨ Thank you for your patience in this transition period.

⇨ We appreciate your continued loyalty, cooperation, and upbeat attitude during this unsettled period.

⇨ We have every confidence you will finally agree that this decision was the only sensible one in light of today's economy.

⇨ We appreciate your courtesy in addressing all your concerns to your immediate manager.

⇨ We look forward to a promising future.

⇨ We think this new plan appropriately places us on the brink of a bright decade for Universal.

⇨ When this turnaround is complete, we believe you'll agree that this decision was the best for all concerned—customers, employees, and shareholders.

⇨ Thank you for your past dedication. Camden offers a challenging future for the most innovative and determined employees.

⇨ Thank you for your hard work and past loyalty. This new direction offers an even more promising horizon.

⇨ We think you will come to appreciate this decision as a major turning point in our company and in the industry.We look forward to increased profitability for all concerned.

⇨ We're glad you're on board for this promising new future.

❖ ❖ ❖

Dear Hosack Employees:

Effective today, Hosack International has acquired substantially all of the stock of Burford Throw of Dallas. With this acquisition, Hosack is now the largest and strongest _____ manufacturer in the Midwest. In a nutshell, this acquisition means that you now work for the industry leader in supplying quality products that span the range of _____ to _____.

Of course, it will be several months before we can arrange all of the day-to-day operational changes throughout the organization. As you have questions about job openings, benefits, or insurance coverage, please direct them through the normal channels. And please be patient with us in getting the right answer to you.

But we also want you to be part of this exciting opportunity to work out creative solutions to our sudden growth and expanded opportunity. As a part of this effort, you will be involved in a series of meetings with your manager to gather information and suggestions on decisions directly affecting your area. Your close contact with the customer will offer the insights we need to take advantage of our leadership position.

We look forward to your help with our operational plans for growth. All of us have an exciting future around the corner.

Sincerely,

❖ ❖ ❖

NEW HOURS/LOCATION/NAME/LOGO _____

Guidelines and Alternate Phrasing

Announce what's new up front—new name, new location, new logo, new hours.

➪ We're growing. As a result, we've taken on a new name that more accurately describes our full product line.

➪ We have a new face and a new name. OLD NAME has now become NEW NAME, with a new direction. We are now able to provide you . . .

⇨ Several clients have told us that they disliked having to take time off from work to keep their appointments; we listened. Beginning October 1, you can now schedule evening appointments with any of our psychologists. We suggest that you call us about their individual weekly schedules, and we'll arrange a convenient time for you to work together.

⇨ Effective May 6, Vivaron, Inc., will offer you longer hours to transact business with us; we'll be open Monday, Wednesday, and Friday evenings until 10:00 P.M.

⇨ We've moved. Come by and see us at our new location: (address) Blythe Services Corporation has changed its name to Flex-Systems—not because name changes seem to be the "in" thing today, but rather because it reflects an important change in our services to you.

⇨ You have known us in the past as Schaper Supplies. Since our inception we've specialized in _____. Now that we've been acquired by ZEX Corporation, we have taken on their name and become an even stronger provider of _____ products.

⇨ Our name has changed, but our superior products continue to get the same high marks from customers. Our new name, _____, will now be the one you see in industry journal ads and product literature. We have a new address also:

⇨ Please make a change on your Rolodex and in your files: Uninex now has a new name and a new address: . . .

Include effective dates if the announcement precedes the actual change.

⇨ All these changes are effective immediately.

⇨ After November 1, you'll be seeing several changes around our offices—all for the better.

If appropriate, take this opportunity to sell. Focus on some new aspect of your service or product, or simply remind readers who you are and what you can do for them. Tell them what the change means in terms of benefits.

⇨ Our new name signifies a new understanding of the market and your changing customer needs. Specifically, our goal is to add value to our current products by giving you new innovative services to accompany them—training and consulting departments.

⇨ This new name and address will involve several changes. Over the next few months, we'll be identifying ways to help you communicate faster and more economically. So, you'll be hearing from us several times in the coming weeks about new branches opening nearer to you, about new rate schedules, and about additional staff to solve your communication problems.

⇨ This new location represents a new attitude on our part. Oh, yes, we've always wanted to provide superior service, but now we don't expect you to have to look so hard to find us. This new location is only three to five minutes from your downtown office.

⇨ We have a new mission as well. Our goal is to improve the quality of your customized graphics by upgrading our software to include such new capabilities as . . .

❖ ❖ ❖

Dear Ms. Henderson:

There's one thing we're not changing—our excellent service to you. But just about everything else around here is new:

> New hours: 7 A.M. to 7 P.M.
>
> New address: 12789 Parkriver Road
>
> New name: Healthshop, Inc.

Why all the changes? If it weren't for the disastrous final analogy, I'd answer as the Big, Bad Wolf did in Little Red Riding Hood's situation: "The better to see you, the better to hear you, the better to serve you."

All the changes reflect an important redirection for the company. We think you should be able to call us for your health needs before and after your normal work hours. We want to be conveniently located for you to stop in for those "little" health-care products that you may previously have had to purchase while doing your routine shopping. You shouldn't have to settle for limited choices and higher prices elsewhere.

Remember, too, that we can provide a complete customized healthcare plan for your entire organization. Our dietitians, fitness experts, and psychologists will be glad to work with you in designing a wellness program that keeps your employees aware of good health habits and makes them more productive on the job.

If you have any other comments about how we can improve or expand our service to you, give us a call at 233-4577. As always, your health deserves serious attention.

Cordially,

❖ ❖ ❖

Dear Customers:

As part of our continuing efforts to ensure prompt posting of customer payments, **there has been a change in the address to which you return your remittance.** The new address is:

(insert)

Herrington and Power, Inc., is pleased to have you as a customer, and we will continue to look for ways to improve your billing and account services. Count on us.

Sincerely,

P.S. By the way, have you been meaning to call us about some of the new services we provide, such as . . .? Now is a good time.

❖ ❖ ❖

NEW POLICY/PROCEDURE _____

Guidelines and Alternate Phrasing

Summarize the new policy or procedure immediately, without getting bogged down in minute details. Include effective dates.

⇨ Beginning October 1, we will implement a new procedure for shipping library materials to our field training sites. All orders for videos, periodicals, audio series, or other packaged courses must be placed through Jan

Graves. After you phone her (ext. 3456) or drop her a note with your order, she will ship your materials to you within 24 hours.

⇨ Effective immediately, we will stop charging entry fees for the activities provided at the Hayen and Bostonian entertainment centers. All activities at these sites will be completely free to employees and their guests.

⇨ The board of directors of the Poppercorn Bureau has adopted a resolution to suspend funding of the Poppercorn Bureau and Affiliates' pension plan as of January 19—. The old plan will be replaced by a money-purchase defined contribution plan. We have finalized plans to computerize all payroll deductions for both hourly and salaried employees. The current pay period will not be affected; rather, all of these changes will go into effect March 15.

⇨ Feel free to make any changes in orders or place any new orders from the current catalog until February 9. After that date, we will no longer print a direct-mail catalog or ship products from this location. Instead, your new orders will go directly to . . .

⇨ Effective with our February tours, a LLC representative will meet each group of clients as they begin their tours and will complete a checklist of details to ensure their security and ours while they are on the grounds.

Use a positive, upbeat tone (rather than a scolding tone) that makes readers feel as though the change is to their benefit or at least to the benefit of the employees or customers as a whole. Giving adequate explanations goes a long way in helping employees and customers accept changes.

⇨ This system is currently being used by only 15 percent of our customer base, and the expense of the extra handling negates any profit on these orders.

⇨ While some of you have enjoyed the convenience of . . ., we think the added value of . . . will more than compensate for the extra time required to . . .

⇨ Although these new guidelines will not apply to every situation, they will address the majority of your concerns about trades, including client proprietary information, discrepancies in order amounts, and breakage reimbursements.

⇨ We think that after you've had time to use the new system, you'll agree that we can offer a much superior service to our customers. And after all, they are our bosses.

⇨ We know this procedure generates more paperwork, and that takes time. But we also are confident that this closer scrutiny of expenses will help us cut production costs in the long run. And, of course, profitability affects all our salaries and benefits.

⇨ We suggest that you try the procedure for six months. If you're not completely satisfied that you're getting better service, let us know. We welcome feedback and will make changes accordingly. Our goal is to provide the best possible service at the lowest cost, and this new procedure is getting high marks in other firms similar to ours.

⇨ There may be some confusion in the interim period, but we think the changes will be well worth any initial frustration with the learning curve.

⇨ We promise you help every step of the way. And we can assure you that this new policy will add value to your membership in the years to come.

Address the most obvious concerns with specific details. Then give readers a source for questions that will arise about exceptional situations.

⇨ Of course, you will have questions about the new commission rates. We've provided an attached listing of . . .

⇨ The specifications for the new equipment sound restrictive and costly. In fact, they are not. In the chart below, I've compared . . .

⇨ You may have questions about your benefits, your rights, and even the advantages of staying in such a business partnership. We have prepared a list of key people with their addresses and phone numbers so that you can direct your questions to the most knowledgeable source. They are expecting you to call and will be glad to calculate for you . . .

⇨ We've added a special hotline number (1-800-334-6666) just for your questions. We want you to understand fully all the implications of the law on this new issue.

⇨ Let us answer your questions fully. Rather than talking to your fellow employees, family members, and other community leaders who may or may not have all the facts of this situation, we encourage you to direct your questions to two top authorities in this field. We have Dr. Tony Gordon and Dr. Marian Harmtle on retainer for the next three months to offer telephone advice and other assistance, as necessary.

Express appreciation for their cooperation.

⇨ You have always been so careful in implementing new procedures that we have no concern that you will have difficulty with this ruling.

⇨ Thank you for your usual cooperative spirit.

⇨ Thank you for helping us help our customers.

⇨ We appreciate your willingness to try new ideas that we hope will save us all time and money.

⇨ Thank you for your openness and cooperation in implementing these new strategies for improving the way we do business.

⇨ Once again, we are depending on your willing cooperation on the front lines. You are the ones who make us look good to our customers.

⇨ With careful attention to detail and a willingness to improve in every phase of our operation, together we can turn this company around.

⇨ Thank you, our customer, for your patience during this transition.

⇨ We've listened to you, and we've made changes. That in itself should show you how much we appreciate your business and your help in offering the finest service available.

⇨ We appreciate your willingness to make changes whenever we receive valuable feedback about how we can run our business more efficiently.

⇨ Thank you for taking the time to learn this new procedure. We think it'll make your job easier.

⇨ Thank you for accepting this new policy as a necessary step in growing a business.

⇨ With special care and a can-do attitude, we can make the difference in this year's bottom line.

⇨ We think this new procedure is just what the doctor ordered for this new product line. Go make your customers well and happy.

⇨ We thank each of you as customers for your loyalty and your cooperation each time we make a change for the better. Here's to our continued partnership under these new arrangements.

⇨ Thank you for your help in making this work.

⇨ We are working for you to help you grow. This new procedure is one more example of our effort to provide innovative products and services in a timely manner at the lowest possible cost.

❖ ❖ ❖

To All Employees:

On March 1, all employees with a Firestone building access card will be eligible to park in the Hyson parking garage after normal working hours. The cost will be only one dollar per entrance, billed directly to the company rather than to you as individual employees. Simply turn in your parking tickets to Charon Jones so that we may verify accurate billing from the parking garage.

This new parking arrangement covers the following hours:

> 5:30 P.M. to 7:00 A.M. Monday through Thursday

> 5:30 P.M. Friday to 7:00 A.M. Monday

We want to remind you also that access cards are to be used only by employees, not guests or family members visiting after hours. Please cooperate with the building guards if they ask anyone entering the building with you after hours for their identification badges.

We are happy to have been able to work out this parking arrangement for those of you working late and on the weekends. Thank you for helping us with the security and billing issues. If any of you have questions about the security provided, please contact the guard on duty (ext. 3456).

Sincerely,

❖ ❖ ❖

Dear Ms. Olson:

Effective May 20, all shipments by Surety, Inc. to our exchange terminals will be made by overnight express. This new procedure will continue through the end of August, at which time we will revert to our normal shipping guidelines. We, not our customers, will bear this additional cost as part of our ongoing efforts to ensure customer satisfaction.

This express shipping procedure should allow us to process the backlog of orders generated by the increased media exposure with regard to the Midland situation. If you have questions about arrival dates on your orders, continue to deal directly with your normal contacts.

We want you to know we truly value you as a customer.

Sincerely,

❖ ❖ ❖

❖ ❖ ❖

Dear Agents:

Effective May 1, you can call extension 7788 for your medical insurance renewal changes. We will enter any changes directly into the system and within two days we will mail your insured a revised or amended renewal declaration and an invoice. If it's necessary to add a dependent to the coverage, we will mail the declaration and invoice within four days.

Such efficient, fast service is a primary concern to both of us, and this direct access will reduce the time for processing these changes. If you have concerns about how this procedure will work, call me at 222-4587.

Cordially,

❖ ❖ ❖

To the Men and Women of AT&T:

In January 1990, we will begin to offer you one of the nation's most comprehensive benefit packages supporting work and family matters. The agreement we signed in May with the Communications Workers of America and the International Brotherhood of Electrical Workers broke new ground. Many believe the scope and variety of the initiatives in our Work and Family Program will set new standards for corporate America.

Providing benefits that are responsive to the needs of employees and their families is a tradition at AT&T. The Work and Family Program not only continues that tradition, but also recognizes the changes in American families that are affecting our lives.

Today many children are living with parents who both work. Many adults are caring for elderly parents. If you face these conditions, you know how tough it is at times to balance work and family. The purpose of this program is simple. We want to make it easier for you to meet your obligations both at AT&T and in your life outside of the workplace.

This booklet describes each of the ten initiatives that comprise the Work and Family Program. I hope all of you will read it carefully. Even if you don't have a personal need for the support they provide, they will no doubt apply to your co-workers, your boss or someone you supervise.

The way we address the family concerns of AT&T people is an important issue for all of us—a competitive issue. Not only will these initiatives benefit you, but they will also benefit our customers, and ultimately, those who invest in our business. The Work and Family Program is an important investment in the future. These initiatives will help us attract and keep the talented workforce we need to win in the marketplace. And they will help all of us maintain a healthy balance between our work and families, so we can concentrate on giving our customers the best we have to offer.

Sincerely,

Bob Allen

Note: Reprinted with permission by courtesy of AT&T.

❖ ❖ ❖

NEW SERVICE/PRODUCT

Guidelines and Alternate Phrasing

Arouse interest immediately—with a provocative question, a startling statistic, a pithy quote, a problem statement, a dream, or a promise.

⇨ If you're like most marketing professionals, you're probably finding it increasingly more difficult and expensive to reach qualified prospects.

⇨ You should be able to cut your check-processing time in half with a new ____.

⇨ We've already proven we can help you eliminate malfunctioning ____ in your large offices—and we think we can now do the same thing for your home. We now have . . .

⇨ Do you know where you plan to be in your organization in five years? Do you want to know? We want to help you answer that question. We're looking for qualified representatives in your area to . . .

⇨ Have you noticed that budgets and goals often contradict each other? We understand. And we think we have a promising solution.

⇨ You can now purchase _____ directly from us. No more waiting and paperwork delays.

⇨ Thank you for asking about our new consulting services. We're pleased to say that we can now provide . . .

⇨ We've just completed a landmark study—the results of which should have an impact on the way your organization . . .

⇨ If you've ever tried to learn a software package without benefit of an excellent learner's guide, you'll appreciate knowing that . . .

⇨ By now, you've read numerous news stories and journal articles about ongoing problems with . . . We can help.

⇨ Why should you go through the usual hassle of changing insurance carriers? Two reasons: one is . . .

⇨ Are you prepared to answer some tough questions? What are you planning to do next year about . . .? And about . . .?

⇨ When you responded to our recent telephone survey about . . ., you confirmed the need for more . . . As a result of your comments about how we can improve and expand our services, you may be interested to know that . . . As the owner of a small business, you know how much effort it takes to succeed. We congratulate you. And we'd also like to help you. I think you'll be interested to know about . . .

⇨ We want to introduce you to a product that in its first six months on the market has captured attention in the most respected industry journals such as _____. Here's why . . .

⇨ Did you see the recent article in _____ about a new method of . . .? If not, I've enclosed a copy of that article and noted in the margin something that should mean direct dollars to you.

⇨ Cost-of-living increases are a benefit that most of your employees expect. Relocation assistance and medical benefits are also key issues with them. But how much is too much? How much is fair?

⇨ If you own a home, please take a minute to read why you might be interested in protecting that investment against . . .

⇨ Consider the convenience of having all your insurance with one company. You'd have only one agent to handle all the paperwork and hassles— along with the biggest advantage of all, an objective look at your real needs.

⇨ Please call us at our new toll-free number (1-800-444-7777) to get your free copy of . . . This is the first such listing you can use immediately to contact . . .

⇨ I'm sending this to your home to alert you to a serious situation developing in the workplace. I'm referring to the recurring accidents during the last few months. We're all fortunate that no one has been seriously injured, but the potential for injury and costly damage is all there. You have two options with regard to your safety and financial protection: . . .

Explain the benefits of what you have to offer.

⇨ We can take the risk out of evaluating new equipment for your factories. As part of our service to you, at no cost we will . . .

⇨ Have you heard of the Huffton line of copier supplies? If not, maybe you're not aware that now you can . . . We have four ways to help you reduce current operating costs and to capture savings on future equipment purchases. First, . . .

⇨ The most compelling reason this program works is that the framework design allows you to . . .

⇨ Almost every organization can benefit from the increased speed in ... and the decreased chance of confusion in . . .

⇨ Our business has grown to serve more than 300 clients in 42 states. What that means to you specifically is the convenience of . . .

⇨ You will find this offer unique to our company. Only our customers have the option of . . .

Either ask for the order—by phone or mail—immediately, or tell readers how they can investigate further. If your product or service is not one they'll make an immediate decision about, then identify the next step for them in the buying process. Should they see a demonstration? Attend a meeting? Ask for literature? Call some references? Visit your trade-show booth? Set an appointment with a local representative? Fill out a survey form for a customized analysis of their situation?

⇨ If you would like to discuss alternatives available to you in manual design, I'd love to drop by and visit with you further (call me at ext. 4589). I can bring along several samples of manuals we've put together for other clients. At the least, you could pick up some ideas for new programs you plan to develop for the upcoming year.

⇨ We will appreciate the opportunity to share with you our professional experience in making the decisions you're facing. May we help?

⇨ We can set up a demonstration in your office so that all your staff will see the results firsthand.

⇨ I invite you to take a risk-free look at the directory. We've copied and attached a few pages of entries so that you can see for yourself what kind of information you'd have at your fingertips. Call us today, and we'll ship out the complete directory tomorrow.

⇨ All you need to do is call 1-800-123-4455 and ask them to put you in touch with your local representative. He or she will be happy to meet with you at your convenience to outline a systematic approach to stocking your various locations.

⇨ Simply return the enclosed response card, and we'll put some additional information in the mail to you. For example, we have some statistics that you can compare to your own in the area of . . .

⇨ If you'll answer the six questions on the enclosed survey, we'll send you information for your specific situation. Then if you're still intrigued about the savings involved, we'll send out one of our agents to sit down with you and go over the costs on an employee-by-employee basis.

⇨ If you'll just attach your business card to this letter and return it in the enclosed envelope, we can give you some information that will help you make that decision.

⇨ For a copy of a special report that contains some of the key industry statistics, simply call us at 1-800-432-0000 and we'll send it by return mail.

⇨ We'll offer you a free estimate on your move and answer your questions at no obligation. What have you got to lose?

⇨ We have other similar events scheduled for the next quarter. If you'd like to be our guest at one of these seminars and learn more about . . ., call ext. 4889 to reserve a seat.

⇨ Just jot us a note on the bottom of this letter and return it. We'll be glad to add you to our mailing list for receiving updated information and prices.

⇨ We have a video that will give you more details about the commitment involved if you decide to join us. Call Andy Reece or me at the above number and we'll put one in the mail to you immediately. Then you can really say you've made an informed decision.

Whatever you're introducing, get to the point quickly, and be clear and specific about the new product or service. Too many readers finish an entire letter with only a vague understanding of what the writer has to offer.

❖ ❖ ❖

Dear Engineering Executive:

Many of you have told us your problem in preparing quality maps, and now we're ready with a solution. Our newest software package, MAPPON, allows you to . . .

What does that capability mean in your day-to-day operations? We think you'll see three improvements in preparing client proposals:

- Faster turnaround time from initial draft to final map
- Improved clarity of blow-ups
- Impressive four-color layout of the proposed design

If you've lost some contracts lately that "should have been yours," then I suggest we talk further. The least I can do is to examine the maps you're now using in your proposals, show you samples of what our software package can do, and give you some figures to help you determine the actual cost per map for your own operations.

Would you please initial the card I've enclosed and return it to me? When I hear from you, I'll phone to see when we can get together. If your need is more immediate because of a more significant pending proposal and contract, you can always phone me at 234-5555.

Sincerely,

❖ ❖ ❖

Dear Mr. Howard:

We have some good news. We've talked with one of your staff members briefly on the phone about your volume of outgoing parcels and then looked at our shipping rates. Comparing what you're now paying and what we charge, we think we can save you between 15 to 20 percent on your monthly shipping bill.

In addition to the lower cost, we can offer a convenient pick-up at your office. You won't have to change anything or go through any long, drawn-out process. Simply call us at 334-4449, and we'll make note to stop by your office every day from now on. That's all there is to it.

If you'd like to check with other satisfied customers about their experience with our dependability, the courtesy of our staff, and our record-keeping and parcel-tracking processes, we will be glad to put you in touch with several people in your neighborhood.

May we work together?

Sincerely,

❖ ❖ ❖

❖ ❖ ❖

Dear Ms. Crocker:

Congratulations on your engagement! There's no question that you're about to plan the biggest day of your life. As with any special event you've hosted in the past, you know the necessity of careful planning and hard work to ensure you and your guests that everything will run smoothly.

We think that a perfect reception begins with a beautiful atmosphere. As you review our enclosed wedding brochure, you'll see that our creativity in decorating, our well-dressed staff, and our formal serving pieces will make your reception one to cherish. Of course, as you glance through the brochure, keep in mind that these photos are suggestions only; we will work with you to customize any theme, setting, and service you want.

At your convenience during the next couple of weeks, I'd love to meet with you personally to give you a tour of our hotel in downtown Fairbanks. If you'll phone (446-9987), I can even make arrangements to stay late one evening or have my assistant here to show you what we can offer. I'll look forward to sharing ideas and making plans with you for that special day.

Cordially,

❖ ❖ ❖

NEW RATES/PRICES/TERMS _____

Guidelines and Alternate Phrasing

Show appreciation for the customer's business.

⇨ We thank you for your long-term business association with us.

⇨ Thank you for your recent order; we are eager to ship your merchandise immediately. We have had a price increase, however, since you last ordered. The price on the items you have selected is now _____.

⇨ We value your business and are continually looking for innovative products that will help you run your operations more efficiently. And, as you know, such state-of-the-art technology is expensive. We've found it necessary to increase the price of our . . .

➡ Thank you for choosing to do business with Horton Parts. We strive to maintain a complete inventory for your every automotive need. But the cost of maintaining such a variety of stock is going up. Because we've had an increase in our leasing costs, we're being forced to raise our prices on several lines of standard equipment, specifically the . . .

➡ Thank you for being such a prompt-paying, loyal customer.

State the new rates, prices, or terms, along with any explanation that you think will make the changes understandable or acceptable.

➡ It's always with reluctance that we have to announce a price increase to cover our increased cost of equipment, supplies, and staff. We trust that our ten percent increase, effective March 1, will still allow you to enjoy the services you've come to expect from an advisory group such as ours.

➡ The enclosed billing for January through June reflects an increase in our collection rates. This rate increase has become necessary to retain the most experienced maintenance staff to service your equipment properly.

➡ Today, we are announcing a six percent increase for our products and services contracted on or after February 14. We always hate to raise our prices, but unfortunately our cost of doing business has also risen accordingly.

➡ The unsettled state of the economy and the difficult times many of our vendors are experiencing in their own businesses have made us rethink our own credit terms and decide to bring them more in line with current reality. Effective March 1, the terms we can now offer are full payment at the end of 15 days. Of course, we still are pleased to offer a one percent discount for payment at the time of purchase.

➡ Rather than increase our annual membership fee to add new services that our members have requested, we have added several minimal fees for activities and privileges we now provide. The enclosed list of fees will allow you to send your children to the center with the appropriate money. Please be assured that these minimal charges will be much less than the expense you would incur were we to raise the annual membership fee. This pay-as-you-go plan, we think, will be more amenable to everyone's budget.

Remind the customer of the benefits of doing business with you, and express confidence that the business relationship will continue.

➡ As always, please note the enclosed list of our official work holidays and mark your calendars accordingly for the remainder of the year. We're looking forward to continuing our service to you—fast, efficient, dependable.

⇨ At Hurstford Ltd. there's only one thing we value more than our new customers—and that's our established customers who depend on us year after year. Thank you for being one of that loyal, long-term group. This increase will allow us to continue to lead the industry in developing new products to help you run your business more efficiently.

⇨ We value you as a long-time customer—and a friend.

⇨ Call on us whenever you think of anything we can do to improve our service to you.

⇨ We invite you to stop in from time to time and chat with one of our senior executives to let him or her know of any new needs you have in the field. Who knows? Together, we may just come up with a new product that will change the way we all do business.

⇨ Thank you for the privilege of providing this service to you.

⇨ Thank you for coming to us with all your _____ product needs.

⇨ We will never take your business for granted. That's why we pledge to you that we will continue to improve our service in all the ways that count for you.

⇨ A quality product is our reason for being in business. Thank you for buying from us.

❖ ❖ ❖

Dear Customers:

We're pleased to announce new terms on discounts for our premium gift items. You can purchase any item in our catalog at 50 percent off the retail price from now until further notice if you order directly from our warehouse.

To take advantage of this new discount, please submit your order on the form provided inside the enclosed catalog. Because of the deep discount, we do require prepayment to save invoicing costs. (We will absorb the postage costs.) As always, major credit cards or personal checks are fine.

We hope these new terms will make our gifts even more attractive to you and more conveniently accessible. When you're happy, we're happy.

Cordially,

❖ ❖ ❖

❖ ❖ ❖

Dear Friends:

It gives us great pride to know that our staff can provide the counseling that makes a difference in a marriage, in a family, in a career. Thank you for your ongoing confidence in our services.

Despite our intention to keep our services as reasonable and affordable as possible, we will have a price increase for appointments scheduled after June 1. The new hourly fee of $_____ is certainly in keeping with established rates of other clinics and will allow us to retain the most qualified professionals to help you in your time of crisis.

We welcome you to continue to depend on us for the help that can save a marriage, save a family, or save a life.

Sincerely,

❖ ❖ ❖

Dear Mr. Forney:

It is that time of the year for us to review and retain services at the Fullerton location in accordance with our ongoing contract.

Currently, your annual payment is $_____. As we have agreed, we are renewing the agreement with Bayden Associates, at a seven percent increase. This increase covers our additional expenses from suppliers involved in producing our _____ products.

Your new contract fee for this year will be $_____. We appreciate your having chosen us as your supplier of _____. We intend to continue *building the quality into our products*, rather than trying to "add it on" when difficulties and inefficiencies of operation occur. Thank you for your continued confidence in our company and in our quality products.

Sincerely,

❖ ❖ ❖

APPOINTMENTS

Because time management has almost become a science to many busy professionals, matters that complicate our own and others' schedules call for precise, clear communication.

Success in securing an appointment often involves convincing someone of either the personal or corporate value in meeting with you. Postponing or canceling an appointment, once scheduled, can often "derail" someone's work and travel schedule for days or even weeks. And declining to meet with someone takes the tact of a diplomat. The important rules of etiquette aside, in the ever-expanding business community your later business dealings and success may depend on how you handle the feelings of those who may perceive you as one who has rejected them or caused them great inconvenience.

Never take such situations lightly.

REQUESTING

Guidelines and Alternate Phrasing

State the purpose of the appointment you're requesting. If you need to "sell" the meeting idea to the other person, be sure to state the purpose in terms of benefits to the other person.

⇨ May we talk? I have a couple of ideas that could save us some money—ideas about how you can . . .

⇨ A colleague of mine and yours, Cheryl Andrews, mentioned that you and I should get together to discuss our mutual interest in distributing our products in the Pacific Rim countries. I have some information that you may find useful, and I'm sure you, too, can share some insights with me about appropriate markets.

⇨ I need to talk to you about the production costs for the Belaire design. You asked me to keep you informed every step of the way, and I think now is the time to go over several key details about our choice of subcontractors and delivery schedules. We want your opinions on these issues that affect your staff so directly.

Suggest a meeting place, date, and time, but show concern for the reader's own schedule by asking for him or her to confirm or to suggest an alternate time.

⇨ How about May 2 at 3:00 P.M. in the lobby of Eduardo's? Since we'll both be attending the ABA convention, it only makes sense that we get together then and save us both air travel elsewhere.

⇨ I can be at your office at 10:00 Friday morning if that's convenient for you. If not, call me with another suggestion.

⇨ I suggest that we meet in the main conference room away from the phones and drop-in visitors. I've checked availability of the room and have it on hold from 3:00 to 5:00 P.M.

Confirm all other details of the appointment, including any preparation that either of you needs to make for the meeting.

⇨ If possible, would you please phone your supervisors and get their input on this issue before we talk.

⇨ Please review the enclosed report as a basis for our discussion.

⇨ I suggest that we both come to the meeting having talked with our colleagues about what they hope to gain from the new program. With that little bit of pre-work, we may find that we already agree on several priorities.

⇨ Would you please calculate your expenses for the past nine months with regard to the Byton project. If you can be as exact as possible, we can identify some specific points for further investigation.

❖ ❖ ❖

Dear Alton:

Could we get together to give some serious thought to my career plans and your intentions for my future here at Clayton and Clayton? As I've read and studied the new marketing strategies that our company has recently adopted, some new ideas have come to mind about how I can contribute to our growth in a couple of innovative ways.

May I suggest Tuesday or Wednesday afternoon at 5:00, April 2 or 3, while I'm in Austin for our new-product training? Our sessions conclude each day at 4:30 P.M., and perhaps by that hour of the day your own phone will have stopped ringing. If that's not convenient for you, I'd be happy to meet you at any nearby restaurant you can suggest for breakfast, during our training-session lunch break, or later for dinner some evening.

I'll plan to bring an updated resume so that you can see the positions I've held and the experience I've acquired during my last five years with the company.

Please let me know (ext. 4779) when we can get together to discuss the issues that are vitally important to both of us.

Cordially,

❖ ❖ ❖

Dear Ms. Graham:

We at National Galleries have just completed a study of _____ that I think can provide some new insights into controlling your organization's personnel costs. I spoke with Frank Smith briefly in your Washington office, who suggested that I get in touch with you about these results to see how we could work together to design a new recruitment plan and compensation package.

Our objective will be to walk away from the meeting with some realistic guidelines for recruiting the very best people at competitive salaries.

Will you be available for a meeting the week of August 9? I'll be in New Orleans then doing some work for another client and would love to take you to dinner Monday or Wednesday evening? If dinner meetings infringe on your family time, I can always arrange to meet you for lunch. I'll phone you next Thursday to see which day or time will be more convenient. Perhaps if you're going to be out of the office that day, you can give your assistant your preferences, and I'll plan my schedule accordingly.

I do think it will be time well spent for both of us. If you have any recent information you've put together internally from your exit interviews, that will be a great starting point for our discussions.

Cordially,

❖ ❖ ❖

POSTPONING OR CANCELING _____

Guidelines and Alternate Phrasing

Tell the reader that you must postpone or cancel the appointment, offering a specific reason.

⇨ I'm afraid that our meeting date about the Hyde proposal is not going to work out for me. I will be away that week and have had to change my schedule.

⇨ Because I'm new in the organization, I'm finding over and over again that my time is still not my own—and it may never be. I'm embarrassed to say that I must postpone our June 2 meeting until I learn more about our organization's strategies and goals for this region.

⇨ Fred Calcant assumed the position of purchasing agent, effective May 5. Therefore, I wanted to let you know that a meeting with him would be much more productive than with me. You can reach Fred by . . .

⇨ I'm in the position of having to curtail some of our activity and spending in the advertising arena for this next quarter. Therefore, I need to cancel our upcoming participation in your video demo session on August 10 and 11.

⇨ We have recently decided to make the advertising theme a committee decision, and I'm writing to let you know that our previously scheduled meeting for May 9 would allow you only an audience of one when you need to convince a committee of 15! I will, or course, pass on to the committee your interest in working with us. Should they decide a meeting at some later date would be mutually helpful, someone from the group will be in touch.

Mention again all the corresponding details of time, place, and purpose to make sure there is no confusion about which appointment.

⇨ I'm referring, of course, to the meeting we tentatively scheduled for September 5 at the Hyatt Grand Ballroom.

⇨ So, perhaps you can find something more profitable to do with your hour on Friday, June 5, than discuss fiber-optic options with me. I'm sorry for having to cancel so late in the month.

⇨ Because Fred Swanke has no further information at this point, our June 9 meeting in my office would be counterproductive.

Show your concern about inconveniencing the other person and take the initiative in suggesting a later contact.

⇨ I'll phone you to reschedule as soon as we have the go-ahead.

⇨ Will you write again the next time you plan to be in town, and I'll do my darndest to see you.

⇨ Perhaps Janet Holcombe can arrange something for you on her calendar. Her department has similar needs to mine, and she has much more flexibility in scheduling that I do.

⇨ I'm sorry to inconvenience you with this sudden change of plans, but I trust that you understand my decision under these circumstances.

⇨ I hate to cancel appointments, and hope you'll understand my need to do so this time. Feel free to call again, however, at the end of the year, and we'll plan to talk in January.

⇨ Thank you for being so accepting of my situation. Will you please phone me again next month about getting together?

⇨ I'll phone ahead when I plan to be in Orlando in the summer. Maybe you can find time to work me into your schedule there.

❖ ❖ ❖

Dear George:

Will you forgive me for having to postpone our April 2 meeting during the TIB convention? You were so thoughtful to call and suggest a get-together for dinner at the Houstonian, but we find the timing is not going to work out with the client commitments we've made during the week. I trust that you understand our wanting to take advantage of being in the city for the convention to see our clients in the region.

I'll phone you the next time I'm in Baltimore and see when you're available for lunch. Your new strategy for Malaysia is timely, and I'll be eager to hear more.

Sincerely,

❖ ❖ ❖

❖ ❖ ❖

Dear Mr. Jakawa:

Our company situation has changed since we arranged to meet in my office July 10 for an overview of the legal services your firm can provide our employees involved in the Baytown incident. As you may have read in the papers recently, a new investor group has purchased both of our Houston divisions. Of course, with this change in management, a decision to retain legal counsel for the rumored lawsuits would be unwise.

If you don't hear from me within the next eight to ten weeks, you can assume that the decision has been made to use our internal legal staff for the situations we have discussed.

Thank you for offering to take the time to meet with me about our current difficulties and your professional expertise along those lines. I wish you every success as you and your new firm put down roots in the community.

Sincerely,

❖ ❖ ❖

DECLINING

Guidelines and Alternate Phrasing

Decline the appointment with a specific reason for the refusal.

⇨ I'm afraid that no matter how hard I try, I'm not going to be able to find a free hour for a meeting on the Boyton project. We are gearing up here for our exhibit for a major convention in two weeks, and every moment is precious.

⇨ I'm pleased to say that we've already selected a vendor that we think can meet our computer needs, and therefore, any further meetings to analyze our tasks would be a waste of your valuable time.

⇨ Cary Sloane, of your office, phoned two weeks ago and gave me a brief overview of your new study; consequently, I feel that I've already received the information of most interest to me. Thank you, however, for thinking to suggest a meeting for that purpose.

⇨ My position within the organization has changed somewhat since we last talked, and I'll no longer be making decisions about transfers and relocation policies. Perhaps Mike Jones or Ann Todd will have the answers you need.

⇨ Since you phoned several weeks ago, our management here has changed priorities for the upcoming few months. I'm going to have to postpone my opportunity to learn more about your company until I can focus more time on the subject of retail displays.

Suggest alternatives to the meeting, if you're so inclined. Can you handle the situation or issue with a phone call, with a letter, or by referral to another individual or group?

⇨ John, why don't we handle this by phone? I suggest that you set up a conference call, and I'll be glad to join you that way.

⇨ Because we have absolutely no budget for that sort of thing, I suggest that you try to see someone much higher in the organization than I. And I'm afraid I don't know who the appropriate person might be.

⇨ If you'll simply send me your information, I'll be happy to add it to my reading stack and make my way down to it as soon as possible.

⇨ Have you thought of contacting nonprofit organizations about these services? It seems to me they would have more inclination to attend these forums than those in organizations such as ours.

⇨ Would you leave me on your mailing list, however, to receive further information. If my situation changes, I'll let you know immediately.

⇨ It occurs to me that a bulletin from your office to all our divisions would accomplish the same objective. Would you consider issuing such a statement?

⇨ I'm attaching here a list of our Atlanta offices that you may find useful in gathering such information. You may use my name and let them know I suggested your call to them.

Mention your openness to other issues of discussion, or state under what conditions you might be willing to meet with the person about the current matter.

⇨ If our budget allocations change next year, I'll be much more receptive to the Carter idea and will give you a call for more information at that time.

⇨ Although I can't say that I have much interest in certificates of deposit, should the Heritage Fund open up again, let me know.

⇨ If your own vice president is agreeable to discussing a mutual sharing of technology in this area, then of course that would be another matter. Let me know if that is the case.

⇨ Should we decide to add staff in the Atlanta office, our further discussion might be advantageous to both of us. When and if that's the case, I'll be sure to phone you to arrange a time to review your plans and interests then.

⇨ Would you write or phone again if you decide to handle a larger inventory of the tools we use regularly.

⇨ Should the political outlook change, I'll be in touch.

⇨ If the economic crisis subsides, there may be more interest in your services, especially in our Denver area. Could you phone me again in about six months for an update on where we stand?

Be courteous, rather than arrogant or punitive, in your refusal. You never know when the situation may change and you'll need to build on this rapport or contact.

⇨ Thank you for thinking of me.

⇨ I appreciate your bringing this opportunity to my attention.

⇨ You never know from one month to the next what twists and turns the market holds. Let's both hang on through this industry crisis.

⇨ I wish I could be more positive in my response. I'm sorry we can't find some mutual project to work on together.

⇨ Thank you for being so understanding of my situation.

⇨ I wish that I had more authority in this area, but I simply can't make decisions of that magnitude without conferring with others.

⇨ Thanks for your patience and many efforts in contacting me about this venture.

⇨ Best wishes in finding a suitable replacement.

⇨ I wish you every success in finding those organizations and individuals that can use your service. You have an innovative idea.

⇨ Thank you for taking the time to contact me.

⇨ I appreciate your effort in phoning, writing, and sending literature on this product line for us to consider.

⇨ Keep us in mind for other projects.

⇨ I trust this letter will clarify management's position on this issue. Thank you for giving us your views also.

❖ ❖ ❖

Dear Mr. Garcia:

Has there been some mistake? I received your letter to confirm our appointment but have no recollection of talking with you about meeting to discuss our financial investments. As a matter of fact, I'm quite pleased with our account executive at Merrill Lynch and have no plans to change brokerage firms.

Thank you, however, for thinking of us in your marketing efforts.

Sincerely,

❖ ❖ ❖

Dear Wayne:

My assistant passed on the message that you would be in the city the week of July 10, but I'm afraid that a meeting during the summer months would be much too early to be fruitful for either of us. As of yet, we still have not completely staffed our new offices in Kuala Lumpur or Tokyo, and any discussion of training needs there would only be a guess at this point.

After all of our new managers have been hired and have spent six months on the job, they and we will have a much better understanding of our needs.

I'll take the liberty of calling you at that time if we identify deficiencies that you can help us remedy. Best wishes in the meantime.

Sincerely,

❖ ❖ ❖

BIDS

We've all heard the maxim, "You get what you pay for." To paraphrase that sentiment in bid situations, "You get what you solicit." If your solicitation letters are unclear and incomplete, the bid responses will usually be equally unclear, incomplete, and off target. So the more time and attention you devote to requesting bids, the more time and attention you'll save in evaluating the responses and making a decision.

The letter of acceptance of a supplier's bid offers an additional chance to make your expectations clear and to express your commitment to the project or purchase.

And in your eagerness to proceed with the bidder who has promised to meet your needs, don't fail to notify those who have not been selected. Your integrity, tact, and forthrightness will go far in retaining their goodwill and commitment to future situations where you may need that bidder's expertise, product, or service.

SOLICITING

General Guidelines and Alternate Phrasing

Invite the reader to bid, giving an overview of the project.

⇨ Following a discussion with Tom Jackson of your firm, I invite your bid on conducting a communications study in early fall. Our board has approved three areas for study: interdepartmental communications, our bulletin-board system, and electronic mail.

⇨ We have in mind a communications project for which we are actively seeking help, and we invite your proposal for consideration. The project will include three phases: . . .

⇨ We need a cost estimate for constructing an additional wing on the Huffines Medical Building at 2455 Park Way. Attached is a line drawing showing our plans.

⇨ We are seeking bids on office furniture for four floors of the Two Riverway Chesapeake Building.

⇨ Carolton and Associates requests your bid for weekly housekeeping and maintenance service of our office suites.

Specify exactly what the bid should include, and make it clear whether the bidder can make substitutions for your stated requests.

⇨ Your estimate should include material, labor, overhead and profit. Please show these as separate line items on your quote, because these four items will be the basis for our comparison of contractors.

⇨ Please overview your study process. We understand your reluctance to reveal your entire method of analysis, but we must understand enough of your process to determine the potential benefits.

⇨ Your bid should include your work plan, resumes of the key engineers on the project, brief histories of similar projects you've completed, and pricing information.

⇨ Please provide the manufacturer's name and model number, the quantity of each item you propose to install, and the cost of ongoing maintenance contracts.

⇨ We have listed our preferences for each piece of equipment; however, we will consider substitutions that you deem of equal quality to those we've listed.

⇨ We have decided not to consider any substitutions on the items we listed here.

Identify the criteria for selection.

⇨ All bidders will be evaluated only on the specified items, with no substitutions. Therefore, our selection will be based on price alone.

⇨ In our decision, we will consider delivery schedules, as well as the previous maintenance record on the reconditioned equipment.

⇨ Our selection will be based, of course, on our subjective understanding of the expertise of the principal consultants assigned to the project. Therefore, please include all of their relevant experience, along with verifiable references who are willing to comment on specific results within their organizations.

⇨ Our timetable is crucial. If you cannot deliver the products by July 31, we ask that you forego this bidding opportunity.

Give the necessary information for submitting the bid, such as time, deadline, packaging details, and a contact person for inquiries. To save both you and the bidders time with certain inquiries, you may also want to mention any information that you are unwilling to provide.

⇨ Please do not include your pricing information in the same envelope with your proposal; instead, forward each separately in the enclosed, labeled envelopes.

⇨ We will not consider any bids received after June 2, at noon.

⇨ At this stage in the survey process, we will not be able to provide information on any equipment we currently use in our remote locations. You can assume it is of equal quality to that used here at headquarters.

⇨ As you prepare your bids, feel free to suggest methods not mentioned in our own description of the problem and potential solution. We are entirely open to your ideas about a better system of management and operation than we have described here.

⇨ Please do not include the cost for reproduction of the manuals. After we select the winning supplier, we will make arrangements to produce and assemble all necessary manuals with our in-house staff.

❖ ❖ ❖

Gentlemen or Ladies:

After reviewing the fact sheets you provided Fairfield Company, we recognize your expertise in the energy-management field. Therefore, we want to invite your proposal to help us reduce our energy cost and improve our efficiency in our four local properties.

The proposal should include the scope of your analysis, the type of information you can supply, the amount of time you would spend on site, and your expectations for what type recommendations your final report would include.

My objective in this project is to determine if there are ways to save enough energy to allow an attractive payback period on the properties before we plan to sell them. I will need to see your suggestions on how to operate the equipment more efficiently without affecting tenant comfort. And, of course, in the final report I will want to compare the approximate cost and savings of equipment and changes in procedure.

As you prepare your proposal, feel free to inspect our four sites at your convenience. Simply let the security guards know that you are here. If you have any difficulty in gaining access to certain areas, ask them to call me or my assistant, John Grimes (ext. 2456), for authorization. We do not, however, plan to conduct formal tours for the bidders before they submit proposals; tours will be at your discretion. After we select the winning proposal, of course, we will be happy to provide you with all energy records and to make ourselves available to answer your questions and arrange formal tours.

If you choose to propose an energy-saving plan, please submit your proposal package to us at the above address by April 30.

Sincerely,

❖ ❖ ❖

Dear Ms. Frazier:

Herrington Corporation is considering suppliers who can provide us with management training programs for our senior executives and our first-line supervisors. This letter, along with its three attachments, constitute our request for pricing and other seminar information.

We reserve the right to reject any and all responses to this request for management training programs and to negotiate further with any supplier.

Along with your pricing information, please include any anticipated price increases for the calendar year and any cancellation or rescheduling policies or terms. Your information should include a complete list of objectives and topics for each of the two training audiences.

Your written quotations must be submitted only in the pre-addressed envelope provided as part of our bid-request package. If we do make a final decision to provide this training, we will be selecting a vendor sometime in the first quarter of next year. If you have questions about this request or the submission process, please phone Helen Graves or Herb Jones (355-478-8890).

Enclosed are copies of all the agreements applicable to the service we are asking you to provide: our standard service agreement, a statement of the work to be performed, and our standard purchase order form with terms and conditions stated at the bottom of the page.

Thank you for providing this information so that we may consider your firm to meet our current training needs.

Sincerely,

❖ ❖ ❖

ACCEPTING

Guidelines and Alternate Phrasing

Announce your acceptance of the winning bid.

⇨ We accept your bid and warranty for installing the computer equipment at our Chicago offices.

⇨ With pleasure, we have selected your firm to provide training programs for our sales staff.

⇨ Your pricing information was exactly on target for our transmission requirements; we are happy to begin plans to schedule delivery dates by your firm.

⇨ Thank you for such a prompt response to our bid request. We are happy to tell you that we have chosen your organization to design and install the irrigation system at 34588 Park Cities.

⇨ Our committee is pleased to tell you that we have identified your firm as the one we'd like to work with in managing our international expansion.

Highlight the primary reasons for your selection to re-emphasize and confirm the bidder's commitment in these areas.

⇨ We are particularly pleased that you could guarantee to maintain spare parts at the Furthermore Center rather than in Waterloo, Iowa.

⇨ Of all the proposals submitted, your approach seemed the most creative in terms of staffing. We were delighted that you estimate the need for only two full-time custodians.

⇨ Our decision became firm when we examined the beautiful photos you included as evidence of your previous results in redesigning facilities while making extensive use of the present structure.

⇨ You are the vendor that seemed most committed to our timetable, a crucial factor in acceptance of the entire project by senior management.

⇨ Your proposal included all the expertise we wanted to hire in the engineering phase.

⇨ I must say that in checking references among your recent clients, we were overwhelmed and entirely persuaded by their glowing comments on your after-the-sale service. That's what we're looking for—an ongoing partnership for the years to come.

Identify the next step in the process such as preparation of contracts, remaining price negotiations, tours of facilities, equipment demonstrations, training, or meetings.

⇨ We will be in touch again when our legal staff has a prepared contract.

⇨ Within the next ten days, our purchasing agent will contact you to supply the necessary ordering information.

⇨ As you begin your work, of course, we expect to arrange an initial meeting for your three project engineers and our six managers whose areas will be affected by the changes you propose.

⇨ As we understand it, your next step will be to install a loaner system while you rebuild ours during the next two weeks.

⇨ Mike Duffy will be calling you shortly to provide a detailed summary of our current objectives and tasks as outlined in earlier sales meetings.

❖ ❖ ❖

Dear Ms. Reyes:

We are pleased to tell you that we have selected your proposal for a film to be titled "The Capable You." Our committee considered your film treatment to be the most comprehensive in the area of self-esteem, the vital ingredient in successful performers in today's market place.

Within the next six weeks, we will be establishing our priorities for all the new titles for this season. After that priority ranking is complete, we will notify you of our production schedule and set up the initial meeting with our director.

Thank you again for preparing a winning idea.

Sincerely,

❖ ❖ ❖

❖ ❖ ❖

Dear Mr. Stockton:

We have received your guaranteed bid of $4,899 to move Mr. and Mrs. Howard Smith's household goods from Dallas, Texas, to Tulsa, Oklahoma, and you are authorized to begin the move. Please insure their belongings for full replacement value with no deductible.

After speaking with other employees who used your services, we are convinced that you will treat the Smiths' goods with care, as if they were your own.

Thank you for making this move for our staff member a pleasant experience.

Sincerely,

❖ ❖ ❖

REJECTING

Guidelines and Alternate Phrasing

Begin on a positive note by showing appreciation for the time, money, or effort spent in submitting the bid.

⇨ Thank you for your proposal to reprocess gravity data on the Macintosh property.

⇨ We have received your price quotes for furnishing our Park City offices; thank you for your prompt response.

⇨ We appreciate your efforts in supplying us with the pricing information on the binders for our training programs for the coming year.

⇨ Thank you for such a detailed proposal; I know it represents much thought and analysis of our situation at Eaglecrest.

⇨ We have reviewed your recent proposal for design and construction of the Magraver wing on our hospital. The photos you included from other projects gave us an excellent opportunity to review several possibilities for use of the existing space.

⇨ We have received your bid for the management consulting project at our Lafayette site. The résumés of the two principals you proposed to assign to the project are quite impressive.

Announce your acceptance of the winning bid, highlighting the reasons for your choice. If you have an ongoing relationship with other bidders and think that you owe them a specific explanation, you may mention why their bid package was not selected. Bidders will be more inclined to put forth another superior effort if they know they can learn from their experience and increase their chances for acceptance in the future. Rejections without reasons discourage later responses, or at the least minimize the effort.

⇨ After reviewing all the excellent proposals we received, we have selected Aerogrunn, Inc., out of California for the work.

⇨ After careful evaluation, we have chosen Universal Incorporated to complete the work because of their outstanding record with similar projects in our community.

⇨ We have finally narrowed our choice to Brighton, Inc., for the consulting project. Their approach seemed to be exactly on target with our management philosophy throughout the company.

⇨ We have awarded the contract to Fullerton of Albany, New York, because of their low price.

⇨ We have chosen Silverton, Inc., as the firm to complete the project. Their understanding of our current economic situation and their willingness to work with us on our timetable affords us the opportunity to progress on an as-needed basis.

⇨ After much deliberation on the many responses to our request for proposal, we liked best the comprehensive approach outlined by Black and Stein Associates and have awarded the contract to them.

⇨ Although we agreed with your problem analysis, we had difficulty understanding how your approach would work with our people and operations being so scattered throughout the nation.

Take care to keep the relationship in tact; on later projects, the currently rejected bidder may be your only source.

⇨ Thank you for taking the time to quote these prices for us.

⇨ We will keep your name on our bidder's list for other similar projects.

⇨ We hope you will give us another opportunity to work with you on a later project.

⇨ We assume you'll be interested in other such projects and will keep your firm in mind.

⇨ We appreciate your prompt and thorough response.

⇨ We'll be in touch again about other work.

⇨ Thank you for the fine job you've done on other such projects for us.

⇨ I'm sorry we could not get together on the price for this work, but maybe the next time we'll be closer.

⇨ We appreciate your attention to the work and our short deadlines for the evaluation and decision.

⇨ Shall we keep you on the bidder's list for later projects?

⇨ We'll keep your organization's name and brochure in our currently active files and hope to have you bid on something else in the near future.

⇨ Thank you for providing this pricing information. We hope to be able to purchase some of your other equipment when the need arises.

❖ ❖ ❖

Gentlemen and Ladies:

Thank you for your very thorough proposal to provide energy management services to us. We appreciate the time you took in preparing such a detailed step-by-step approach to the work you projected; it sounds as though you really know your business and have excellent experience in this arena.

However, after our staff met with all the vendors, we have decided to use Energy Source Forever, out of Nebraska. Their focus seemed to be more in line with our perspective on the changes we would like to incorporate. In addition to their offering a lower price, we noted that their approach dealt with the full scope of the buildings rather than simply the computer operations.

We thank you for your interest in the energy-management issues and value our on-going relationship on other projects.

Sincerely,

❖ ❖ ❖

COMMENDATIONS

Half the pleasure in doing an outstanding job is that others know of our achievement. That's why it's important to commend employees in writing—a letter that you also send to their boss or that they themselves can show to family, friends, and colleagues. For those days and weeks when things aren't going so well, the written commendation for accomplishments serves to remind individuals of a successful past, regardless of their current state of mind.

An oral pat-on-the-back is always welcome; a written one, even more so.

TO SPEAKER

Guidelines and Alternate Phrasing

Mention the occasion of the speech or the presentation.

⇨ Thank you for the excellent talk you presented last evening at the Forum Club.

⇨ Your remarks last week at the Tunisia meeting were exactly on target for the group gathered to hear them. Thank you for being so forthright.

⇨ We appreciate so much your speaking to our group of CPEs last Tuesday about the need for continuing creativity in the field.

⇨ Your topic "Eighteen Ways to Stay Well" certainly made a hit with our CVA group last evening—or could you tell by the boisterous laughter? What fun!

⇨ Thank you for making yourself available to our graduates last week in their tenth session this semester.

⇨ We have read the evaluations—you were a real favorite with the attendees at this year's Boston convention.

⇨ We appreciate your sharing your expertise with us at our Tenth Anniversary Celebration in San Antonio.

⇨ Thanks so much for the outstanding presentation you made to our group this past week as we launched our organization into what we hope will be our finest year ever.

⇨ I appreciate so much your taking the time out of such a busy schedule to speak to our group.

⇨ From the comments that continue to come into our office, your presentation last week at the IBA convention was a tremendous success.

Express your appreciation as specifically as possible. Single out one or two things that were particularly helpful to you personally or to your company. In other words, let the reader know you still remember the presentation!

⇨ I heard so many members on the way out comment about the thought-provoking issues you raised—issues that we've feared to face in the past.

⇨ What a superb speaker you are! Your delivery style is captivating—who could dare not listen to a message wrapped so beautifully with all the right words and gestures?

⇨ Your analogy of the malfunctioning elevator will stay with me for a long time. What a memorable way to present your "me-first" obstacle to good customer service.

⇨ Your ideas were basic to the industry, nothing we haven't heard before. So why haven't we carried them out successfully? An interesting question you raised. And the answer is just as you said: We're not convinced of their value. Well, I won't let myself get caught in that mode of thinking anymore.

⇨ The slides you used to illustrate our key points looked so professional. I'm sure they're evidence of the long hours you spent in making the presentation meaningful to our group specifically.

⇨ Your cartoons, while giving us several good laughs throughout the day, brought some sharp points home. I'll remember them.

⇨ Your levity added just the right mix to the seriousness of our situation.

⇨ Particularly to your credit was your ability to keep the audience tuned in, despite so many distractions outside in the hallway.

⇨ The statistics you quoted certainly impressed upon me the urgency of taking action now.

⇨ Your five how-to's were as instructive as your stories were motivational. And I've been one to say we need both—know-how and inspiration. Thanks for delivering large doses of both ingredients to our plan for success.

⇨ I was overwhelmed by your knowledge of the subject. You handled the audience's every question with accuracy, honesty, and brevity. In fact, the multitude of questions should underscore again to you the audience's genuine interest in your ideas.

⇨ To put it succinctly: You fired us up.

Mention the ongoing value of what the speaker had to say.

⇨ I had no idea that what you planned to say in last week's New Orleans session would change my career goals, and in fact, my life.

⇨ Fred Graysonen came up to me after your presentation and said simply, "Powerful. Let's do it." That comment from him can be the start of an entire new direction for our company.

⇨ For so long, we have needed to hear from a peer in the field who has actually made these strategies work in the local office. Your words will carry a lot of weight in our goal-setting sessions next month.

⇨ I plan to make my notes on your presentation a permanent part of my sales manual.

⇨ Your ideas are going to work for me; my desk is looking better already.

⇨ Our group will never be the same. We can't help but realize some return on the ideas you planted.

⇨ I think that we will see a real turnaround in the attitude of our service department because of the genuineness of your message.

⇨ It's been a week now, and I still hear comments in the cafeteria and hallways about your presentation. I think your ideas have already become a permanent part of our culture.

Offer to refer the speaker's name to others, if you're in a position to do so.

⇨ I plan to pass your name on to the program chairman for next year. Even in two programs, we won't begin to hear all you know about this most important topic.

⇨ Several other regions could certainly benefit from this program. I intend to forward information to them about how they can contact you directly.

⇨ I'll assume you don't mind that I want to drop my regional directors a note, suggesting that they contact you directly for other follow-up programs.

⇨ If you ever need a reference for someone who has had his head in the sand for the past decade and doesn't know who you are, give me a call. I'll be happy to tell him or her what you've done for our organization.

⇨ Your name will be on the tip of my tongue for others looking for a unique presentation on this subject.

⇨ I plan to keep your brochure and my notes on your session permanently so that I can share them with colleagues in the months to come.

❖ ❖ ❖

Dear Vernon,

What a special treat it was to hear you at BNA! Your outstanding program had to be a convention highlight for the entire audience. The program content was packed with an incredible amount of usable information. I particularly found helpful the "Ten Ingredients of a Successful Proposal." That formula should certainly improve my sales ratio in the immediate future!

Your delivery style, too, was both captivating and powerful. I could tell within the first thirty seconds that the audience became instantly eager to hear what you had to say, recognizing the immediate payoff of the ideas.

I plan to keep in touch with you and your contributions to the industry. Specifically, I intend to make my own local chapter aware of your availability and your strong message. In the meantime, best wishes for outstanding success in your groundbreaking work.

Sincerely,

❖ ❖ ❖

TO YOUR OWN STAFF

Guidelines and Alternate Phrasing

Begin with your overall commendation for the reader's effort, attitude, or results and then get specific in your praise.

⇨ If you're learning to ride a horse and you fall off, you must climb right back on and try again. It appears that that's just what you've done. Your sales record has never looked better—your sales in July were 20 percent above quota!

⇨ I want to take this opportunity to say how much I've appreciated the initiative you've taken in new roles over the last few months. As coordinator and receptionist, you've shown a sense of responsibility, a dedication to accuracy with scheduling, and resourcefulness in handling conflicts.

⇨ Under your excellent leadership, the team has continued to shine as the most capable of the region. Your record of completed projects is outstanding.

⇨ Thank you for your empathy, sound judgment, and skill last week in handling the unfortunate situation at the Cordell site. With no time to prepare, you immediately took control of the dazed visitors, minimizing the potential for panic and even legal liabilities.

⇨ Your persuasiveness is to be commended. Until you assumed the position, we had great difficulty in getting participation from community volunteers. This year, I understand that 70 percent of the staff were unpaid adults and teenagers interested in seeing this program work in our city.

⇨ I want to commend you on the excellent job you did in evaluating our recent purchase of property in the Allen community. You exhibited unwavering commitment to the stated goals while aggressively pursuing a new way of looking at the revenue potential.

Name the various individuals involved if commending a large group or department. At the least, list their names specifically on your distribution list rather than using an "all-purpose" label.

Avoid any negative comments about the situation that may detract from the praise. For example, if you're commending the reader for an excellent proposal presentation to a customer, don't mention that the key decisionmaker didn't bother to glance through it in the briefing meeting.

Stay focused on the reader and keep yourself out of the picture. You don't want to sound as though you are tooting your own horn of leadership. Use the "you" approach rather than "we."

⇨ You have certainly made us all look good.

⇨ Your professionalism was quite evident in this tense situation.

⇨ You used sound judgment that signifies clear thinking.

⇨ Your integrity and honesty in all such situations impress upon our customers again and again why they should return to our doors.

⇨ Your individual talents will always make the difference in how successful the company becomes.

If you can say so truthfully, mention any personal or career benefit for the reader that you think will come of the effort.

⇨ I'm very pleased to contribute my support to your efforts in other locations. Please call on me for any help I can provide.

⇨ Sing your praises around the region, I will.

⇨ I think this new experience will enable you to handle far more responsibilities than we've thus far given you. I'm looking forward to giving you other assignments that will continue to stretch your abilities.

⇨ I will not hesitate to recommend you in any capacity that requires your expertise and self-motivation.

⇨ You have the dedication and drive that we like to see at Hilton Associates.

⇨ Such effort can't go unnoticed and unrewarded in our organization. In my way of thinking, the sooner the better.

⇨ We're looking forward to the opportunity to increase your responsibilities to match your talents.

⇨ We have exciting plans for your future here at Bechtel.

❖ ❖ ❖

Dear Silvan:

I want to express my sincere appreciation for the outstanding manner in which you have performed your usual duties during these recent weeks, as well as the responsibilities for the day-to-day operations since Mr. Nizte's sudden resignation.

Your cheerful demeanor and enthusiastic personality, combined with an exceptionally positive work ethic, have won you the respect and admiration of all your co-workers. We all noted the long hours required to cover the extra telecommunication equipment installations and the accompanying operator training.

Especially, I want to mention how you flawlessly orchestrated the April 5–6 Region IX management meeting. Your meticulous attention to every travel and meeting site detail made this function a totally enjoyable and productive session for the 28 managers who attended. This was, by far, the most successful meeting in recent memory.

Please accept this letter as a slightly more tangible expression of the esteem and gratitude with which I view your work here at Hartbro.

Sincerely,

❖ ❖ ❖

Dear Marty:

Congratulations for winning over Fenton Lybrand, Inc. I understand that the key players over there on the account had all but taken our proposal out of the running until you edged your foot in the door and initiated the series of meetings to all three levels of management involved in the decision.

From those of our own team who sat in on your presentations, I've heard that your technical knowledge of the AATC configuration and the potential applications for their software choices wooed them immediately to reconsider us. I know such technical presentations can be overwhelming for lay decisionmakers, so obviously you had the correct mix of technical information and day-to-day operational benefits.

Please pass on my comments to Shirley Tellspen and Drew Howard for their support in actually drafting the proposal.

As you can imagine, several senior executives have been watching the progress of this effort during the past 18 months. I plan to see that you and your team get as much recognition for this as you deserve.

Sincerely,

❖ ❖ ❖

Dear Silas:

On behalf of the organization, I thank you for your time and effort in resolving the five-month Drayton situation. Drayton is a very technical and demanding customer. But through your continuous efforts in helping them to articulate their problems and concerns and to identify and correct their diagnostic procedures, they are now aggressively purchasing our newest products.

Additionally, our suggestion to them to stay current with maintenance has significantly improved their operations, and they have the productivity figures to prove it.

We appreciate your follow-through and sincere commitment on the customer's behalf. Employees like you keep us in business.

Sincerely,

❖ ❖ ❖

TO OTHERS FOR OUTSTANDING SERVICE

Guidelines and Alternate Phrasing

Commend the outstanding service performed. Get specific with details about that service so that the reader knows what you consider "extra" effort. You may also want to mention why you are in a position to recognize superior service. Such a statement makes your comments more credible and more valuable to the employee. Remember that these letters often go in an employee's personnel file and, at the least, they are shared with colleagues and supervisors.

⇨ You do excellent work. My attendance at your seminar was most enjoyable primarily because of the fine service and accommodations in your resort facilities. The physical fitness center is equipped as well as most membership gyms.

⇨ Your service was exceptional last week when I dined in your restaurant, arriving half hour late for my reservations and with two extra guests. Not only did you seat us without complaint on this busy evening, you also saw to it that we were served promptly so that we could still make our later appointment.

⇨ Your people obviously take the quality issue seriously. Two days ago I was in your store and spoke with Marge Hatfield about . . .

⇨ I recently attended a four-day meeting at your site August 9–12. From the moment of my registration to my departure in the hotel's complimentary shuttle, it was evident that you and your entire staff "had your act together." Even during the Friday morning electrical storm, you seemed genuinely concerned for the comfort and safety of the guests.

⇨ I wanted to let you know how much I appreciate the extra time and care you put into preparing my graphics for the development study we recently submitted to SynTech on such a short deadline. With little more than a day's notice, your staff (Jim and Janet) created a special application of their software to give the special effect necessary.

If you're commending a group of several people, try to include the name of each. People like to feel that you have remembered and singled out their individual contribution.

⇨ Please pass on my comments to George, who also took care of several publication details on the project.

⇨ I know that your capable staff, specifically Margaret Hanson and John Blakeley, contributed to your effectiveness with their behind-the-scenes coordination.

❖ ❖ ❖

Dear Ms. Warner:

I echo the congratulations that certainly must be coming to you from many of those in the industry who recognize superb journalism when they see it. The recent article you contributed to *Insight America* represents the best of our U.S. efforts to inform and educate the families of disaster victims. Although I read widely and have, as a result, devoured numerous stories on such work done by the agencies you highlight in your article, yours by far was the most thoroughly researched and accurate feature.

My sincere thanks for *not* doing the usual journalistic fluff piece.

Sincerely,

❖ ❖ ❖

❖ ❖ ❖

Dear Mr. Kakawa:

It is not standard procedure that I write letters of appreciation after I return from conventions, especially to those outside my organization; however, neither was your effort on my behalf standard procedure in your position. I'm referring to the excellent service you gave when I had difficulty with my rental car while staying at your hotel.

After my inability to persuade the rental car agency to replace the car at 2:00 A.M., you left your cozy desk in the middle of a rain storm to pick me up in your personal vehicle. And I was 45 miles from your location! Not only would you not let me pay you for the trip, you made special arrangements with room service, after hours, to bring a warm snack and coffee to my room. And then much to my surprise the next morning, you had been able to coordinate the replacement of my rental car.

Believe me, in all my travels around the country, this excellent service has not been matched anywhere. Needless to say, you have my business any time I'm staying overnight in your area. I also plan to send a copy of this letter to your hotel management in case they are unaware of your fine attitude and dedication to customer service.

My sincere thanks,

❖ ❖ ❖

Dear Ms. Crawford:

Thank you for taking the time to meet with us last Tuesday and give us a tour of your facilities. We certainly appreciated the opportunity to see your set-up firsthand and to learn of your current procedures.

I especially want to mention the helpfulness of your assistant, Sharon Summers. She was most accommodating in pulling our files to show us what information she had retained on our various product lines. And then as a big time-saver to us, she provided the necessary forms to add our organization to your source list for the upcoming Hile project.

You have both been genuinely helpful and positive in allowing us to offer our services to your organization. We appreciate that sincerely.

Yours truly,

❖ ❖ ❖

RESPONSE TO A COMMENDATION

Guidelines and Alternate Phrasing

Acknowledge your pleasure in receiving the commendation.

⇨ Thank you for letting us know of the exceptional service you received in our hotel.

⇨ We are so pleased that you received your merchandise on time and at a reasonable cost. As you noted in your letter, Jeff Herman cares about customer service.

⇨ We appreciate so much your time in dropping us a note about how well Mark Jones took care of cleaning your damaged apartment last week.

⇨ This morning's mail brought your letter and a smile to our face.

⇨ How nice of you to write and let us know of the manner in which Nell Johnson has been servicing your account. She's been with our organization for 12 years, and her comprehensive knowledge of the business certainly works to the client's advantage.

⇨ Commendations such as yours of Margaret Frazier's help on the Boyton property certainly contribute to management's morale in our slowing economy.

Thank the reader for taking the time and making the effort to let you know about the exceptional service.

⇨ Your letter took time, and we appreciate your letting us know of your experience here.

⇨ Your effort in dropping us the nice letter is appreciated.

⇨ Thank you for writing to let us know how we're performing.

⇨ Feedback such as yours—though time-consuming for you—is an invaluable part of our staff training. Thank you so much.

⇨ We appreciate your time in writing. Although we want our excellent service to be commonplace here, we do appreciate knowing that our customers recognize the extra efforts.

Promise to pass on the comments if they were intended for subordinates or other colleagues.

⇨ We will let Mr. Hartford know of your letter.

⇨ We will pass on your comments to both the employees involved. Thanks to you, they will have a nice day when we call them in to commend them on the effort you mentioned in your letter.

⇨ Such letters in their personnel files mean a great deal at review time.

⇨ We like to reward our employees for looking after the customer's needs in an exceptional way. Your letter helps us take note of these efforts.

⇨ We have mentioned your comments in this week's staff meeting. Be assured that they were meaningful and much appreciated by those involved.

❖ ❖ ❖

Dear Mr. Rae:

Thank you for your kind remarks about one of our employees, Ms. Sandy Vermuellen. It's nice to know that you have taken the time from your usual tasks to acknowledge Ms. Vermuellen's attention to good customer service. We agree that she exercised sound judgment in handling your communication needs at such a late hour. We're equally pleased that the matter turned out so well for you with your client.

I can assure you that we value Ms. Vermuellen as an employee and will let her know of your nice comments.

Cordially,

❖ ❖ ❖

❖ ❖ ❖

Dear Ms. Monroe:

I received your letter about Gustavus Emory's actions on the TRAB project in Miami last month. We agree with you wholeheartedly that he has accomplished much in a very demanding and critical situation. Yes, he was entirely responsible for the success of the work, and we have placed your letter of commendation in his personnel file.

We also want to take this opportunity to thank you for writing to let us know how the community feels about the completion of this project. Those displeased are always most vocal in their complaints, and the average citizen tends to be silent when things are going well. Thank you for voicing your support. Our day will be brighter because you wrote.

Sincerely,

❖ ❖ ❖

COMPLAINTS

If your idea of a complaint letter is "to tell someone off," then that kind of letter is not difficult to write. Your adrenalin is usually flowing and emotionally charged words come all too easy.

But if your purpose in complaining is to get corrective action, to leave the relationship intact, and even to build goodwill, then a complaint letter is difficult to write. Consider the complaint letter a request for action, and your tone will generally be much more effective than otherwise. A clear statement of the problem and a firm, yet pleasant, request for *specific* action will go a long way in resolving unpleasant situations.

ABOUT POOR SERVICE/DELIVERY/ PERFORMANCE/PRODUCT/ADVERTISING/COMMUNICATION

Guidelines and Alternate Phrasing

Summarize the problem briefly, specifically, and clearly. Include enough detail so that a previously uninvolved reader can understand what has happened, but avoid irrelevant detail that will only obscure the real issues. In most situations, a once-upon-a-time format is not an appropriate arrangement of facts or issues.

State what specific action you want from the reader. If you are writing to a superior within your own organization, suggest a suitable arrangement or resolution in terms of benefit to the company—reduced costs, increased profits, improved productivity or quality, and so forth.

⇨ Please send a replacement part immediately.

⇨ Our position is that your organization should reimburse the entire amount of $4,550.

⇨ We ask that you correct the situation by closing the old account and establishing an entirely new one.

⇨ We suggest that you discuss with your staff the importance of a prompt response in such emergency situations.

⇨ Please credit our account for the entire $489, along with the shipping charges of $42.98.

⇨ We will appreciate it if you will confirm to us in writing your plans for future work on our site.

⇨ I'm simply asking for your investigation of the situation and a response from your organization about your position on the matter.

⇨ In the future, please send all the authorizations directly to me for my signature before beginning any work projects on our behalf.

⇨ We have written you about these subscriptions on two previous occasions. If the changes cannot be made by the next issue (March), please cancel all three subscriptions.

⇨ If we can make these two changes in the printed form, I'm confident that we can reduce our internal costs by as much as 50 percent.

⇨ Please designate only two representatives from your division to attend future meetings; this limited number of participants should decrease the time necessary for discussion and improve the overall quality of the decisions made by our most experienced staff members.

Assume a confident tone about a suitable resolution. Avoid aggressive or sarcastic statements. Your letter should sound firm and factual, not emotional. If it becomes necessary to write additional letters, become stronger in stating your next course of action while maintaining an objective tone.

⇨ We feel confident that you can correct the structure with minimal expense.

⇨ You have always been fair in your dealings with our organization, and we have every confidence that you will decide to make an adjustment in this situation.

⇨ I'll assume you will rectify the problem unless I hear from you otherwise.

⇨ If we haven't heard from you by August 5, we will assume you prefer to cancel the project altogether. I hope that's not the case.

⇨ We appreciate your attention to this detail.

⇨ We are eager to hear how you think the problem can be corrected.

⇨ Let us know if you need further information to verify the claims we have presented here.

⇨ We are looking forward to continuing our relationship on future projects.

⇨ Huffco expects to work with your organization until the situation is resolved.

⇨ We believe that we can count on your best efforts in this regard.

⇨ May we count on your attention to this detail in the future?

⇨ Thank you for your usual attention to our concerns.

Be sure to attach any necessary documentation for your claims such as invoices, receipts, canceled checks, order numbers, authorizations, and so forth.

❖ ❖ ❖

Dear Mr. Horton:

On June 9, I damaged my car at our 2390 Fairview headquarters when making a left turn near a brick island with sharp-edge steel cones protruding from it. The cones are not high enough to be visible from the driver's side of approaching vehicles. In my opinion, the garage entrance is hazardous and has caused problems for several employees, who have also filed incident reports such as the one I filed on June 9.

Would you please investigate the hazardous island and authorize some corrective change to its structure?

The Security manager says he has no authority to correct the problem and has suggested only that I file an insurance claim. The insurance company contends that because the brick island is stationary, I am at fault. Consequently, I have had to absorb the $168 dollar auto repair bill.

Thank you for helping to make this a safer parking garage for all our employees.

Sincerely,

❖ ❖ ❖

Dear Mr. Winger:

We are experiencing problems with several Hobart valets' reckless driving in our garage—problems such as spinning tires, speeding, and driving with car doors open. To date, there have been no accidents or injuries reported by our tenants, but we want to notify you formally of your responsibility in this situation.

Please see that your valets are reminded of the safety hazards involved. Also, we ask that you no longer park cars in more than one entrance ramp on week days and that you leave at least one entrance ramp open at all times during the weekend.

I have every confidence that these problems can be remedied with both your attention and mine.

Sincerely,

❖ ❖ ❖

Dear Mr. Hightower:

We are very concerned about the quality of the plumbing fixtures and condition of the drain lines at our St. Louis offices. On two previous occasions our offices have been flooded because of leaks. On March 9, a third leak occurred that caused considerable damage to our printing operations, our printing equipment, and the office furnishings. The total repair and replacement costs amounted to $3,459.

We have attached all the invoices for your reimbursement. Please let us know immediately if you prefer that we follow some other procedure for handling the damage claims.

Additionally, as a matter of precaution against a reoccurrence and possible injury to our employees, we ask that you do the following: replace the old drain lines above our printing operations, and recheck the newer lines in other locations.

Would you please notify us immediately when the work is complete and let us know of other precautions that you plan to take.

Sincerely,

❖ ❖ ❖

❖ ❖ ❖

Dear Martin:

One of my employees, Winston Walkman, attended your June 6 class in St. Louis and was very disappointed with the quality of the course. Specifically, the content did not match the course outline in your advertisements. Although the agenda listed three topics having to do with conflict resolution, less than half an hour was spent addressing those issues. Additionally, the instructor's knowledge was inadequate to deal with the technical questions from the class.

I spoke to the instructor briefly at the end of the class, and he agreed that the questions and customer situations brought up in the class situation were beyond his experience.

In light of the expectations raised by your course announcement, I think we are entitled to a refund of our $350 registration fee. A copy of that registration form is attached.

Should you need to discuss the class situation with me or Mr. Walkman in more detail, you may reach us at 346-2209.

Sincerely,

❖ ❖ ❖

Dear Sir or Madam:

The four lamps we ordered from you on May 9 were shipped with improperly fitting globes. I'm returning the lamps for an immediate refund of $826.78. Because our first order took three weeks to arrive, we have decided to make an alternate selection at a local store rather than to wait for your replacement shipment.

Attached is a copy of our May 9 order, the customer receipt, and our canceled check. Thank you for processing this refund immediately.

Sincerely,

❖ ❖ ❖

RESPONDING TO A COMPLAINT WHEN ADMITTING FAULT _____

Guidelines and Alternate Phrasing

Focus immediately on any positive action you have taken to solve the problem. Even if you have had to turn the situation over to another person or department for handling, let the reader know that and promise to follow up.

⇨ We have now corrected the situation you mentioned in your July 7 letter.

⇨ Your letter arrived May 2, and we immediately went to work to correct the missing-authorization situation you detailed.

⇨ By the time you receive this response to your concern about the Fuhtii matter, you should have received our replacement shipment of tubing.

⇨ As soon as I got off the phone with you, I located Mr. Hytacci to investigate the situation you mentioned. As a result, we have already been able to verify the information you gave us and have corrected the misunderstanding about our clean-up schedule.

⇨ We were concerned to learn of your disappointment with our construction work at the Overton facilities and have passed your comments on to our subcontractor, Schwartz Inc. They have promised to send their crews back to your site on Friday, May 12, to . . .

⇨ We have forwarded your letter about the performance of our spot remover to the distributor who sold you the product. As you may know, we have no control over how various merchants advertise the product, but we are definitely concerned about misleading our customers. I'll be in touch with you again after I've spoken to the distributor about . . .

⇨ Your claim for expenses has been forwarded to me for handling; we have, therefore, enclosed our check for $478 to cover the cost of the damaged windows.

Give a brief explanation of how the mistake happened or the situation occurred. An explanation adds credibility to your resolution; at least, the reader knows that you have made the effort to investigate the problem. That in itself gives confidence about a resolution. And don't hesitate to admit an error when that's the case. Such honesty often diffuses the customer's anger more than excuses and vague platitudes about customer service.

⇨ The incident revolved around our attendant's tardiness in picking up the registration ticket that you left at the front desk.

⇨ One of our secretaries inadvertently mislaid the forms in another customer's open file. We regret that error.

⇨ We simply did not follow through as we should have with repeated phone calls to make you aware of the possibility of severe weather conditions and possible delays.

⇨ Our investigators have completed their research and simply were unable to locate the items you reported missing. We're at a loss as to what could have happened to them. Nevertheless, we . . .

⇨ Our team leader had an emergency personal situation to develop late Thursday and rushed out of the office without remembering to tell anyone of the pending authorization. I'm sorry for the confusion.

⇨ With so many people having input into the decision, it's often difficult to know exactly who was to inform you of the outcome of our deliberations. Regardless, the responsibility was ours—someone should have phoned you immediately that day.

⇨ There is certainly no excuse for the difficulties you encountered while trying to have an iron sent to your room.

⇨ We made a mistake and we ask for your understanding.

⇨ You are correct; we did make an error in your last billing. The correct amount should have been $1,489. We can either credit your account or send a refund check. Phone us at 344-9999 to let us know which you prefer.

⇨ Unfortunately, in our efforts to get the funds to you faster, we failed to take the time to verify the address against your latest payment coupon mailed to our Shreveport office.

⇨ Our ultimate goal is to automate the entire process to improve the accuracy and speed with which we can respond to your questions. In the meantime, we are experiencing some confusion during our learning process. We hope you'll understand and forgive us for the inaccurate information on this occasion.

Empathize with the reader about the difficulty or frustration of the situation. Avoid vague generalities; instead, add one or two statements that show the reader that you really understand the specific inconveniences involved.

⇨ I do know that you have had to make four long-distance calls to our headquarters to get the matter corrected. May we reimburse you for these?

⇨ Certainly, you must have been disappointed in the delay and the missed deadline for your report.

⇨ You probably have been frustrated to no end, trying to find the appropriate person to address this concern!

⇨ Of course, this mistake has probably caused you several hours of rework, and I'm sure that increased your distress.

⇨ Can we in some way alleviate the burdensome chore of reviewing the employment paperwork that our error caused?

⇨ The malfunctioning doors must have created a major traffic jam during your peak customer hours.

⇨ I'm sure the two delays created frustration around your office for several days.

⇨ I regret that your final report had to be delayed while we collected the correct data for you.

Be sure that your tone and comments underscore to your reader that you value his or her goodwill. Specifically, that means to avoid "fight" phrases such as "you must assume" or "evidently, you were unaware" or "I'm sure you'll have to agree"; readers don't like to be told what they know, feel, and must do.

⇨ This service—or lack of it—is certainly not typical of our organization, and I sincerely hope you will give us a future opportunity to show you the true meaning of hospitality.

⇨ We will make every effort to ensure that your next transaction with us is handled efficiently and courteously.

⇨ We want to assure you that the next time you do business with us, we'll be eager to show you how much your business means to us.

⇨ We promise to make your next visit to our store an enjoyable one.

⇨ We are concerned that the poster insert created controversy. It was not our aim nor intent to offend any individual's moral viewpoint or sensitivities. Evidently, we unknowingly did so, and we apologize.

❖ ❖ ❖

Marion:

Today I have completed your application for tracking petroleum technology, and I will begin training your staff to use the program on Wednesday, July 21.

Please accept my apology for the delay. After I determined my estimated time in completing the project, my supervisor asked me to concentrate on two other developmental projects necessary to the critical drilling work going on in the Gulf. Quite honestly, I just had to lay your project aside for three days. I realize the significance of your own application to you and your department's schedule, and I regret that my own delay wreaked havoc with your schedule! I appreciate your patience.

I do look forward to the staff training and think we can make great productivity strides for your team.

Sincerely,

❖ ❖ ❖

Dear Ms. Crump:

I have read your February 9 letter and understand your distress. Your fine article made a notable contribution to our journal, and I'm sorry we have not returned the favor. I realize that we cannot undo what was done, but rest assured that any inquiries made to our office in reference to the article have been directed to you and will continue to be referred to you.

We have a public relations firm on retainer, and the firm selects one or two articles from each issue to publicize. Although the press release based on your article did not claim that our journal had conducted the research study mentioned in your article, apparently many editors of other journals who picked up the piece inferred that we had. Obviously, the results should clearly have been attributed to your organization, and I apologize that they were not. This incident is a vivid reminder of the need for effective communication. We have now discussed the matter with our PR firm, and they are aware of the importance of attributing research to the correct source.

Again, my apologies. If you would like us to include a notice in an upcoming issue about the continuation of your research project, we will be happy to do so.

Sincerely,

❖ ❖ ❖

❖ ❖ ❖

Dear Mr. Stockton:

I am pleased to say that we have been able to get your son's check-cashing privileges restored at both Avis and SuperMart, effective immediately. Of course, we've also waived the penalty charged for returned checks; we'll simply hold the voided check until the new one from your son arrives.

Thank you for bringing the situation to our attention. Upon investigation, we found that because of a clerical error on our part your son's two checks were never presented to the Duncanville Bank for payment. The checks were mistakenly placed in the "Return" batch rather than the "Forward" batch.

I realize our error caused embarrassment on your part, not to mention the time it took to go to both merchants and retrieve the checks. I hope our phone calls to these two merchants to accept responsibility for the error and to restore your son's check-cashing privileges have somewhat restored his confidence in our bank.

We take great pride in maintaining a reputation for excellence, and you, our customer, should never experience such situations. When they happen, we do our best to set things right because we sincerely appreciate your relationship with our bank.

Sincerely,

❖ ❖ ❖

Dear Mr. and Mrs. Shawn:

I have just received your letter about your embarrassing experience at the Saturday Breakfast Brunch hosted by our organization on October 5.

The club manager and I had a very lengthy and detailed discussion about the incident, and I can assure you that she now understands the proper way to have handled the situation. She herself will be writing you a letter shortly to apologize.

But thanks to your comments, I feel certain that the service has improved. Should you not receive the attention you deserve on your next visit, please phone me directly at 333-0098.

Please accept the enclosed brunch coupons for a date and time of your choice. We are eager to show you that we value your patronage.

Sincerely,

❖ ❖ ❖

RESPONDING TO A COMPLAINT WITHOUT ADMITTING FAULT _____

Guidelines and Alternate Phrasing

Acknowledge the complaint even if you don't consider the problem your fault.

⇨ Thank you for the January 10 letter about the Fairfield incident. We appreciate the opportunity to respond to your observations.

⇨ We have received your letter describing the difficulty you are having with your NRT system.

⇨ We've reviewed your letter about how your Finley account has been handled by the Atlanta office.

⇨ We appreciate your taking the time to write us about your views on our plans for developing the Grayson property.

⇨ Your letter arrived this week just as we have completed our test-marketing on a new irrigation system, similar to the one you have had some experience with at your own location.

⇨ We were sorry to hear of your frustrating experience while touring our facilities last week.

⇨ We were distressed to learn that you were disappointed with the way in which your equipment was serviced at the Dejon Center.

⇨ Heton and Kline Associates welcomes letters such as yours on the experiences customers have while evaluating our training facilities and resources. Such comments give us opportunity to review how and why we do things the way we do.

State your views on the situation.

⇨ The loss of the manufacturing system is directly related to the fact that the software does not provide the necessary functions required by your evaluation committee.

⇨ We believe that part of the problem stems from the original analysis reported to us. . . .

⇨ As a result of our investigation, we could find no cause for the problems you described in your letter.

⇨ We do not agree that the misunderstanding developed from a lack of technical expertise on the part of our representatives.

⇨ We've investigated the situation, and frankly we can't find the culprit in this incident. We have eliminated several possibilities, however. The _____, _____, and _____ are certainly working properly in all our tests on the system.

⇨ Definitely, there are discrepancies in the details recalled by our own service department. Our two technicians on duty still insist that . . .

Offer anything you are willing to do to improve or correct the situation, but be careful about admitting fault if you could be held liable for damages or promises.

⇨ Although we do not agree that it is our responsibility as a distributor to replace the merchandise, we are making an exception in this case.

⇨ Regardless of where the problem originated, we have decided to reimburse you for the damage.

⇨ We can write a letter on your behalf to explain to your investors the necessity for this additional verification procedure.

⇨ Even though the warranty with this product does not cover the labor charges, we are not billing you for this $679 amount.

⇨ While I appreciate the difficult situation in which your organization must operate, we cannot assume the responsibility of . . .

Try to retain the reader's goodwill and re-establish a "business as usual" relationship.

⇨ We hope you will reconsider your intention to close your account with us.

⇨ Please let us know the next time you're on our grounds, and we will make a special effort to show you the appropriate product lines.

⇨ We hope you'll give us another opportunity to serve you.

⇨ We want to invite you and your staff for a return visit under more pleasant conditions.

⇨ We fully expect to have improved service upon your return visit.

⇨ Mark Hatford looks forward to working with you on another project, should you need our services again.

⇨ Thank you for your cooperation during this transition time.

⇨ We appreciate your patience and loyalty when things like this happen.

⇨ We value your business and want you to know we will do everything in our power to provide the service you deserve.

⇨ It's our intention to make all the possible improvements while continuing to provide this service at such a low cost.

⇨ With your feedback and our concern, our procedures should be much improved. We thank you.

⇨ Thank you for allowing us to review the procedure.

⇨ Thank you for your efforts in letting us know of the situation. As a result, the future working relationship between our organizations should be much improved.

⇨ A better product at the lowest possible cost is our goal.

⇨ Thank you for letting us hear from you. We value your comments and will act accordingly.

❖ ❖ ❖

Dear Ms. O'Connor:

Thank you for you letter about the delays in receiving your orders from our company. I think I can identify some areas for improvement in processing your emergency orders that are occasionally faxed to our Rourker office.

Upon my investigation of the situation, I've discovered that your Maxwell office has frequently held or returned invoices to us due to incomplete purchase order numbers on the faxes you've sent us. We will appreciate your help in including on your faxed orders all the necessary numbers your purchasing department requires to pay the invoices. Then, we can ship your orders of the stock items almost immediately and bill that same day.

Another suggestion is to designate one person from your office to act as liaison on the emergency orders faxed to us. That should prevent duplicate and burdensome paperwork for both of us.

My main concern is to fill your orders quickly and accurately. Thank you for your help and patience in working out an efficient processing system between our companies.

Sincerely,

❖ ❖ ❖

Dear Mr. Hartley:

Thank you for your comments on our customer feedback card about your recent visit to our resort. Customer opinions are the one valuable source of identifying situations that need improvement within our programs.

Our limited number of available ski instructors during your stay was due primarily to the extra-large, holiday-weekend crowd. Even though we called in our contract instructors to fill the demand, I'm sure some guests such as yourself were disappointed in their availability schedules. On your next trip, if you will write ahead about the number of guests and your intentions to take instruction, we will make every effort to meet your needs.

We are now discussing with the reservations office assistant the need to give very complete information when callers ask about ski conditions and the classes offered here. We also try to clarify to our callers that we cannot predict a last-minute change in weather conditions. Our employee has been reminded that courtesy is in order at all times, no matter how stressful the situation.

Again, thank you for your comments. Just drop us a note or phone before your next visit, and we will see to it that you have reservations for your personal ski instructor.

Sincerely,

❖ ❖ ❖

❖ ❖ ❖

Dear Keith:

To alleviate the inconvenience of being unable to locate an engineer on site, we have now provided all engineers with a digital pager. When necessary, you will be able to page them at #4444. If you are unable to get in touch with someone, call base at #4889, and someone there will contact an engineer and have him or her return your calls.

I hope this resolves most, if not all, difficulties in trying to communicate with our engineering staff. Thank you for your feedback.

Sincerely,

❖ ❖ ❖

Dear Mr. Taylor:

Thank you for your January 2 letter and the photographs showing the Relon being used on an elbow. The excessive shrinking visible on your photos does indeed make the product look poor by comparison to the Fulgate material shown adjacent to it. I can imagine how frustrating it must have been to watch the tape pull back as you added heat.

In any case, we will be happy to refund your money on the tape your purchased from us. We'll simply issue you a refund check, or you may use the enclosed credit voucher against your next order with us. Please let us know which alternative you prefer.

I want to try to shed a little history on the evolution of our tape product so that you will have a better understanding of its shrinking characteristics. . . . This new product, then, seems to be a good compromise for the uses our customers normally cite, and we've been able to price it much lower than the Fulgate tape. Of course, with uses other than those we had in mind with the product's design, problems do arise, such as the one you mentioned.

I have forwarded your letter to our product engineering section, and I will phone you when I have a response from them. In the meanwhile, we suggest that for your purposes you try a wider roll of tape with at least a six-inch overlap.

In closing, let me again say how much I appreciate your bringing this matter to our attention. We realize that it would have been much easier just to stop buying our product than to write a letter and send photos. We certainly appreciate customers such as you, who often offer ideas for innovative improvements for our products.

Thank you.

Sincerely,

❖ ❖ ❖

CONDOLENCES

To offer condolences at the time of sorrow gives us an opportunity to add the human touch in a high-tech world.

When we are genuinely moved by another's loss, we often find it difficult to put that emotion into words to a colleague or an associate we've known only in a formal, business relationship. Our dilemma revolves around several issues: We want to show personal concern without stepping over the bounds of our relationship. We don't want our words to create pain for the reader, yet we want to show our emotions to the degree that the colleague knows we sincerely empathize. Consequently, at an uncomfortable loss for words appropriate to our relationship and the situation, we tend to lapse into cliches, thus sounding insincere or even cold.

Letters of condolence, instead, should be sincere personal statements of our feelings of concern and/or loss.

TO BUSINESS ASSOCIATE UPON DEATH OF A LOVED ONE

Guidelines and Alternate Phrasing

Express your regret over the death, but avoid dwelling on the details of the illness or tragedy.

➪ We were sorry to hear that your precious wife had passed away after such a long illness.

➪ John, how can we tell you how shocked and upset we are over your daughter's accident.

➪ Selena gave us the news about Larry's tragic accident. The situation has been on our mind ever since. We are so upset.

➪ We heard of the plane crash last Monday, but didn't learn that Tom was a passenger until late last night. We are so sorry.

➪ I was so sorry to hear about your husband's death. You must be devastated by the news, and we want you to know we are thinking of you in this difficult time.

➪ Please know that our thoughts have been with you ever since the word came about your son and his family.

Honor the loved one by offering some specific praise. When you're unacquainted with the deceased, you may simply pass on comments from others or comment on the loss of the relationship in a general way.

⇨ Although we had not had the opportunity to meet your daughter, we've heard you say the relationship was a close one. You can be grateful for that love between you and those memories.

⇨ I've heard you comment often about how supportive Mac was when you had to travel so much with your job. He must have been the kind of understanding husband most women hope to have.

⇨ As a couple, you always looked so lovingly happy when I noticed you together at company functions. You must feel the loss very deeply.

⇨ She was always so pleasant and helpful to me the times I found it necessary to phone your home after hours.

⇨ The photographs you have on your desk reveal what a beautiful young woman she was. I know she understood how proud you always were of her achievements throughout her schooling and beyond.

⇨ The years you've had together, I'm sure, will always seem too short. Happy marriages are a blessing some take for granted.

⇨ The glow on your face daily as you reported to work tells me that your home situation was always a happy, supportive environment. How much you will miss that, I'm sure.

⇨ Please take comfort in the fact that you did everything you could for him during the long illness. I recall your devotion in so many ways—the phone calls, the cards, the weekend trips. Parents always know when they are loved, as yours were.

Offer any help you or the organization can provide.

⇨ If we can help with any hotel arrangements for out-of-town relatives traveling to the memorial service, let us know.

⇨ If I can provide assistance through our legal department, please call on me.

⇨ I'm sure the estate details are complex and varied. If you need assistance, we have an expert on staff who can possibly offer you advice when the time comes to make further decisions.

⇨ If we can provide temporary assistance for the children's care while you must be out of town, both Joan Black and I are free for the weekend. I'll phone you later in the week to see what you decide.

Handwrite your letter on personal stationery to add a warmer touch.

❖ ❖ ❖

Dear Conroy:

The Atlanta office called this morning with news of your wife's tragic accident. I am so sorry.

During our recent time together at the Orlando convention, I recall your breaking away early from our dinner several evenings to phone her. You two must have been very close, and it should give you some comfort that you made such an effort to stay in touch with your family as often as possible even while traveling.

Please don't worry about the upcoming appointment we had scheduled for next month. Your schedule, I'm sure, will need to be reworked, and I can get any necessary regional reports from other sources.

I'll pray God's comfort for you and the children in this time.

Sincerely,

❖ ❖ ❖

Dear Ms. Phillips:

Tim Johnson mentioned in our staff meeting this morning that your husband had just passed away after such a long illness. Please accept my sincerest sympathies.

I've heard others around the office who knew him comment on his jovial nature. And they also recall your telling of so many weekend golfing tournaments that you both participated in. I understand he was quite a golfer and made the game enjoyable for all who played with him. You will miss him, terribly, I know.

We have asked Margie Turner to take over the pending projects on your desk. Take the time you need.

Sincerely,

❖ ❖ ❖

TO FAMILY UPON DEATH OF A BUSINESS ASSOCIATE _____

Guidelines and Alternate Phrasing

Express your regret over the death, but avoid dwelling on the details of the illness or tragedy.

⇨ I was sorry to hear of the tragic accident.

⇨ The news of Vera's death came to me early yesterday morning. I was overwhelmed with sadness.

⇨ We learned of your husband's death when a manufacturing rep called on us last week. I'm so sorry we didn't hear sooner, in time to attend the memorial service.

⇨ We regret so much the news about your wife's illness and death.

⇨ Our entire staff has asked me to express to you our sincerest sympathies in the death of your husband.

⇨ Although we have expected to hear the news of John's death for the last several weeks, we were still struck with sadness when we received your call today.

⇨ Our thoughts are with you during these days of sadness. We were so sorry to hear of your grandson's accident.

Tell the family one or two things that you appreciated about the loved one.

⇨ Freda's pleasant attitude was contagious to us all.

⇨ Silvan's talent was exceeded by very few professionals in the industry.

⇨ His leadership and direction for the department went unquestioned. We had that much respect for his judgment.

⇨ We wish we had other employees like her, those who give their best every single day and don't care who gets the credit for the results.

⇨ I never heard her complain about anybody's work or attitude while here. That in itself is remarkable.

⇨ She was kind, sensitive, and considerate of others' needs.

⇨ Although a quiet person, he was always listening for opportunities to support our ideas when the occasion arose.

⇨ Although Ellen was never a "life of the party" person, her thoughtfulness ran deep. When she did offer her opinion, her ideas were always well grounded and sensible. We depended on her a great deal.

⇨ She was thorough, capable, and courageous.

⇨ To the very end, we never heard her offer a comment that indicated she felt sorry for herself and her circumstances. She loved her family and every minute of her life with you.

⇨ She spoke so frequently around the office of you and her children. You all three were the light of her life. That must give you some comfort that she felt loved and loved you in return.

⇨ He recounted story after story of your weekend outings and family get-togethers. Obviously, you were the biggest part of his life, much more important than his job. That's as it should be.

Mention any memorial (book, flowers, monetary donation, memorial plaque or stone) that you are making on behalf of the deceased.

⇨ The flowers represent the beautiful memories Carol left behind.

⇨ We are sending flowers as an expression of our esteem for Ralph.

⇨ Our staff has placed a volume of _____ in our company library in Harvey's memory.

⇨ Gene's portrait will be hung in our executive meeting room as a constant reminder of his leadership in our organization.

⇨ Our check to the museum that Sherry so diligently worked to support should arrive shortly.

⇨ In honor of Kevin, we are forwarding a check to the American Cancer Society.

⇨ The flowers you have received are a small expression of the great loss we feel.

⇨ Please accept our small donation to the art fund as our way of saying thank you for the community pride Bill exemplified with his life.

Handwrite your letter on personal stationery to add a warmer touch.

❖ ❖ ❖

Dear Ms. Pelena and Children:

We want to express our deepest sympathy in the death of your husband and father. The heart attack was such a shock to us all in the office that we have gotten very little done since hearing the news.

In our office, there is the one individual that everyone gets along with and enjoys having around, no matter the occasion. Whether it was his constant reminders to drive carefully as we left the office, his welcome-back hug after our vacations, or his "now if I were in your shoes" advice on career moves, he acted like a father to us all. We will miss him.

As a small gesture of our admiration, we are sending a donation to the Heart Fund in his honor. Our thoughts are with you in this difficult adjustment.

Sincerely,

❖ ❖ ❖

Dear Mr. Graves:

I heard of Mary's death on the TV news, as soon as the hospital released the list of those involved in the accident. I want you to know how sorry I am; words can't express, I'm sure, how much you will feel the loss.

Although I didn't work closely with Mary, she had a fine reputation as a talented engineer who had contributed greatly to our organization. Her project team frequently commented on her creativity, her knack for reading a client's mind, and her willingness to work long hours to get the job done. I'm sure she was an equally devoted wife, mother, and friend.

We are sending flowers as a token of our memories of her. Please accept our sincere sympathy on your loss.

Sincerely,

❖ ❖ ❖

Dear Mr. Paton:

Last week while attending a management meeting in Hartford, I heard that your father had passed away after a long illness. I didn't want to let the news go by without expressing to you how much I appreciated him during our long years together at Texaco.

With any new job, there are always difficult adjustments, relationships that cause conflict, assignments that build stress. I had my share during those first few years, and your father was the individual who offered encouragement, support, and even advancement opportunities and referrals when it was within his power to do so. More than that career advice and networking, he became my friend, with all the camaraderie that label entails. Even though we hadn't stayed in close contact since his retirement, I drew great comfort in knowing he "was there" for me should I need to talk. My only great regret is that I didn't phone him more often in his last year or two.

Would you please express my sympathies to the other family members.

Sincerely,

❖ ❖ ❖

CONGRATULATIONS

A major part of any accomplishment, career milestone, or happy personal event is recognition from others. A letter from a colleague on such an occasion encourages, affirms, and rewards us for our labor, talent, or good fortune.

Be sensitive to times when a congratulatory note can cement a relationship, as well as allow you to recognize another's achievement or good sense. Such letters should be brief, specific, and genuine. Handwritten notes add that special warmth that wraps the sentiment with individual care.

AWARD/HONOR/DISTINCTION

Guidelines and Alternate Phrasing

Commend the reader on the award or honor.

⇨ Congratulations on being named "Woman of the Year."

⇨ We are so thrilled to learn that you have been recognized by your professional association for your contributions to the field.

⇨ We understand that your organization has been awarded the Fenmore Prize for its outstanding customer service, and we are so pleased.

⇨ I couldn't be happier to know that you have been named to the list of Fenmore's "Most Talented Professionals."

⇨ The "Manager of the Year" honor is quite a distinction—one you obviously have deserved for several years now.

⇨ Your father mentioned to me that you had been selected as UTA's "Senior of the Year." How pleased your parents are. My congratulations on an outstanding four years of diligent work.

⇨ Just a note to comment on your selection as "Customer Representative of the Month": I wholeheartedly agree with that choice.

⇨ You have finally been recognized for the talent I've observed in you for years now at ATC. Congratulations on making the list of ....

Mention one or two specific reasons he or she deserves the distinction.

⇨ You have taken a difficult situation and turned the tide against overwhelming odds.

⇨ The politics of the situation have been difficult to overcome; yet, I knew that eventually talent would win over high visibility.

⇨ I can't believe you have accomplished such a sales record in such an economically depressed industry.

⇨ For months, I've watched your work—creative, on-target, insightful.

⇨ Your professionalism is always evident in your dress, your communication, and your demeanor with clients—no matter what their attitude and behavior.

⇨ You have astonished us with your knowledge of the growing software applications for the industry.

⇨ We here have all commented on your resourcefulness in finding solutions to the problems we faced, specifically the Kline conflict and resolution.

⇨ Your pleasant attitude, your ability to get along with people in all walks of life, and your personal integrity make you the ideal choice for this award.

⇨ You have a clever way of motivating people to stretch them to their fullest potential—the highest evidence of leadership.

⇨ Your leadership and management skills, your amiable personality, and your commitment to hard work have made you the ideal choice.

⇨ You have worked long and hard on the membership drive this past year, making countless phone calls and walking many miles on our behalf.

⇨ No detail has been too small for your personal attention. That concentration has been the difference this year in the success of your programs.

Be enthusiastic and personal; don't make your letter sound like the typical boilerplate message sent to everyone.

❖ ❖ ❖

Dear Carey:

I received word last week that you have been named "Outstanding Engineer" for Bell-Plainview. That honor has been given to some outstanding talent in the past, many of the recipients having gone on to the ranks of senior management, where all of us in the industry can benefit from their expertise and insights.

Congratulations on having built that kind of reputation for yourself so early in your career. I understand that your project team has been extremely productive, as well as creative. Under less-than-desirable circumstances, you have undertaken and completed both the Fortenberry and Johnson City projects to many accolades from the two clients.

I couldn't be happier about your selection for this award. My best.

Sincerely,

❖ ❖ ❖

BIRTH

Guidelines and Alternate Phrasing

Congratulate the reader on the birth.

⇨ We've heard the good news—the stork has delivered as promised!

⇨ We're so happy for you and the new baby.

⇨ Congratulations on your little darling—isn't Timmy the name I heard?

⇨ From all of us in the office, congratulations on the birth of your nine pound boy—he sounds so healthy and full of life already.

⇨ We're so thrilled to hear that the baby is healthy and beautiful.

⇨ I know you must be so proud to have a beautiful daughter, Mandy.

⇨ Congratulations on this happy occasion—we are so pleased to hear that you and the baby are doing just fine.

Add a personal note about the joyous occasion, but don't be overly familiar with associates you don't know well. Humor or sentimental comments about what the future holds is often the perfect touch.

⇨ I know you've longed for this moment for years. Enjoy every minute with him and his father.

⇨ I guess that by now you've given some thought to how your life will change—dirty diapers, smashed green beans, noisy nights, and outgrown next-to-new clothes. But you won't regret a moment.

⇨ Spend the next few weeks at home enjoying every coo and hug. Those moments are going to be precious as the years go by.

⇨ Being parents ourselves, both Mark and I know what happiness is in store for you two—the missed golfing tournaments notwithstanding.

⇨ I know you'll give Jimmy the nurturing—both emotional and spiritual—that a child needs to grow up healthy and happy in today's world. You are special people, who will make great parents.

⇨ That baby will be the source of much pride—and many sleepless nights—around your house.

⇨ On March 2 at 3:00 A.M., the waiting, the hoping, the pacing ended. On second thought, maybe they're just beginning.

⇨ Enjoy your time together—the cuddling, the talking, the play. I'm sure you feel the responsibility of bringing a baby into this world, but it's a responsibility that you'll cherish for a lifetime.

⇨ Well, it's now your time to brag, to pull out the pictures, to show off David. (And it's also your time to drag the playpen to the park and cut a slice of roast beef into one zillion tiny bites.)

⇨ Babies are so much fun. You're headed for a wonderful adventure.

Wish the baby and family future happiness.

⇨ Best wishes for a lifetime together.

⇨ Here's to your continued health and happiness together.

⇨ We wish you many fun-filled days ahead.

⇨ Give the baby a hug for me.

⇨ You and Todd take great care of that littlest angel.

⇨ We pray that all three of you will be as happy as you are now.

⇨ We wish for him good health, a happy family, a bright future.

⇨ This relationship is so special—best of everything as you build a family together.

⇨ That little glow around the baby's head is my special wish for protection and a rich life.

⇨ We wish you all—parents, Amy, and Todd—a wonderful lifetime together, starting now!

❖ ❖ ❖

Melba,

Congratulations on your newest family member. We were all so thrilled to hear that Melanie is healthy and that you are both doing so well.

Your two older children are so well-behaved and respectful that I'm sure this one will pick up their habits quite easily—thanks to your constant attention and caring. (Now, notice that I didn't expect Melanie to be reading by age three months. Even yours will probably not be that precocious!)

We wish you so many fun days ahead.

Sincerely,

❖ ❖ ❖

BIRTHDAY

Guidelines and Alternate Phrasing

Mention the occasion, but don't be overly familiar in counting. A humorous approach adds a nice touch.

⇨ Today is special—it's your birthday.

⇨ Someone around here dropped the word that today is your birthday.

⇨ Happy birthday from an admirer—or two . . . or three . . . or ten.

⇨ Didn't we celebrate your birthday about this time last year?

⇨ I've been counting—isn't this the tenth anniversary of your 29th birthday? Oh, well, close enough.

⇨ We're both getting older these days—one of us is also getting better! Happy birthday to that one!

⇨ This week marks a special occasion, your birthday.

⇨ Happy birthday from all of us on the staff.

Tell the person one specific thing you appreciate about him or her, or the relationship in general.

⇨ You're always so accommodating when I'm in your office that I couldn't let the day go by without notice.

⇨ Your sunny disposition is the "fix" we all need every Monday morning.

⇨ You're the kind of person we always depend on—even if we rarely say so.

⇨ You always make such an effort to help out when we need extra coverage here that I wanted to let you know how much we appreciate your cooperation.

⇨ Your flagrant use of large doses of courtesy has been affecting the entire office—thank goodness.

⇨ You're always here when we need someone with that extra commitment.

⇨ Your loyalty and commitment are unequaled around here.

⇨ Your friendship is one of the nicest things about working here.

⇨ Your smile is a welcome sight each time I return from the cold, cruel world out there.

⇨ You know how to do your job—and because you do, that makes mine so much easier.

⇨ Thanks for being so super and amiable as a working partner.

Wish the reader a happy celebration and many more years.

⇨ Celebrate long and hard—birthdays come only once a year.

⇨ You may not have another birthday for a year—party heartily.

⇨ I hope the day brings fun and happiness.

⇨ I wish you the best today and the rest of your life.

⇨ Here's to many more such occasions.

⇨ Our best for many more happy years together here at Arvark.

⇨ Many, many, many more.

⇨ One wish for you—not a wasted day or year of your life. You deserve to enjoy every minute ahead.

⇨ Much happiness as you celebrate today.

⇨ Much happiness as you enter the next year and forever.

❖ ❖ ❖

Susan,

I noticed a sheepish grin when you arrived at work today—could it be that you thought we would do something lavish and embarrassing like send you around the world on a cruise? It's a good thing, because I'd hate for you to be so disappointed on your birthday.

But the second best thing we could come up with is lunch and this sentimental consensus: You're special. Celebrate like it!

Our best,

❖ ❖ ❖

Terri,

My calendar tells me that August 2 is your special day—happy birthday. You're not one to call attention to yourself, so it's best we all keep our own calendars of those who mean a great deal to us. Consider this a bouquet of warm wishes for a great day and a great year.

Best regards,

❖ ❖ ❖

Dear Mr. Milton:

I just wanted to drop you a note to say "Happy Birthday." Calling on you every month is an enjoyable routine—all my customers should be so pleasant and full of life! Have a good time with family, staff, and friends—may you have many more years with them.

Cordially,

❖ ❖ ❖

CIVIC ACHIEVEMENT _____

Guidelines and Alternate Phrasing

Commend the reader on the achievement.

⇨ We want to take this opportunity to recognize your important contribution in . . .

⇨ Our community has been honored by the national attention your efforts have garnered for the cause of . . .

⇨ I was so pleased to hear of your success in . . .

⇨ You have made us proud—through your leadership, we as a community can now boast that we have . . .

⇨ Few people of your talent and caliber are so disposed to share themselves as you have done recently in your efforts with the _____ program.

⇨ Thank you so much for lending your support to the drive to establish . . .

Highlight the significance to the community of the reader's achievement.

⇨ The citizens of this community will never be the same after having heard your ubiquitous appeals on behalf of the homeless. We have learned to care and share.

⇨ Through your efforts, children will be fed, clothed, and in a warm shelter tonight.

⇨ Your untiring travels and appearances before the necessary agencies have put our city in the forefront of the minds of our national leaders.

⇨ Your work on this project means that our school system has the potential to become the finest in the nation.

⇨ Your work with the tutoring program means fewer tax dollars funneled through the various governmental assistance programs that have already proven so ineffective in this regard.

⇨ In a phrase, we now can grow.

⇨ Our community now has a safe place for our young people to gather, thanks to your leadership and caring commitment.

⇨ As a fairly long-term community member, I can say that for the first time in years I feel safe to walk the downtown streets. I thank you.

⇨ We can all be proud of the parks and recreational sites that this BYZER project has now funded.

Stay focused on the individual rather than on others who may also be involved.

❖ ❖ ❖

Dear Larry,

I was so pleased to hear of your success in exceeding your goal of $2,000,000 for the Lowery Art Museum.

In these days of high-tech and low-touch, so much attention is given to the wizardry of new machines and faster processes. What our younger generation, as well as those of my age, needs is the opportunity to reflect on the spiritual side of life—to feed the mind and soul on the beauty and artistic efforts of our time.

Your long hours, your undying faith in the community's economic ability to respond, and your rousing speeches carried on the cable TV networks have brought us to this success. Yes, I say "us" because your success flows to all community members, who will enjoy your efforts for years to come.

Thank you for your caring and hard work.

Sincerely,

❖ ❖ ❖

ENGAGEMENT\WEDDING _____

Guidelines and Alternate Phrasing

Express your congratulations on the engagement.

⇨ We've heard the good news—you and Matt have married.

⇨ Congratulations on making that big decision.

⇨ You're smarter than I thought you were—talking Regina into marrying you before you even got a vice president's title. Way to go!

⇨ Congratulations on your upcoming wedding. We were so pleased to hear of your engagement.

⇨ Engaged, no less? Such a whirlwind romance sounds intoxicatingly exciting. We should pass the elixir around to the rest of the dreary world! Congratulations.

⇨ We are thrilled to hear of your marriage to Mark Hayes.

⇨ The wedding will be perfect—congratulations on your choices of bride and groom.

⇨ I was delighted to hear that you have become engaged.

⇨ Your wedding sent off all sorts of sirens at our office. We never thought you'd do it.

⇨ Best wishes to you both on your upcoming wedding.

Comment positively on one or both of those involved.

⇨ You both are such special people—you deserve each other.

⇨ Michael always said he was waiting for the perfect woman—I think he found a close second to that non-existent dream in you.

⇨ You two are perfect for each other—motivated, positive, fun-loving, and successful. What a match!

⇨ Your mother tells me that Barry was her reward in a son-in-law—for keeping her mouth shut about all those throwaways you dated in the process of finding the right one!

⇨ Your husband-to-be is a gem. I've known him for years and you couldn't have made a better choice.

⇨ If the past 28 years have been any indication, Tom will be that successful provider that dreams are made of.

⇨ You two are starting a trend—nice people finding nice people.

⇨ Can you tell me how you two were so lucky to find each other? The special people of the world are almost always taken.

⇨ Although I don't know Jill personally, she has to be a sensitive and warm person to have captured your love.

⇨ I've heard of Bill by reputation only—but, wow, what a reputation in our business circles! I understand he's headed for a really bright career in his organization.

Wish the couple happiness.

⇨ We wish you a lifetime of happiness.

⇨ Have a great life.

⇨ Many years of love and fun together.

⇨ For you both, we wish nothing less than the best life has to offer.

⇨ We wish you long days of bright sunshine.

⇨ We are praying for your good health, personal and professional success, and a warm relationship that nourishes your souls.

⇨ We want you to know that we've found marriage to be God's gift to us on earth. Enjoy each other for a lifetime.

⇨ Have a special wedding day and a long, happy life together.

⇨ Enjoy each day from now on—you've made a wise decision.

⇨ Life begins now. Enjoy it hand in hand.

⇨ Join hands and don't ever let go.

⇨ Walk together and you'll smile all the way.

❖ ❖ ❖

Sheila,

We are so thrilled to hear of your recent marriage. Mark Laney was spreading the good news at a convention dinner last weekend. Although we don't personally know Todd, common sense tells us that he's a peak performer and a super nice guy—or else he wouldn't have won your love.

We wish you the very best for many years of success, health, and happiness together.

Our best regards,

❖ ❖ ❖

NEW JOB/PROMOTION

Guidelines and Alternate Phrasing

Congratulate the reader on the promotion or new job.

⇨ I read yesterday of your promotion to executive director—I'm so pleased to hear the news.

⇨ We in the Southern Region are delighted that you have accepted the promotion to divisional director.

⇨ The title of executive director sounds so right for you—I'm glad they've made it official.

⇨ Your promotion is such good news.

⇨ I hear that they finally made you an offer you couldn't refuse—and I'm glad to hear you didn't.

⇨ With regard to promotions, you're about due. And this was a big one at that—deputy assistant.

⇨ I was so impressed to see your photo and name in the local paper this weekend. Your promotion comes not a minute too soon. We have needed you desperately in such a leadership position.

⇨ Belton, Inc., has made a marvelously sound business decision in asking you to join them.

⇨ I couldn't be happier for you in your new position, Kenneth.

Comment on past achievements, skills, or personal attributes or attitudes that have contributed to the new success.

⇨ You are one of the most highly motivated individuals I've had the privilege to work with.

⇨ Your record here has been outstanding, first as a sales rep, then as a manager, and finally as regional director.

⇨ Your inclination always to go to bat for the customer has been the crux of your success.

⇨ Your determination in reaching goals, your drive and physical stamina during the required travel, and your willingness to work long hours have set you apart.

⇨ Your second degree, your Lanney Award, and your commitment to the

Frazier project—all provide evidence that you are the right person for the job.

⇨ Not only have you always been at the right place at the right time—you've done the right job in the right way.

⇨ Your personal integrity and moral courage have made you a clear choice for this post.

State your confidence in the abilities of the person to perform well, and wish him or her success.

⇨ I know I'll hear much of you in the years to come.

⇨ We all will be eager to read of your successes there.

⇨ Best wishes as you continue to rise in the organization.

⇨ Go get 'em, Mac.

⇨ We expect great things from you.

⇨ We have every confidence that you will not let us down in this challenging position.

⇨ I'll watch with excitement as you reel in the big fish.

⇨ We promise our support as you assume this responsibility.

⇨ It's a big task—one you're certainly capable of handling.

⇨ With confidence, I wish you my best.

⇨ Your future here remains wide open.

⇨ Your future here is going to be a bright one.

⇨ This is the first of many promotions that we have in mind as you grow with us.

⇨ Your work has been outstanding; we have reason to believe it will continue to be so.

⇨ The job might be overwhelming for a less-capable individual. With you at the helm, we feel confident about the future.

⇨ I want to express to you my sincerest best wishes as you lead your people to new horizons.

⇨ You have my very best wishes with the challenges that lie ahead.

⇨ The challenges ahead deserve all your attention, and we have every confidence that you have what it takes.

❖ ❖ ❖

Dear Wendy,

Yesterday's Chronicle says that Arco has a new vice president of marketing. I don't know if I'm pleased or perturbed to see that our competition has wised up and tapped such a star performer in the industry. Congratulations.

I've watched you break sales records year after year, heard you give workshops at industry meetings, saw your visibility hit its zenith as you published several articles during these past two years. You evidently set some high goals for yourself, and have even greater things in mind to offer your new organization. They have outdone themselves this time in their recruitment efforts.

I have no doubt whatsoever that I'll be reading great things about you in the years to come. My best to you as you build your sales team at Arco.

Sincerely,

❖ ❖ ❖

Dear Tyron:

I was so pleased to learn that you have been selected to go to Seattle to open our new offices there. With each new promotion, there always comes a new challenge, along with the responsibility. As I understand it from my corner of the world, this new position will entail acquisition of property, staffing, and a marketing strategy for the unique situation in the area.

Evidently, I'm not the only one who has admired your work to date and who has complete confidence in your skills and judgment for such an assignment.

You have my best regards as you bring this new profit center into the organization.

Cordially,

❖ ❖ ❖

OPENING NEW BUSINESS _____

Guidelines and Alternate Phrasing

Mention the occasion for your writing.

⇨ Did I see your sign on the door at 2234 Post Oak? Congratulations.

⇨ Your business is off to a great start. Or, at least the ad in *Today's Architecture* certainly got my attention.

⇨ I'm so happy for you—opening one's own business is quite a momentous occasion.

⇨ Congratulations on opening your new store at such an enviable location.

⇨ Your new store front, ads, and window displays are breathtaking.

⇨ Your practice is one we've needed in the community for a long time.

⇨ Just what we need—a new restaurant that serves calorie-free food. Or did I misunderstand your intention?

⇨ Congratulations on your new venture; opening your own business certainly is a mark of distinction.

⇨ I admire your foresight in opening your new _____ business in such a booming area.

⇨ The floors are carpeted, the windows are clean, the merchandise is displayed—it's a great feeling, I'm sure. Congratulations on your efforts.

Comment on past achievements, dreams, or personal traits that have led to the new endeavor.

⇨ Your years at Wilhelm have paved the way for sound buying decisions.

⇨ Your achievements in all the usual slots the large corporations could offer have been a valuable training ground. You have acquired the training and the insights to successfully fly solo.

⇨ Your genuinely warm personality, I know, will attract clients and build the relationships into long-term ones.

⇨ I feel certain that it's your persistence and rugged determination leading you on this exciting new path.

⇨ Your unique approach to problem-solving as a team leader will make you an excellent small-business owner, a situation where every player counts.

⇨ I know this has been a life-long dream, and few of us have the courage to act on our dreams.

Wish the reader success.

⇨ You and Margie have worked hard to position yourselves to take advantage of this new opportunity. You deserve to succeed.

⇨ Frankly, I'm envious—though you still have my best regards.

⇨ I wish you every success as you build the business.

⇨ Here's to your success in the years to come.

⇨ I look forward to seeing a multi-million dollar corporation shortly.

⇨ We'll be seeing great things from your efforts.

⇨ If anyone deserves to succeed, you do.

⇨ Your idea is a splendid one—I wish I'd thought of it myself.

⇨ My hat's off to you.

⇨ Your timing looks great, your location seems logical, and your product sounds superb. Congratulations!

❖ ❖ ❖

Dear Twyla:

Your new address on Jackson Drive is quite impressive. Yesterday's mail brought your announcement about the practice you and your two colleagues have established.

Although I couldn't say from personal experience, it seems to me that hanging out your own shingle takes courage, creativity, and commitment. And from my associations with you, you have just those ingredients in quantities enough to be successful in whatever you choose.

I wish you a most rewarding first year and future as you build your clientele in the community.

Cordially,

❖ ❖ ❖

PUBLICATION

Guidelines and Alternate Phrasing

Commend the reader on publication, mentioning the prestige of the journal, magazine, or book or the difficulty of getting published.

⇨ Writing is a task I found very difficult, yet your article in last month's *Digest* made the whole process seem so simple.

⇨ Congratulations on being published in such a prestigious journal as . . .

⇨ I read with interest your excellent article on molecular biology.

⇨ I'm glad to see that the editorial review board of *Science Today* recognizes the significance of the subject you covered so adequately in last month's issue.

⇨ Your newsletter article was a tremendous hit around our office. We just love motivational success stories from one of our own!

⇨ Thank you for the thought-provoking article recently printed in *Personnel Journal.*

Comment on the uniqueness of the article or book information or why you think it will have value for other readers. If you can do so sincerely, mention some specific usefulness of the information to your personally.

⇨ Your ideas about time-management and our new "desk-stress" syndrome make so much sense. Particularly helpful to me personally was the idea-wheel construction.

⇨ I found the idea of . . . intriguing.

⇨ I've always followed the research being conducted on this subject and I continue to find it fascinating.

⇨ You've done such a thorough job of outlining all the options open to business owners today.

⇨ Your analysis of the customer-service problem was right on target.

⇨ Your conclusions make sense.

⇨ Your style is so conversational that I read the complete article in five minutes—and felt as though I'd been through a six-week course.

⇨ You are articulate and precise in your pronouncements. I hope the leaders in our industry listen.

⇨ I plan to use your information about ... in a presentation to management next month.

⇨ The data included in your article certainly add credibility to the premise. With your permission, I'll include your findings in my own presentation to our senior executives.

⇨ Your general premise has been treated before, but never so adequately, with so much supporting documentation.

⇨ The information is immediately useful to me in my own work here at the center.

⇨ Your article alone was worth the annual subscription price.

Thank the reader for his or her dedication to the industry, field of study, or subject.

⇨ Thank you for your timely exposé.

⇨ Thank you for taking the time to argue the other side of the coin.

⇨ I appreciate what your work has contributed to my own professional growth.

⇨ The article will be remembered as one of the year's best.

⇨ Your ideas capsule the future of our country.

⇨ Your ideas should ignite the fuel that sparks our industry out of its lethargy.

⇨ Thank you for your contribution to the field.

⇨ We appreciate your willingness to share your insights with those who have not had the travel and research opportunities your position provides.

⇨ Please take this letter as a sincere expression of my admiration for your contributions to the medical field.

⇨ I regret that the article will probably not be read by the entire industry.

⇨ Our leaders will do well to take note of your recommendations for the future.

❖ ❖ ❖

Dear David:

How excited I became when it dawned on me that the byline under "The Chosen Few—Antibiotics That Kill" in the *New England Journal of Medicine* was yours.

I must say that the title was also a grabber. Neither was I disappointed when I read of your recent research and the unique perspective you set forth. This is an area worthy of much more study, and you're just the colleague who might find that breakthrough. I admire your work tremendously.

Thank you for taking the time to publish such controversial theories; I wish more professionals had the moral courage to raise such questions.

Sincerely,

❖ ❖ ❖

RETIREMENT

Guidelines and Alternate Phrasing

Mention the occasion of retirement.

⇨ Your time of leisure, travel, and rest is fast approaching; I'm so envious.

⇨ Congratulations on such a long and varied career.

⇨ Congratulations on such a successful, forty-year record!

⇨ What a record—thirty years of hard work, commitment, excellence.

⇨ I am so pleased to have had the opportunity to work with you through the years on so many joint projects. On this your retirement, I have very mixed emotions. On the one hand, you deserve the well-earned years of leisure; on the other hand, I'll miss you greatly.

⇨ From my distinct vantage point as a competitor, I can't say how glad I am to see you retire—you've put most of us to shame with your accomplishments. Seriously, I hate to see you go. Leaders who've exhibited the courage you've shown are difficult to replace.

⇨ My colleagues tell me that you're retiring after 30 remarkable years.

⇨ After twenty-eight highly productive years, you think you're really going to get any rest on the sidelines?

⇨ You've had such a spectacular career that I find it shocking to think you will not be leading our organization to new records.

⇨ I understand from mutual friends that you will be retiring at the end of the month, and I didn't want the occasion to go by without a special note to let you know how much I've enjoyed our association.

⇨ If our records are right, you've been showing up for work here every morning for the past 20 years. Now, that's consistency!

Comment specifically on the career achievements, skills, or personal attributes of the retiree.

⇨ You have spread your fatherly interest to include me so often.

⇨ Your business acumen has been noted so often in the press that I feel at a loss to comment further other than to say that I've learned more from you in our six-month relationship than in all my earlier years with the organization.

⇨ Your punctuality, your dependability, and your loyalty have been exemplary.

⇨ Whenever there has been a technical problem, I always had the confidence that given enough time and the proper assistance, you would have us back in operation.

⇨ Your sound judgment, your can-do attitude, and your management skills have contributed more than I can say in this short letter.

⇨ You have so faithfully performed every task assigned, without complaint and with excellence.

⇨ Your record of attendance, your skill development, and your attitude have been marvelous through the years.

Wish the reader well with any announced plans for the retirement years. Remember, however, that not everyone is pleased about retiring, and in those cases, your comments should only be general.

⇨ My very best wishes for your future years.

⇨ My thoughts and prayers go with you as you leave us.

⇨ Have fun as you travel the globe, meet new people, and enjoy your family.

⇨ Many years of health, happiness, and fun to you.

⇨ Thank you for making us part of your life; we wish you many more years with the people who matter most—your friends and family.

⇨ Your plans for retirement sound exciting. Make the most of every moment.

⇨ Godspeed as you go.

⇨ You have earned the thorough rest that only retirement provides. Enjoy.

⇨ You have worked long and contributed much. We hope your retirement brings you equally as much contentment.

⇨ Our best wishes go with you as you face those exciting days of pure leisure—long conversations, unhurried visits, uninterrupted rest. You deserve to enjoy life to its fullest.

❖ ❖ ❖

Dear Douglas:

Rumor has it that you're going to be deserting us here in the Eastern region for greener pastures—golf courses, tennis courts, hunting leases in Wyoming. Congratulations on your planned retirement.

But before you leave for those greener pastures, let me recall for you the outstanding successes you've had here with us. It seems like only yesterday that you were breaking sales goals and had set the bell curve on edge. Then, as my mentor in the field of management, you showed me what it meant to listen to your team members and really give their ideas a chance, to work long hours for a common goal, to envision the future as you want it to be and then make things happen. Thank you so much for what your career has meant to me as both a friend and an observer.

Your retirement has come too soon to suit me; nevertheless, I wish you the very best in the years ahead.

Sincerely,

❖ ❖ ❖

SERVICE AWARD

Guidelines and Alternate Phrasing

Mention the occasion and length of service, stating anything you plan to do to commemorate the occasion such as a certificate, luncheon, or gift.

⇨ We are pleased to note that you've been with us at United Carolton for ten years now.

⇨ This is a special month for both you and us at United Carolton; our records show that you've been giving us long hours of hard work for 15 years.

⇨ United Carolton is pleased to commemorate your twentieth year with us by asking you to join your co-workers and friends for lunch at the Barrymore Loft, August 5, at noon. You are our guest of honor.

⇨ For the past 20 years, you have been committed to our goals here at United Carolton. We are committed to repaying you in some small way with a token of our gratitude for your excellent performance. Please accept the enclosed watch as a symbol given to special people here—those who have excelled in their careers.

⇨ The enclosed certificate commemorates your fine performance at United Carolton for the past five years.

Comment on the reader's specific contributions to the organization so that the letter doesn't sound like a boilerplate document sent out routinely to all long-term employees.

⇨ Your shop runs smoothly with little supervision.

⇨ Your supervisor has commented that she can depend on you totally to carry out any assignment in the most efficient way.

⇨ Your resourcefulness, your judgment, and your vision have led your staff to exemplify what a divisional team should accomplish.

⇨ Given little direction and less budget, you have performed next-to-miracles with the Woodhaven store.

⇨ Under your management, we have seen sales double in two years—a remarkable record.

⇨ Your candor, your commitment, and your caring have paid off for both you and the company.

⇨ Your talent and creativity have provided just the kinds of design work we envisioned for your team.

⇨ We can't thank you enough for your attention to the minutest details that make the difference in customers coming back to us again and again.

Express your appreciation for continuing service in the past and in the years to come.

⇨ Employees like you keep us in business.

⇨ We wish every employee had the commitment that you've shown over the years. Thank you.

⇨ We hope you'll serve with us for many years to come.

⇨ We believe that employees such as you make the difference in our profit or loss. Keep up the good work.

⇨ You're an excellent performer, who will continue to contribute to our success for years to come.

⇨ The future here is wide open for employees of your caliber.

⇨ The future here is unlimited for employees with your performance records and abilities.

⇨ The future here is bright for employees who have your attitude of commitment and dedication to excellence.

⇨ United Carolton hopes to send you a paycheck for many years in the future.

⇨ We will do everything possible to keep employees like you happy.

⇨ We expect the second ten years to be equally as successful for you and for the company.

⇨ Thank you for your commitment. We owe you our gratitude.

⇨ Your loyalty and excellent service will not be forgotten for years to come.

⇨ Thank you for working with us here to do the best job possible for our community.

⇨ Customers deserve the best. It's quite evident that you are committed to that goal. We thank you.

❖ ❖ ❖

Dear Dwayne:

This month marks your twentieth year with United Carolton—20 years of hard work and commitment to keeping our customers happy.

To commemorate your long-term service, we are shipping to your home a painting of the local landscape by artist Harold Pitone. We hope that every time you, your family, and friends look at the painting, you will think fondly of your years spent here together and that your work life will be a big part of that sense of contentment.

This gift represents only a small sense of the gratitude we feel for your loyalty through the years. You have contributed greatly to our customer service department, keeping our records up-to-date, handling the phone so capably, and coordinating our work schedules so that customer repairs are completed on time and as promised.

You ARE United Carolton to the customer. Your work has kept us in business these many years, and we hope to have you with us for many more.

Sincerely,

❖ ❖ ❖

RESPONSE TO A CONGRATULATORY NOTE

Guidelines and Alternate Phrasing

Thank the reader for his or her thoughtfulness in taking the time to recognize the achievement or mention the occasion.

⇨ Thanks so much for taking the time to drop me your kind note.

⇨ How thoughtful of you to write about the Draper Award.

⇨ Your note about the Draper Award was particularly special to me.

⇨ The primary benefit of publishing that article was to hear from old friends like you—thanks so much for writing.

⇨ You're always so thoughtful to take note of what others are doing in the industry.

⇨ Your letter came today. Thank you so much for recognizing our efforts toward the Fullerton cause. I do think it's a worthy effort on the part of the community here.

⇨ With your busy travel schedule, how did you ever find time to drop me a note about this special time in my life? Thanks so much for thinking of me.

⇨ You have such class—how nice of you to write me about the sales record.

⇨ Thanks for your vote of confidence. From your kind words, it's too bad you weren't on the award selection committee years ago!

Avoid "telling your story" about the achievement or distinction. Be modest.

⇨ As you well know, such work is not the result of solo efforts.

⇨ We all had a part in the results; I simply was the one lucky enough to be singled out this time.

⇨ It was a team effort, I can assure you.

⇨ As you may have guessed, I had much support from our organization.

⇨ From the very beginning, your advice and direction were invaluable in turning me on to this job.

⇨ Colleagues like you make the work so worthwhile.

If appropriate, extend your own hospitality or wish for further contact.

⇨ Maybe we can visit further when you have the time.

⇨ Would you call me when you get caught up from your travels?

⇨ Please feel free to drop in on me whenever you're here in the area.

⇨ Let me know when you have time to chat about your own situation.

⇨ Perhaps we can get together before too long. I'll be in touch.

⇨ Give me a call when you have the time to sit down for a long visit.

⇨ I welcome any further ideas from you on the subject; your insights have been invaluable to me in the past.

❖ ❖ ❖

Dear Virginia:

Thank you so much for your nice note about the Draper Award. The recognition takes on another special meaning when colleagues like you are so complimentary and supportive. I'd love to renew our acquaintance with a luncheon date when you're in town again.

Sincerely,

❖ ❖ ❖

Dear Matthew:

How nice of you to take the time to write about seeing the *Futura* article on our company. We just hope that reporter is a prophet. Best wishes to you and your staff also, and keep me posted on how the Middle East project shapes up.

Cordially,

❖ ❖ ❖

COVER LETTERS

Cover letters are ubiquitous. They transmit everything from greetings from the IRS . . . to your new credit card . . . to your annual mail-order Christmas catalog.

Effective cover letters should say more than "Here it is." Consider them an overview of the entire document that is attached. They should summarize all the vital issues, benefits, facts, and figures that the primary readers will be most interested in.

Second, they should move the action forward. That is, they should contain detail necessary for the reader to understand and respond to the attachment.

If you're routinely using the same cover letters and simply "filling in the blanks," take a critical look at them. Do they accomplish a purpose more than to say, "Here it is"? If not, rework them according to the following guidelines and models.

FOR INVOICES/EXPLANATION OF FEES

Guidelines and Alternate Phrasing

Mention what you are enclosing. If you have attached several items, be sure to list them specifically either in the body of the letter or with an enclosure notation after the signature block. If for some reason the items get misplaced or inadvertently omitted from the package, your reader will know that documents are missing.

⇨ I am enclosing copies of . . .

⇨ You will find enclosed . . .

⇨ Attached is . . .

⇨ Our invoice for the recent Guttenheimer work is attached.

⇨ The laser products have been shipped to your site (invoice enclosed).

⇨ The enclosed invoice shows work performed to repair the irrigation system at your Guttenheimer location.

Tell what the invoice is for and give any special instructions for payment that are not included on the invoice itself.

⇨ The invoice includes a breakdown of hours by day and by assigned consultant.

⇨ You'll notice that the invoice is for $457; we can offer a 2 percent discount for payments received within seven days.

⇨ Please forward your payment directly to our Accounting Department at the Silford address.

Anticipate and answer questions your reader will have about anything unusual regarding work, products, fees, payments, or terms.

⇨ As we agreed, we have added the latest maintenance charges to this invoice so that you can make payment from this quarter's budget.

⇨ Our invoice covers parts and materials, but not labor. Those labor charges will be billed at the completion of the total project.

⇨ Because we pay our subcontractors at the completion of each day's project, we ask for immediate payment of these charges for the Silbon address. We will be happy to carry the charges for parts and materials for our usual 30 days.

Add the name and phone number of the person to contact with any further questions. Be specific about which questions to direct to which person when others are involved.

⇨ Bill Jones is available for further discussion at 222-2345.

⇨ You can reach either Sue Tony or me at ext. 3467 to provide further information about the completion schedules.

⇨ I'll be back in the office next week if you need any elaboration on these alternatives or terms.

⇨ For engineering concerns, please phone Bill Gatz at ext. 223, and for billing matters, contact Marge Harvey at 1-800-628-4461.

Thank the reader for the opportunity to do business.

⇨ We appreciate your confidence in our products.

⇨ We thank you for letting us complete this work for you.

⇨ Your business is important to us. Thank you.

⇨ Your business represents a significant part of our current projects. Our goal is to meet your needs on time and within budget.

⇨ We appreciate the opportunity to do business with you.

⇨ Thank you for thinking of us for your computer needs.

⇨ Please call on us again if we can help you in any way.

⇨ We appreciate the chance to design this system for your Belco office. You won't be disappointed in the results.

❖ ❖ ❖

Dear Mr. Hightower:

We have prepared and attached the settlement statements for the sale of Loboy, Inc.'s, Hammerly and Simon gas plants to NRT Fuels. These statements were prepared according to the proposal submitted by Loboy, Inc., on August 30, 19—, and contain all the revenues and expenses allowed by that agreement.

After our analysis of the revenue and expenses associated with these plants during the interim operations, we have determined that NRT Fuels owes Loboy, Inc. $3,098,448.48. Therefore, we have attached for your payment our invoice #09-3349 for that amount.

Attached also are the following support documents:

- Summary statement—Hammerly and Simon plants
- Charges processed through Accounts Payable
- Salary analysis
- Interim accounting service charges
- Net revenue settlement

If you have any expense- or revenue-related questions, you may contact Bill Bynum at 390-200-8909. For questions about the support documents, please direct them to Shirley Akins at 390-200-8926.

Very truly yours,

❖ ❖ ❖

FOR PROPOSALS/PRICE QUOTES _____

Guidelines and Alternate Phrasing

Begin with an overview statement of what you are proposing or what pricing information you are providing.

⇨ Thank you for the opportunity to quote Bordelon products for use in the Shnook laboratories.

⇨ This proposal outlines a comprehensive plan for training all your management and supervisory staff at the headquarters location.

⇨ The pricing information provided here covers the computer needs you outlined in your August 6 request: installation, maintenance, and training. We are proposing to install 39 Model 30s, a comprehensive maintenance plan, and two days' training for 42 operators.

⇨ We are pleased to propose to you . . .

⇨ We are submitting our proposal for . . .

⇨ Thank you for allowing us to bid on the linen needs for your hotel chain. We are suggesting an arrangement whereby we would . . .

⇨ We have detailed below the pricing information you requested on the Buggrin furnishings for your field office at Luzanne.

Summarize the key benefits in doing business with your company. If you are selling on price—low price being your key strategy—then highlight that in your cover letter. This overview may be the only part of the proposal that the key decisionmaker reads.

⇨ We believe that this arrangement will allow you maximum use of your currently installed machines.

⇨ We think this decision is a sound one because of the . . .

⇨ Our proposal will allow you to take advantage of your own in-house expertise in the design phase.

⇨ We offer low prices, volume discounts, and free delivery.

⇨ This system should virtually eliminate your check-back authorization problem.

⇨ I don't think you'll find anything currently manufactured that will meet your needs at such a low price.

⇨ From our experience with clients in similar situations, we expect you will be able to decrease your processing time by 38 to 45 percent.

⇨ We don't think it's unrealistic at all for you to expect a productivity increase of 20 percent in all four lines.

⇨ Improved reliability, lower maintenance cost, and superior quality—all are good reasons to adopt this new way of handling your transactions.

⇨ We can promise improved efficiency, clearer work orders, and high-impact visuals.

Ask for the order, or at least suggest the next action in the buying process.

⇨ May we go to work for you?

⇨ May we begin installation?

⇨ We're ready to order the materials as soon as you give us the go-ahead.

⇨ If you think it appropriate, I will be happy to meet with your committee as they review and discuss this proposal. Perhaps I can help to alleviate their concerns about availability dates.

⇨ We are eager to work with you on this project. When may we expect a decision?

⇨ With our receipt of your signed agreement, we will begin the scheduling process immediately.

⇨ Simply sign the enclosed agreement page, and we will begin preparing the formal contracts.

⇨ I'll phone next week to see where you are in the review process.

⇨ As we discussed in your office, we will be more than happy to present the proposal to your managers as a group. I'll phone Friday to talk about that possibility.

Thank the reader for the opportunity to quote prices or prepare a proposal, mentioning any help they provided in supplying information.

⇨ We appreciate your allowing us to quote Canary products for your needs.

⇨ Thank you for your help in supplying the data about your operations so necessary to an accurate price quote.

⇨ We appreciate the time your staff took in showing us your operations there at Seaside. Their comments were quite informative. As a result, we think we have provided a comprehensive plan of attack. Thank you for the opportunity to study your situation and the improvements you want to make.

⇨ Please pass on my regards to Tim Trimmer, who provided all the model and serial numbers for your equipment. We do appreciate all your efforts in allowing us to quote prices.

⇨ We were pleased you included us on your bidders list.

⇨ Please keep us in mind for other similar projects, and thank you for allowing us this chance to show you what we can do.

⇨ No proposal is completely satisfactory that does not include key customer data such as you were able to provide us. We appreciate your efforts in helping us prepare a quality plan of action.

⇨ Thank you for thinking of Westheimer for your cleaning needs.

⇨ We hope you'll find this proposal thought-provoking, immediately practical, and cost-effective. Thank you for your part in its preparation.

❖ ❖ ❖

Dear Mr. Zortzman:

Enclosed is our proposal for the computer-controlled chemical irrigation systems for your Plano site. Specifically, we are proposing our Model D-440.

The immediate benefits will be a reduction in the staff needed to care for the property and improved efficiency of your operations. As also detailed in the proposal, the $300/month lease price should easily be recovered through the chemical savings alone. You'll also notice a measurable maintenance savings as well.

A signed lease agreement is all we need to put the system in service. I'll phone you next week to see when you may be ready to schedule the installation.

Thank you for your help in supplying the maintenance records and the tours provided by your staff as we gathered the necessary information for this proposed work.

Sincerely,

Enc: proposal
       lease agreement
       manufacturer's spec sheets

❖ ❖ ❖

❖ ❖ ❖

Dear Dr. Everett:

Thank you for requesting our bid on support services for the 784 Cartmands at your location. We are offering to maintain your equipment under the terms and conditions outlined on the attached service agreement. To overview that arrangement succinctly: a Hitachi customer engineer will repair any and all contracted units, including parts, labor, and materials that have been taken to your specified site.

The total monthly price will be $2,983. This pricing is valid for 30 days, and subject to change thereafter without notice.

Please review the enclosed servicing information carefully. You'll notice that we require 30 days lead-time to guarantee that parts and services will be available to accommodate your immediate service needs.

If the pricing, terms, and conditions meet your approval, please sign and return both copies to me for further processing. We'll return an original to you for your files.

Finally, you'll find enclosed a listing of the models and serial numbers required for identification purchases. Please complete these forms.

If I can answer questions, Dr. Everett, about this pricing information, I'll be available at 330-0909.

Sincerely,

Enc: service agreement—two copies
        forms for listing models and serial numbers

❖ ❖ ❖

FOR REPORTS

Guidelines and Alternate Phrasing

Mention the report you are enclosing.

⇨ I've enclosed our activity report for . . .

⇨ Enclosed is the feasibility study you requested on the possibility of . . .

⇨ I've attached my conclusions about the work to be done on . . .

Summarize the key conclusions and recommendations. This overview may be the only part of your report that the executive decisionmaker reads.

⇨ After careful study of the area, we have concluded that extending the gas lines to this Keystone development would not be economically advantageous.

⇨ Our audit shows a serious problem with inventory control; our calculations suggest an excess of $250,000 in out-of-season inventory.

⇨ Our analysis of the staffing needs reveals a shortage of at least four field engineers and two equipment operators.

⇨ Our primary recommendation is to terminate the contract.

⇨ My suggestion is to begin study immediately on the feasibility of . . .

Suggest a next action, if appropriate.

⇨ If you think these preliminary results are inconclusive, I suggest that we contract with Belton Associates to complete a brief study of . . .

⇨ I suggest that your office draft a letter to the would-be buyers to make them aware of the extenuating circumstances.

⇨ If you think more work should be done in this area, we can always . . . before making a final decision.

⇨ If you agree with these assumptions and conclusions, I suggest that we seek budget allocations of $10 million to . . .

Close with your opinion, if appropriate, about the work undertaken and its benefit to the organization.

⇨ I think we should hire the staff necessary to complete the project by year's end. With that information, we should be able to budget more accurately for the coming nine quarters.

⇨ With this information in hand, I think we are in a superior position to make an offer on the Haverty property.

⇨ The results of this study should considerably minimize the risk in our moving ahead with the marketing plans.

⇨ With this latest data, we should have solved our processing problems for the Ohio regions.

Thank a client for the opportunity to conduct the work. If you're submitting an internal report, you may want to acknowledge help from other sources within your own organization.

⇨ Thank you for the opportunity to be involved in this project.

⇨ I appreciate your seeking our expertise before making the final decision.

⇨ Thank you for funding this study—the results should be far-reaching for our employees and the community-at-large.

⇨ I also want to take this opportunity to make you aware of the help our Marketing Department (John Turner and Kay Tibbs) provided in gathering this information.

⇨ Mark Fritz also contributed valuable insights on these figures and the related issues. Both he and I have appreciated the opportunity to look into this situation further.

❖ ❖ ❖

Dear Mr. Schwartz:

I've enclosed my initial report on the property loss at 2897 Barbagallo Street. This loss occurred as a result of the heavy snowfall on January 16 in the foothills near Santa Fe, New Mexico. Our insured's large warehouse and showroom collapsed as a result of the heavy build-up of snow.

We have paid the insured's contents claim of $128,344. On the building itself, however, we have reserved $335,000, pending further investigation. Recent information leads me to believe that this claim is overstated. Ned Rosoff Independent Adjusters is involved in handling this claim. We are in the process of requesting bids for the demolition and repair of the structure and will report to you again as soon as the information is available.

If you want to discuss this claim further, Scott Andrews or I can answer your questions.

Sincerely,

❖ ❖ ❖

❖ ❖ ❖

Dear Mr. Ruyon:

I am forwarding to you a list of current work in progress on the Barton project. To date, we have expended 422 hours in surveying sixteen sites. Of these sixteen sites, our conclusions are that six will require a complete replacement of all structures; five sites can be handled with "built-ins."

We estimate that our survey will be complete by the end of the year. In my opinion, the additional staff required to attempt to rush completion will not be cost-effective for your purposes.

I suggest that a representative of your office label and arrange shipment of the replacement materials for each site. Because we are referencing so many past drawings, this cataloguing should begin only toward the end of the project.

As always, we are finding it a pleasure to work for you and a challenge to help you identify your construction alternatives. Please keep us in mind as a source of expertise on other similar projects.

Sincerely,

❖ ❖ ❖

FOR RÉSUMÉS

Guidelines and Alternate Phrasing

State specifically what position you're interested in, mentioning how you learned of the opening or heard of the organization.

⇨ I saw your ad for a receptionist in yesterday's Star Telegram and have enclosed my résumé for that position.

⇨ Joe Burke in your Chicago office suggested that I contact you about the program analyst position that will be vacant at the end of this month.

⇨ Your organization keeps coming to mind as an excellent place to work.

Would you please consider me (résumé enclosed) for a position in your accounting area?

⇨ If you want to increase your visibility in the oil and gas industry, I think my skills as a trade association manager can contribute to that goal.

⇨ Have you given thought to having your basic wordprocessing needs handled by a freelancer who pays his own salary and benefits? If that idea sounds appealing, I would welcome the opportunity to talk to you about such a freelance arrangement, whereby I would pick up and deliver daily your reports, correspondence, and proposals.

Summarize your specific experience, talents, or attributes that apply to the job, emphasizing the contributions you can make to the company rather than what you want out of the job.

⇨ With 14 years' experience in corporate law, I think I could contribute significantly to your company's positioning itself as legal advocate for the causes we discussed yesterday.

⇨ My excellent sales record, my selection as this year's Storman Award recipient, and my position on the board of directors for the AEEC, I think, evidence my commitment to customer service.

⇨ It's not unrealistic to expect that I could increase your media exposure by placing two or three articles per month in various industry journals.

⇨ My academic credentials, I feel, would be an impressive part of a BVI proposal to prospective clients.

⇨ My willingness to travel, my flexibility on job assignments, and my communication skills with clients could pay off tremendously in a widespread operation such as BVI's.

⇨ My four-year work history with no direct supervision serves as a training ground for the position you now have open.

⇨ My time-management skills and my organizational skills should be directly useful in coordinating the consultants' schedules among so many job sites.

Suggest an interview.

⇨ May I suggest an interview?

⇨ If this experience is on target for the kind of trainer you need, let's talk further.

⇨ I'll phone next week to see if we can talk further about your BVI plans for the coming year.

⇨ May I have an interview?

⇨ Would you please phone me at 304-440-5789 if you think we should talk further? I'd certainly appreciate the opportunity to meet with you personally about this position.

⇨ May I visit with your selection committee personally to discuss how we can work together?

⇨ I'll be in Philadelphia for the entire month of May and will phone to see when you have a few moments to talk about your plans for this position.

⇨ Please consider this résumé carefully in light of your current needs, and let me know if you see a match with my experience.

⇨ I'll look forward to scheduling an interview with you.

❖ ❖ ❖

Dear Mr. Wainwright:

If you anticipate a need in the near future to increase your marketing, public relations, and advertising activities and results, please take a look at the enclosed résumé.

My most recent position as director of corporate communications for Bolton, Johnson, and Frezzer ended on November 1, when the company reduced its workforce by 30 percent. My work there included developing promotional materials, providing marketing support to sales reps in the field, and drafting speeches for our senior executives. Additionally, I served as the company spokesperson to the media. My experience at previous companies has included writing responses on governmental affairs issues and writing ad copy.

If you think you can put my communication experience to work at Universal Park Cities, then I would most definitely welcome a call. Effective communication and media contact can be a direct channel to your profitability as a service company.

Sincerely,

❖ ❖ ❖

CREDIT AND COLLECTION

To paraphrase Thomas Paine: "These are the letters that try men's souls." Almost nothing pushes a person's "hot" button more than talking about his or her finances; the ego seems buried shallowly beneath.

To refuse someone credit, to cancel an established credit line, or to remind someone of payment due is often an insult long remembered. Delivering such a negative message in a subject so closely attached to another's ego takes great finesse.

And, of course, the time for finesse turns to firmness when legitimate accounts become long overdue. Generally, you should consider the first occasion of late payment as an oversight; invoices do get lost or delayed in the mail and credit departments do make billing mistakes. When gentle reminders do not bring results, then firmer, yet matter-of-fact, letters should give the reader all the details to pay the account immediately.

Finally, firm letters must necessarily turn to demand letters, even to the point of threatening legal action. On occasion, when threats fail to motivate empty-handed borrowers to action, a return to the appeal letter may produce results.

Almost like a parent on various occasions, you must remind, plead, push, and unfortunately punish. The appropriate tone to such letters is most important if your intention is to retain or regain the customer's goodwill and business in better financial times.

BILLING DISCREPANCIES/ERRORS

Guidelines and Alternate Phrasing

Summarize the information you have and any apparent discrepancy or error. If the error is yours, state your corrective action immediately. If the error is your reader's, suggest an appropriate resolution.

⇨ We have discovered an error in our records—we owe you $28.

⇨ Our records show that you have not returned your credit application and that your order for four sofas is still pending credit approval. Would you please let us know if we have misplaced the application?

⇨ As you requested, we have reviewed our records and can find no discrepancies. Our investigation still shows an outstanding balance of $2,339.39. We are enclosing a complete record of all transactions so that you can compare our records to yours. If these are your purchases, would you please forward the balance to us in the enclosed envelope.

Include all the details—amounts, dates, invoice or order numbers, account numbers, check numbers, copies of previous correspondence.

Give any other available, relevant information about how the discrepancy or error occurred, expressing regret if the error was yours.

⇨ We regret that our clerk transposed the numbers when she entered them on the computer.

⇨ Human error again. As much as we would like to blame the error on the computer, we can't in this case. We inadvertently mislaid the check you sent and discovered it only after we mailed this month's invoices.

⇨ Possibly Bill Hughes from your office did not pass on to anyone his directions for us to reinvest the credit balance. We regret the confusion—we should have verified those directions with you again. Your payment did not arrive until two days after our billing cycle closed.

⇨ We have no record of having received your return shipment of the merchandise.

⇨ One other bit of information that may be useful to you in investigating the problem: Our proof of delivery states that Kay Smearson signed for the package.

⇨ We suggest that you talk further with the engineer who placed the order, to verify the extent of the damages. It was our understanding that only the glass was broken, a repair we can make easily and inexpensively.

Reestablish a business-as-usual tone to close.

⇨ Thank you for helping us resolve this issue.

⇨ Thank you for reviewing your transactions once again.

⇨ We appreciate your help in correcting our records.

⇨ We will appreciate anything further you can tell us about the situation.

⇨ We appreciate your business and your effort in bringing this error to our attention.

⇨ We are pleased to correct this error for you and value your future business.

⇨ Let us know immediately if we can expect your payment.

➪ Let us know if you have some further information of which we are unaware.

➪ Let us know if you have other details that might clarify the discrepancy.

➪ Do you have any other information—names of people with whom you spoke, for example, or dates of your calls—that would help us investigate further?

❖ ❖ ❖

Dear Mr. Trayvert:

Upon researching your account with our bank, we find that you have a credit balance of $432.88. Because your account has been closed since January 4, we are sending the attached cashier's check to clear this credit from our files.

We have appreciated your past business, and should you return to our area, we would be pleased to serve you again.

Sincerely,

❖ ❖ ❖

Dear Ms. Mitaka:

Thank you for your letter about the invoice we sent you upon delivery of our computer to your office. You are quite correct; we delivered the computer to the wrong customer and billed you by error. Please return the computer to us COD, and we will credit your account for the $6,322.48 immediately.

We have enclosed a copy of our invoice #TVB3882 and a proof of delivery. According to our information, Fred Carson of your receiving department signed for it.

Thank you for your patience and help in resolving this matter. Without your phone call, our search for the missing computer would have been a time-consuming mystery! We regret the error, and look forward to a future opportunity to deliver your next *correct* order.

Sincerely,

❖ ❖ ❖

VERIFYING CREDIT RECORDS

Guidelines and Alternate Phrasing

Request the credit information immediately. When writing to a third party, state that the credit applicant has given the reader as a reference.

⇨ Bob Jones has asked that we contact you for verification of his credit records.

⇨ We are in the process of opening an account for Bloomfuller, Inc., and this organization has given your name as a reference.

⇨ Would you help us by supplying some credit information on Mr. and Mrs. C. J. Seltman. They have listed your names as a reference on our credit application.

⇨ Would you help us with credit information on Ms. Cecelia James? She has suggested we contact you about her credit history with your organization.

Identify the information you want specifically from the individual or from the third-party reference.

⇨ She has plans to purchase merchandise amounting to $4,550. Do you have any reason to think she could not repay this amount?

⇨ Would you give us details about the promptness of his last six payments?

⇨ Can you give us the amount still owed your organization and the average monthly outstanding balance?

⇨ Would you please send us your income tax returns for the past two years.

⇨ We need these documents from you: 1) . . .

Make the response easy. Suggest a phone call or a margin note on the bottom of your letter, or supply a form and a return envelope.

⇨ Please respond by completing the attached form and slipping it into the postage-paid envelope enclosed here.

⇨ Simply jot us your answers in the margin and return our letter in the enclosed envelope.

⇨ If a phone call is easier for you, please ask for Joanne Summers at 325-444-0987.

Promise confidentiality.

⇨ We will, or course, keep any information you provide confidential.

⇨ This information will not leave our offices.

⇨ This information is for our use only, of course, and the customer will not be privy to your comments.

⇨ We can assure you that this information will remain confidential.

❖ ❖ ❖

Ladies or Gentlemen:

MacNult and Associates has asked to open a credit account with us and has given your name as a reference.

Would you please help us with some credit information on this organization? Has this company been prompt in their payments to you? What is their credit limit? What other information do you have about their history that might help us determine their ability to repay an account of approximately $56,000?

We, of course, will keep any details you can give us completely confidential. Thank you for your willingness to share this information in serving our mutual customer.

Sincerely,

❖ ❖ ❖

❖ ❖ ❖

Dear Buell:

In our recent attempts to reconcile our investment system to the bank statements, we discovered that we did not have sufficient information. We have been able to reconcile all security types except collateralized mortgage obligations. We need the bank to provide us with a supplemental statement each month that will reflect this information.

I've talked to several people in Treasury and have been unable to resolve this problem from my position. Consequently, I need you to please help me by requesting from your own contact at the bank this additional information.

Collateralized mortgage obligations are unique because these security types frequently have unscheduled prepayments of principal. However, these prepayments are not reflected in the bank's monthly statement.

A draft letter is attached as a model; feel free to use this one or your own.

Sincerely,

❖ ❖ ❖

Dear Ms. Cox:

A review of our files indicates that we have not received the year-end 19—financial data for your company. Therefore, we will appreciate your sending us your latest statements.

And in the event you issue interim statements, we would also like to receive them on an ongoing basis. If, for some reason, financial data is not available, please let us know. Would you also place our name on your mailing list to receive future reports as they become available.

Thank you for forwarding these statements to us so that we can continue your credit line without disruption.

Sincerely,

❖ ❖ ❖

❖ ❖ ❖

Dear Mr. Fritterbux:

We want to take this opportunity to thank you for your patronage. In an effort to serve our valued customers better, we are attempting to extend the maximum credit limit permissible for your purchases here. Would you help us by supplying the following information:

- Bank references, account numbers, addresses
- Trade references, account numbers, addresses
- Financial statements
- Statement of Exemption and Current Tax Status

The above information will be kept confidential. Thank you.

Sincerely,

❖ ❖ ❖

OFFERING CREDIT

Guidelines and Alternate Phrasing

Tell the reader that you are extending credit.

⇨ We are pleased to tell you that our investigation has verified your fine credit standing, and we are happy to open an account for you.

⇨ We will be opening an account for you immediately; your credit history is exemplary.

⇨ Today International Engineering and Equipment has approved your credit line for $300,000, based on the financial information you provided us, dated March 9, 19—.

⇨ We are happy to extend credit to you for the purchase of the software packages you have ordered.

⇨ Your credit record is excellent, and we have now opened your account with Rorger, Inc.

Explain the terms of the credit—credit limit, payment plan, invoicing cycle, and so forth.

⇨ You will receive your statement shortly after the sixteenth of each month.

⇨ You may charge up to $800.

⇨ Our terms are 30 days with no interest charge. A monthly service charge of one percent will be added to any outstanding balance.

⇨ We will require updated financial information periodically.

State your confidence in a positive future business relationship.

⇨ We look forward to having you with us.

⇨ We are pleased to have you as customer.

⇨ We're looking forward to a mutually positive business partnership.

⇨ Thank you for doing business with us; we look forward to meeting your needs.

⇨ Thank you for your interest in our products; we look forward to servicing your account.

⇨ Our business partnership should be highly rewarding.

⇨ Our business partnership is an excellent idea—we're happy to go to work for you.

❖   ❖   ❖

Dear Mr. Carter:

Thank you for the opportunity to provide a financing alternative for the copier you are evaluating. Blaycox International has been approved for both our "Lease with Option to Purchase" and "Deferred Payment" plans. The approval is subject to a down payment of 15 percent of the amount financed. The rates and terms for both plans are summarized on the attached page.

The monthly payments are based on financing the total amount of the quote you received from us. These payments also include personal property tax, but do not include insurance or sales tax.

Thank you for considering our copiers; we think you'll be very pleased with their performance and dependability.

Sincerely,

❖ ❖ ❖

Dear Mr. Hume:

On the basis of financial information dated August 1, 19—, from your company, we are pleased to extend to you a line of credit of $250,000. In conformance with the industry, credit limits under normal circumstances are extended for a period of one year from the date of the financial information provided.

In order for us to continue to extend a line of credit, we will require that you forward to us your most recent fiscal year-end balance sheet and the related statements of income and expenses on an annual basis. Please make a note of this necessary update.

Thank you for depending on us for your financial needs, and for your usual fine cooperation with our procedures.

Respectfully,

❖ ❖ ❖

Dear Ms. Canfield:

Welcome to Buford's as a preferred charge customer! Your credit application has been approved, and you can begin enjoying the convenience of your preferred charge status today.

To make sure you don't miss out on a moment of shopping, we've already assigned you account number 45812IT so that you can charge up to $1,000 immediately. Please use your account number every time you place an order or inquire about your account, because it helps us serve you more quickly and efficiently. You'll also soon be receiving a Buford credit card to use when shopping by mail or in our stores.

Enjoy your new Buford preferred charge and thank you for shopping with us.

Sincerely,

❖ ❖ ❖

REFUSING CREDIT

Guidelines and Alternate Phrasing

Thank the reader for his or her interest in doing business with your company.

⇨ Thank you for forwarding your credit application to us.

⇨ We appreciate your cooperation in completing our credit application.

⇨ Thank you for allowing us to review your credit application and history.

⇨ We were pleased to know that you are interested in buying our products.

State your refusal of credit in a tactful way, giving your reasons, if appropriate.

⇨ We have received information that we cannot ignore in making our credit decision. This information leads us to believe that because your monthly expenses are very near your monthly income, the financial burden for you would be excessive.

⇨ We think that it is in the interest of both Sevelle and you that we decline to extend credit at this time.

⇨ With the current economic situation, we have had to set and abide by strict guidelines for credit. We are sorry that your situation did not fall within the acceptable limits.

⇨ Because we cannot find record of any previous credit references, we are unable to open an account at this time.

⇨ Our research shows some information that has caused us to decide against granting credit in this instance.

Mention under what conditions, if any, you will review your decision.

➪ If you think that your credit information as provided to us is incomplete or inaccurate, please let us know.

➪ We suggest that you write us again if you think you have further information that would make a difference in our credit evaluation.

➪ Perhaps after another year of prompt payments on the accounts you now have outstanding, we can take another look at the situation.

➪ If you have a considerable increase in monthly income ($500, for example), please let us have that information and we will re-evaluate the decision at that time.

Ask for the business on a cash basis.

➪ We hope you choose to deal with us on a cash basis.

➪ Thank you for expressing interest in our products; may we send them to you on a cash basis?

➪ If you can pay cash for the equipment, we would love to have your business.

➪ We will, of course, appreciate the opportunity to have your business if you can send us cash for the products.

➪ We hope you can purchase the equipment with cash. We think you'll be very pleased with the machine's performance.

❖ ❖ ❖

Dear Mr. Portelo:

Thank you for your interest in Arrow's products and services. After carefully considering your credit application and history, however, we find that our stringent guidelines will not allow us to extend credit at this time because of your past difficulties.

If you have some further information that we have not yet considered or if you feel the credit history supplied to us is erroneous, please feel free to write us again and we will reopen the credit investigation.

Our products are reliable and effective; we do hope you can make other arrangements to buy and use them.

Sincerely,

❖ ❖ ❖

CANCELING CREDIT

Guidelines and Alternate Phrasing

Summarize the poor credit history and situation in a tactful manner, including the unpaid balance.

⇨ We show five unpaid invoices dating back to March of this year. The total now due us is $982.34.

⇨ We have extended credit to your organization on three previous occasions for a total of $6,300 and still have received no payment according to the terms to which you agreed.

⇨ For several months now, we have been trying to work with you to resolve the outstanding balance of $890.34 on your account with us. We fear the situation is not improving for you or for us.

⇨ Our records show a lawnmower purchase June 8 for $456.57, a power-tool purchase on June 16 for $389.39, and lawn furniture purchased on July 30 for $1230.90. All of these items are still outstanding now after seven months.

Offer any alternative arrangement that you will accept for future business, and suggest some follow-up meeting or method to repay the balance. Be clear about your decision to terminate the current credit arrangement.

⇨ We cannot extend further credit and have closed your account. We are willing to work with you, however, to repay the unpaid balance over a longer time period.

⇨ Have you thought of contacting an agency that would help you consolidate all of your monthly bills into one payment and get the credit situation under more formal control? Whatever you decide about going this route, we will have to refuse further credit with our organization.

⇨ Perhaps your local bank could assist you in a loan that would minimize the burden of such unpaid accounts. In any case, we have had to close your account with us until the situation changes.

⇨ We simply cannot extend credit any longer. Your account has been closed. We will be willing to change your repayment structure, however, so that the monthly payments are lower and less burdensome.

Avoid an aggressive tone. Try to sound matter-of-fact or even positive, possibly suggesting that the customer tell you if there's some mistake in your own records.

⇨ If by some chance we have made some egregious error in our records, please contact us immediately.

⇨ If we do not hear from you with some further information, we will assume our understanding of the current situation is accurate.

⇨ Thank you for your understanding of our decision.

⇨ If you can make prepayments on further orders, we will be happy to ship them immediately.

❖ ❖ ❖

Dear Mr. Hyde:

You currently have three outstanding invoices amounting to $7,893.35 against your agreement, with no payment toward any of them.

Our policy is to cancel an agreement once three invoices have been generated with no payment. Unless we receive payment for the enclosed, past-due invoices within the next ten days, we must cancel your line of credit.

Please let us hear from you so that we can keep your credit line open and your records clear.

Sincerely,

❖ ❖ ❖

Dear Mr. Tiedt:

I have not received any response from you to my May 2 letter. Our records show that your account is still delinquent in the amount of $782. Your credit agreement requires that all balances be fully paid within 30 days.

While I can sympathize with your situation, you understand that we must also keep our records current to meet our own obligations. If necessary, I suggest that you talk to your bank about a loan to cover the payment to us. This may protect your credit rating and future freedom to purchase products and services in the community. In any case, we find that we can no longer extend credit to you.

Thank you for your past business, and when your situation improves, we hope you will again consider our products.

Sincerely,

❖ ❖ ❖

SERIES OF COLLECTION LETTERS

Guidelines and Alternate Phrasing

Ask for payment of the specific amount immediately.

Adopt a neutral tone on the first notice, gradually getting stronger with each letter. Your first letters are simply reminders—your own records could be in error, or your invoice may have gone astray; you don't want to anger customers unnecessarily. If it becomes necessary to write again, you should inquire about the reasons for the late payment. On subsequent letters, you may resort to an appeal to the reader to contact you and make some attempt at even partial repayment. Finally, you must demand payment in lieu of further legal action. In other words, your letters should remind, then inquire, then appeal, then demand.

Make the response simple—give all the necessary details, include a return envelope, provide a name and phone number for questions or explanations (if these are not already on your letterhead).

❖ ❖ ❖

Dear Ms. Markwardt:

Whether your payment was sent by pigeon, runner, mule train, or the U.S. Post Office, the service is lacking. Your check has not yet arrived in our office! Would you please let us know when we can expect it?

Your balance is $426.81.

Thank you,

❖ ❖ ❖

❖ ❖ ❖

Dear Mr. Birnbach:

After posting all payments received through August 1, we show no record of having received your check for $922.28 which was due on July 3. If our letter and your check have crossed in the mail, please ignore this reminder.

A printout of items we show as unpaid is attached. If you have not yet sent your payment, please do so now.

Yours truly,

❖ ❖ ❖

Dear Mr. Stein:

We appreciate your call in response to our last reminder about the overdue balance on your account. Our records indicate that your check #2624 dated Oct. 4 for $250.00 in payment for our invoices #1369 and #2699 has not been received.

Would you please assist us by verifying with your bank that this check has cleared. If it has, please forward a clear photocopy (front and back) to me. If it has not cleared, please send a replacement check.

Thank you for following up on this matter.

Sincerely,

❖ ❖ ❖

Dear Mr. Ta Hong:

As you have requested, another copy of your September 5 invoice is enclosed.

Should there by any reason why this invoice cannot be processed for payment, please contact me immediately at 456-9986.

Sincerely,

❖ ❖ ❖

❖ ❖ ❖

Dear Mr. Sharron:

Thank you for your recent payment on invoice #681955 for $6,420, leaving an outstanding balance of $2,125 on this account.

If the reason for the short payment was tax, please forward a copy of the appropriate tax certificate to my attention. We can reconcile this account only upon receipt and verification of tax-exempt status.

We'll appreciate your cooperation in clearing this outstanding balance.

Sincerely,

❖ ❖ ❖

Dear Ms. Kline:

Attached is a statement of items we show to be unpaid as of March 1 and past due on your account. Please review our statement for correctness and let us know of any discrepancies.

If there are no problems associated with these items, we request that you expedite your payment to us within the next ten working days. Thank you.

Sincerely,

❖ ❖ ❖

Dear Mr. Warella:

Are our records in error? We show your last payment of $428 is past due. According to the terms set forth in your purchase agreement, payment was due August 1. Payments received through July 31 have been credited to your account. A printout of the items we show to be delinquent is attached for your review.

If our information is incorrect, please contact me so that I can properly credit your account. If you have not yet sent your payment, please do so today.

Sincerely,

❖ ❖ ❖

❖ ❖ ❖

Dear Ms. Gomez:

We recently received your payment on our invoice #12134958 for $622.58, which results in an amount of $320.62 still owing.

Attached for your review is a photocopy of this invoice.

We will appreciate your cooperation in clearing up the remaining balance.

Sincerely,

❖ ❖ ❖

Dear Mr. Buschmann:

We recently sent you a reminder that your payment of $829.45 had not been received. As of Oct. 1, we have received neither your payment nor a reply.

Perhaps our previous letter was unintentionally overlooked or went astray in the mail. In either case, your account is now several weeks past due. If you have not already done so, please send your remittance today.

Sincerely,

❖ ❖ ❖

Dear Ms. Figurski:

We received your check for $426.99 on Dec. 1. While we thank you for the payment, we want to remind you that your purchase agreement requires that all minimum balances be paid monthly. Our records indicate that you remain delinquent in the payment of $668.22.

Please mail your check for $668.22 within the next five working days.

Sincerely,

❖ ❖ ❖

❖ ❖ ❖

Dear Mrs. Jernigan:

Our records indicate the following invoices have not been paid and are past due as of July 31:

Invoice#   Date   PO#   Amount

. . . (insert data) . . .

Should you have any reason for withholding payment on these invoices, please let us know immediately so that we may assist you in clearing these items promptly.

If no problems exist, we would appreciate payment by return mail at (address).

Thank you.

Sincerely,

❖ ❖ ❖

Dear Ms. Hull-Ryde:

We wrote you on March 15 regarding the $728.66 payment that, according to our records, has been past due for 30 days. As of today's date we are still showing the items on the attached report to be outstanding.

If you have not already done so, we ask that you please take care of these charges now. If further action is required on our part to expedite payment, please contact me or my assistant, Joan Hughes, at 449-5526.

Sincerely,

❖ ❖ ❖

❖ ❖ ❖

Dear Mr. Tamasy:

On April 2, I wrote you a letter detailing all of the services that I'd performed on your behalf regarding the potential claim against Orfin Corporation.

I am at a loss to understand why I have not heard from you about the payment due. Please let me know immediately if there was some problem with the services I rendered. Otherwise, I will appreciate your remitting my $450 legal fee at once. Again, your file is available for your review if you have questions.

Very truly yours,

❖ ❖ ❖

Dear Mr. Thorstenson:

Just a short note to confirm our conversation of May 6 concerning your past due account. You agreed to the following:

- Pay $2,000 immediately (payment to arrive in our office by no later than April 15)
- Pay the balance of your monthly payment of $325 by May 30
- Pay your total monthly payment of $782 by June 30
- Pay your total monthly payment of $782 by the twentieth of each month without interruption

I trust you are on schedule and will be able to meet the above commitments as indicated in our conversation.

Regards,

❖ ❖ ❖

❖ ❖ ❖

Dear Ms. Sheldon:

Please see the attached copy of the Proof of Delivery requested on our invoice #99826. I have also attached a photocopy of the invoice for your review.

We ask that you process this invoice for payment immediately.

Yours truly,

❖ ❖ ❖

Dear Mr. Scherf:

I understand from our phone conversation of April 22 and my further discussions with your accounts payable department that your company pays invoices on a 55-day cycle. Brighton consumer payment agreements have a net term of 30 days, with discounts allowed for early payment. Thus, your account has consistently been past due 30 to 60 days and, in some cases, 90 days.

The discounts are two percent for Electronic Funds Transfer prompt payment and one percent for payment received on or before the fifteenth day following the invoice reference date. A late payment charge is assessed if payment is received beyond the 30-day net period.

I'm enclosing some information on Electronic Funds Transfer (EFT) that you may find helpful in deciding how best to meet the terms of your consumer payment agreement. I hope we can work together to eliminate the past-due balances and to keep payments within Brighton's 30-day guidelines.

Sincerely,

❖ ❖ ❖

❖ ❖ ❖

Dear Gish:

Your check #926 dated June 6 for $792 has been returned unpaid by your bank. Once it has been returned, we cannot resubmit your check for payment. Therefore, we must ask that you make arrangements to replace this check with a *cashier's check or money order* within five days.

While we trust that the return of this check was only an unintentional accounting oversight, we are required to advise you that there will be a $20.00 charge for any checks returned in the future.

Please return your remittance in the enclosed envelope to my attention.

Yours truly,

❖ ❖ ❖

Dear Ms. Sawai:

The enclosed invoices are 60 days delinquent.

Please review your records and let me know if there is a problem with approval on these invoices. Otherwise, we would appreciate your putting these items through for immediate payment.

If you need additional data, please call me at 321-4444.

Thank you for your immediate attention to this balance.

Sincerely,

❖ ❖ ❖

Dear Mr. Ouellette:

As of January 31, we have received no response on our previous requests regarding the short payment on invoice #987544.

Since this invoice is now past our terms of net 30 days, please remit your check today.

Sincerely,

❖ ❖ ❖

❖ ❖ ❖

Dear Mr. Jarzynka:

I can find no record of your response to my May 6 letter concerning your check #2832 for $789.62, which your bank refused to honor. The amount is seriously delinquent and must be paid **immediately!**

To avoid further action, your payment by cashier's check must be received in my office by August 1. A pre-addressed envelope is enclosed.

Sincerely,

❖ ❖ ❖

Dear Mr. Luck:

Your fifth monthly payment of $426.98 is now due, and our records show that you are two months delinquent in payments for a total past due of $1,280.94. Your purchase agreement requires that your payment is due on the fourteenth day of each month.

We are concerned that you have allowed this situation to develop. Unless payment is already en route, we must insist that you pay the delinquent payments within five working days of receipt of this letter. Failure to do so will be considered a serious breach of your purchase agreement.

If you have any questions regarding this matter, please contact me or my assistant, Ted Aimes, at ext. 2977.

Sincerely,

❖ ❖ ❖

Dear Ms. Jeffries:

Several attempts have been made to reach a resolution for the open invoice on your account now totaling $3,280. Due to the extreme delinquency of your account, we must have payment in full within ten days from the date of this letter.

If we do not receive payment, we will pursue any avenue available to secure our interest.

Sincerely,

❖ ❖ ❖

Dear Mr. Gackenbach:

Despite several previous collection attempts, we still have not received your last three payments, for a total of $1892.68.

We view this as a serious breach of your purchase obligation. If full payment is not received immediately, we may be forced to seek recourse as provided for under the terms of the agreement.

Sincerely,

❖ ❖ ❖

Dear Ms. Gaerty:

Your check #9264 dated May 10 for $2,192.68 has been returned unpaid by your bank.

Because you have previously had checks returned for insufficient funds and have been advised of the fee for subsequent returned checks, we must assess a charge of $20.00 to offset our costs in re-processing your payment.

We now make formal demand of you for the payment (by **cashier's check** or **money order**) of $2,192.68, plus the insufficient-check fee of $20.00, within ten days of receipt of this letter. Further, we can no longer honor your company checks and can accept only cashier's checks or money orders. After ten days, outstanding insufficient funds checks may be referred for collection to the District Attorney's office without notice.

Please send your payment now to my attention at the address listed above.

Sincerely,

❖ ❖ ❖

❖ ❖ ❖

Dear Ms. Callesen:

Once again we find it necessary to write you about the seriously delinquent nature of your payments. Our records show that you have not made the last three payments and still owe us for several invoices billed in June. The total past due as of today's date is $6,202.64.

In fact, our records show that you have been in an almost constant state of delinquency this entire year. To be quite frank, our patience is at an end. Unless the entire $6,202.64 is paid before year's end, we intend to apply full legal pressure against you to enforce payment.

I sincerely hope such unpleasantness can be avoided, and you can make the necessary financial arrangements to bring your account up to date. The decision is yours.

Sincerely,

❖ ❖ ❖

Dear Mr. Gwynn:

Despite our previous collection letters and conversations, I find that you have made no progress in bringing your payments up to date, and, in fact, are now delinquent in three months' payments totaling $3,106.

I am aware of your situation, and while I sympathize, under no circumstance could I consider your check for $200 as adequate evidence of "good faith" efforts to retire this delinquency.

Demand is hereby made upon you for the immediate payment of $3,106. The attached printout lists charges remaining unpaid as of September 30. If payment in full is not received in my office by Monday, October 12, I see no alternative other than to recommend that you be sent the legally required notice of default, and thereafter that we initiate such legal action as is required to fully collect the monies due under our purchase agreement.

Yours very truly,

❖ ❖ ❖

❖ ❖ ❖

Dear Mr. Guardsmitz:

In discussing the July 6 letter to me regarding Mr. Bruce's claim for the attached invoices, Mr. Bruce has indicated that unless we can resolve this matter in some reasonably short time frame I should institute suit on the matter.

Certainly, your original letter did state that you intended to return the equipment you removed from his shop on November 5. But you have neither returned the equipment nor paid his invoices, despite his many requests to hear from you.

Unless a reasonable effort is made on your part to pay Mr. Bruce for the equipment within the next 14 days, he has authorized me to file suit in the proper court and pursue judgment against you.

I will appreciate your immediate action.

Very truly yours,

❖ ❖ ❖

RESPONDING TO COLLECTION LETTERS

Guidelines and Alternate Phrasing

Tell the creditor that you intend to pay the amount owed but must do so with different arrangements—for a lower amount each accounting period or over a longer time frame.

⇨ We are making every effort to repay the outstanding balance with your company, but we need your understanding about the minimum amounts due each month.

⇨ Our organization does plan to remit the balance of $5,600 on our account with your company, but we must ask for an extension of 90 days.

⇨ We have reviewed our account with your company and the outstanding balance of $2,239.45. Although we have full intentions to remit the complete amount, we must ask for your patience in changing the terms of our agreement to allow us to resolve some current cashflow problems.

⇨ With your flexibility in payment terms, we are going to be able to pay you the full amount of $457 owing on our account. However, in light of a drastic reduction in income because of my wife's current unemployment, we must have a lower minimum payment each month.

Enclose some amount, if at all possible, to show your intention to pay in full on a delayed schedule.

⇨ Please consider the enclosed check for $50 as my best effort in beginning repayment of the loan.

⇨ We have enclosed $5,000 toward the full balance of $30,000. We intend to forward the remainder of the money over the next six months.

⇨ The attached check for $250 will show you our good intentions in reducing the outstanding balance as soon as possible.

Explain your situation and reasons for past nonpayment.

⇨ Our industry has experienced a tremendous downturn within the past two months, as I'm sure you've read in the newspapers.

⇨ We have recently moved, and your invoices did not reach us at the new address for almost three months, at which time we were out of the country.

⇨ Two of our major accounts are late with their payments to us, and although we're embarrassed to say so, we are caught short in the middle.

⇨ Due to the recent illness of the principal of our firm, we have had to postpone work on several of our major consulting projects. As soon as we resume that work and complete those contracts, we will be able to take care of our account with you.

⇨ My husband has recently lost his job, and we simply are unable to meet our current obligations. As soon as he finds work again, we will contact you and begin payment again on this account.

Remind your creditor of your past business and suggest that you plan to give them future business when times improve.

⇨ We have enjoyed doing business with you over the years, and hope this temporary situation does not affect that partnership.

⇨ We appreciate your patience in allowing us to extend our payments over a longer period. We trust that when we buy from you in the future, we will not run into this embarrassing situation again.

⇨ We have enjoyed using your services in the past and hope to continue to do so after this current matter is resolved.

⇨ After this temporary setback, we intend to return to our past volume of business with you.

⇨ We appreciate your bearing with us during the next three months, and we will remember your loyalty.

⇨ Thank you for agreeing to work with us on this credit matter; we want to resume our orders with you as soon as possible.

❖ ❖ ❖

Dear Mr. Nebraskan:

Your letter about the outstanding balance of $4,300 on our account arrived today. Yes, we do intend to pay the full amount; however, we do need to discuss with you a different payback schedule. As evidence of our intentions, we have enclosed a check for $500 against the remaining balance.

As you can imagine in a small family-owned business, every client counts. During this past quarter we have had three major clients reduce the volume of their orders to us during this economic downturn. Their actions have drastically affected our cash flow, and we are in the process of restructuring and streamlining our own operations to reduce overhead and meet our current obligations.

Thank you for your understanding of this temporary situation; we do hope to pay you in full within the next 12 months and to continue to use your services. We do want to continue our five-year relationship on a favorable note.

Sincerely,

❖ ❖ ❖

DECLINING TO DO BUSINESS

Occasionally, you'll find yourself in the difficult position of having to turn your back on an opportunity to do business because of ethical issues, your own lack of expertise, time, or product, or any number of other reasons.

An individual's expression of interest in doing business with you is a compliment; turning down that business opportunity often comes across as an insult. Therefore, such letters demand special care in presenting the reasons for that decision. To suggest an alternative action and to imply that you're thinking of the other's welfare as well as your own softens what could be a blunt message.

DECLINING TO DO BUSINESS

Guidelines and Alternate Phrasing

Thank the reader for his or her interest in your product, service, or organization.

⇨ Thank you for contacting us about the research work you have underway.

⇨ We appreciate your writing us about the products you saw advertised recently.

⇨ Thank you for phoning us about the availability of your staff to complete the Sycon project.

⇨ We appreciate having the opportunity to review the materials you sent us about your organization.

⇨ Your interest in Sycon Inc. is flattering.

⇨ Thank you for inquiring about our bidding process and the projects now underway.

⇨ Your offer to help us complete the Lybednon work is generous and tempting.

⇨ We've heard a great deal about your organization and are flattered that you would think of contacting us about ....

⇨ Your information arrived today; thank you for considering our products and services in your marketing and distribution plans.

⇨ Your future plans sound exciting; thank you for offering to make us a part of them.

Lead into your statement of refusal by first outlining your reasons for the decision. Then state your turndown as positively and tactfully as possible.

⇨ We have already made prior commitments for contracting such work.

⇨ We think a decision to narrow our focus to one company such as yours would limit our future plans. Therefore, to keep our options open with regard to . . ., we have decided to . . .

⇨ The information you provided on your work with valves interests me a great deal; however, there is currently no formal procurement requirement or open solicitation for this effort.

⇨ The research you mention in your letter has to do with hydroponics and greenhouse systems. Our emphasis here is primarily on solid substrate mediums rather than hydroponics. The bulk of the work you mentioned is being conducted at other locations.

⇨ As you may imagine, we can foresee a possible conflict of interest in that . . .

⇨ Therefore, to avoid all appearances of favoritism, we have decided to . . .

⇨ Our experience in similar situations tells us that there could be legal ramifications if we were to join hands in . . .

⇨ Because of the politics of the situation and the impression that this relationship might leave with our own employees, we must decline the opportunity to . . .

Suggest that it may not be in the best interest of your reader to do business with you under the circumstances or that he or she should devote efforts elsewhere.

⇨ We believe that you could formulate a much better arrangement if you contacted some of our competitors who do not perform this work in-house. The price compares very favorably with other products of lower quality than yours; I suggest that you raise your price before offering the product line to a more suitable distributor.

⇨ I'm afraid that we simply do not do the volume of business that you would expect for your profit margins on an exclusive arrangement.

⇨ If I were you, I'd refurbish the equipment and housing and offer it to a buyer in the local market. Possibly such a buyer could pay you more than we could because of the logistics and distance involved.

⇨ We think that you'll find our philosophies too restrictive for your future plans.

⇨ We fear that our structure here would be limiting to your creativity in solving many problems.

⇨ You deserve freedom to make pricing choices, and our current arrangement would limit that freedom.

⇨ I'm sure you would be concerned with copyright infringement possibilities, so rather than create confusion over these issues, we think it best to decline.

Offer any referral, if possible, for the product or service.

⇨ In the event you want to contact other divisions, I have attached a list of names.

⇨ Perhaps you can check listings in the Dallas area for nonprofits in a position to take advantage of your work.

⇨ I want to take this opportunity to wish you well in your efforts to contact other interested organizations.

⇨ Elaine Turnbolt may be more interested than I in such a program.

⇨ Perhaps Booker and Charles Ltd. could offer you more exposure than we could. Feel free to use our name in contacting them.

⇨ Let me make one suggestion: Humbolt, Inc., would seem a likely candidate for this service.

⇨ Have you thought of offering your service to Humbolt, Inc.?

⇨ Despite our inability to work out clear, unambiguous arrangements, we wish you success with the project.

❖ ❖ ❖

Dear Mr. Abrams:

Thank you for your interest in submitting a proposal for the construction work to be done at our Brownsville plant.

The project requires very specialized equipment and technical expertise available from only a few sources that we've currently identified. The limited information you provided in your letter does not justify delaying our decision on this project in order to receive your full proposal. However, if you would like to discuss your ideas with agency representatives before expending extensive preparation time on later projects, we suggest that you contact Raymond Fraiar at ext. 3458. If he considers your capabilities to be in line with our needs for this project, he then can add your name to the bidder's list for similar projects.

Our company fosters and encourages new and innovative ideas relevant to our mission requirements, and we encourage you to contact other branches of our agency to identify other ventures that you may be interested in pursuing.

Sincerely,

❖ ❖ ❖

Dear Mr. Sanchez:

Thank you for contacting us once again about your information service, *Direct Communications.* We recognize the quality improvements and cost reductions that your organization has achieved over the past few years within many companies around the nation.

After reevaluating your material, we still believe that the content is "nice to know," but we have difficulty in measuring its value to our organization in light of our production cost of the series. Most of the information has become available to us through other channels.

We know, too, that obviously you have some costs in offering the information to us even on a complimentary basis; at the least, the coordination of new issues takes your valuable time. Therefore, our decision to no longer accept, produce, and distribute this information will probably afford you opportunity to apply your efforts on companies that can and will schedule workshops based on your series.

You have our very best wishes with the series. We hope your complimentary arrangement leads to many profitable training sessions in organizations with a budget larger than ours.

Sincerely,

❖ ❖ ❖

EMPLOYMENT

Anyone who advances to the ranks of management will find himself or herself dealing with letters regarding employment matters: to accept or refuse job applicants, to issue or interpret statements of company policy, to offer or decline promotions, and, unfortunately, to reprimand or dismiss nonproductive employees.

Aside from the employment issues, you have to be mindful of numerous legal implications. With such letters, you must walk the fine line between praise and promises, tact and truth, and company and court.

ACKNOWLEDGING RECEIPT OF RÉSUMÉS

Guidelines and Alternate Phrasing

Thank the applicant for his or her interest in your organization.

State your intentions with regard to the résumé: Will you file it for future reference? Forward it to someone else? Review and evaluate it with your staff? Call later to arrange an interview if you are interested in talking further?

❖ ❖ ❖

Dear Mr. Graves:

Thank you for forwarding your résumé to us; we are always pleased to hear from those who have high regard for our organization and consequently seek employment here.

We will be reviewing your résumé, along with several others received after our *Wall Street Journal* ad appeared last week. If, after our review process, your experience and expectations seem to match those of the position we want to fill, we will call you to discuss the possibility of an interview.

We appreciate your letting us review your résumé.

Sincerely,

❖ ❖ ❖

150

ANNOUNCING PROMOTIONS/TRANSFERS _____

Guidelines and Alternate Phrasing

Announce the promotion or transfer, including the new title, effective date, and reporting line.

⇨ Barbara Stedman has recently assumed the position of director of Human Resources, reporting directly to Michael Treadwell.

⇨ We are pleased to welcome Harvey Malone to the position of controller, effective October 15. Harvey will be reporting to the vice president of operations here in Atlanta.

Outline the major new responsibilities.

Highlight some of the past accomplishments that led to the promotion or transfer.

⇨ As you may remember, Marla has led our team to record sales on the Fusia products for the last two years.

⇨ In past positions, David has developed policies and procedures on personnel issues and negotiated client contracts for gas purchases.

⇨ Harold comes to us from United Ferris, where he held several internal auditing positions.

⇨ Carol led the effort to restructure our European division, a turnaround that within three years resulted in a 428 percent increase in gross revenue.

Express confidence in the newly promoted or transferred employee's future success.

⇨ We have every confidence that Joanna will do great things in this capacity.

⇨ We are watching eagerly as David establishes new client contacts in this region.

⇨ We have great expectations for Marla as she assumes this new role.

⇨ Our support is with you, Marilyn, as you forge ahead into these uncharted waters of Waverly accounts.

⇨ We look forward to his leadership in this new position.

⇨ We welcome his creativity with this new assignment.

⇨ I'm anticipating great things from John with this challenge.

⇨ John, welcome and good luck.

⇨ Our best to you, Marla, as you assume the reins of this new challenge.

⇨ The opportunities and the challenges are great. We wish Foster well.

⇨ The challenges and the rewards are there—we're excited about what Rob can do and wish him well.

⇨ Joanne undoubtedly is the right person for this "mega" assignment.

⇨ With great confidence, we want to express our best wishes to Seiko as she masterminds our division's future success.

❖ ❖ ❖

To All Employees:

We are pleased to announce the promotion of Donna Sizemore to vice president of marketing for our European operations, effective September 1. In this new position, Donna will be reporting directly to Richard Chambers.

This assignment will involve a challenge starting from the ground up, with a plethora of opportunities to excel in a totally new arena. Donna will be setting up distributorships in England, Spain, Sweden, Portugal, and Italy for our automotive products. Then she will be opening retail centers for the remainder of our product lines, with all the accompanying responsibilities that entails.

Donna has proven her mettle, even in a weak and unstable economy, having come to us 15 years ago as an eager sales rep fresh out of the University of Texas. Her career has taken her through several positions throughout the eastern and southern divisions as local, regional, and divisional manager.

Please join me in offering your congratulations and support to Donna in this new challenge. We're expecting her to take Europe by storm.

Sincerely,

❖ ❖ ❖

EMPLOYMENT OFFERS

Guidelines and Alternate Phrasing

Make the job offer, including position title, salary, and starting date.

⇨ We are happy to offer you a position as accounting clerk with BTI, effective May 1, at a starting salary of $22,000.

⇨ BTI is pleased to say that we have selected to serve as manager of health facilities with our organization. We'd like to make you an immediate offer of $46,000 annually, with a first salary review scheduled six months later. Your starting date would be April 15.

⇨ I want to confirm our offer to you of a position as systems analyst here in Tulsa, effective June 15. The annual starting salary is $32,500.

⇨ John, after the two recent visits with you and your wife while you were here in Detroit, we have had time to assemble our group and discuss your excellent qualifications for the managerial position in our Louisville center. We'd like to make you an offer of employment (Director of Testing), effective February 1, at a starting salary of $72,000.

Summarize again, with key management employees, the primary job responsibilities to avoid later misunderstandings about goals and performance standards.

⇨ As we discussed, we want you to assume responsibility for our entire marketing operations in the Southern Division, including staffing, distributorships, promotional support literature, and visibility in the local media.

⇨ You will be responsible for all data-processing and telecommunications functions within the headquarters location.

⇨ Our primary goal for you over the next year will be to identify European markets for our two latest product lines.

⇨ Your assignment will be a rough one—to identify and recommend cost-reduction measures, with a goal of reducing our total workforce by approximately 50 percent.

Ask for a response by a specific date if the job offer has not already been accepted by phone or in person. If the job offer is rather open-ended, suggest a general time frame for some further contact.

⇨ If you decide to come to work for us, we need an answer by December 1.

⇨ Please call Mike Douglas with your answer by the end of the week.

⇨ We hope to have a positive answer from you by May 9.

⇨ If you are interested in this position, we'd like to hear from you within the next two weeks.

⇨ We need your decision by May 20 so that we have time to process the paperwork for your overseas trip with the next group of inspectors.

Give any necessary details about orientation, health records and testing, or forms processing.

⇨ On your first day of employment, we will handle all the paperwork with regard to insurance and so forth.

⇨ On your first morning, we ask that you report directly to Employee Relations, where they will give you information about the required health testing and certification procedures.

⇨ When we receive your positive reply, we will forward a new-employee packet to you with all the necessary paperwork and reporting details.

Welcome the employee to the company and express confidence in his or her future.

⇨ We are eager to hear from you about this job—it seems the perfect match.

⇨ We are so pleased to have you as an employee.

⇨ We're looking forward to many years together as you grow along with the company.

⇨ We're excited about the possibility of your coming to work with us.

⇨ We believe you can make a great contribution to the company; we hope you'll see the relationship as mutually beneficial.

⇨ May we look forward to your putting your talents to work here?

⇨ We can't wait to get you on board, Marilyn.

⇨ The staff is eager to have your answer; they enjoyed visiting with you tremendously and expect great things together.

⇨ We can certainly profit from your leadership. We hope your answer is positive.

⇨ We'll hope for a quick, yes response.

⇨ Your experience will allow you to hit the ground running on the projects we have underway. Welcome to the team.

⇨ We look forward to a long and productive relationship for us both.

❖ ❖ ❖

Dear Mr. Hyde:

We are pleased to offer you a position as an associate programmer in our Colonade offices upon completion of your degree this semester. In line with our latest salary increases, we can offer you a starting salary of $36,800. Although we have some flexibility to work with you in scheduling a starting date, we would like to have you report to work by May 15.

If you decide to accept this position, we will begin immediately to schedule you for our three-week orientation program in Cleveland. The details of that and other forms processing we'll forward to you later.

Please call Mark Spencer directly at 214-555-0494 to give him your response by Friday, May 6. We look forward to your decision to go to work with us because we believe your background and interests will make your association with us mutually rewarding.

Sincerely,

❖ ❖ ❖

NONSELECTION OF APPLICANTS—NO OPENING

Guidelines and Alternate Phrasing

Thank the applicant for his or her interest in the position. If you have reviewed the résumé, you may want to comment on the applicant's experience, skills, or achievements.

➪ Thank you for allowing us to review your résumé. We were most impressed with your academic achievements—you must be very pleased.

➪ Thank you for taking the time to send us your résumé.

➪ We appreciate your interest in investigating job possibilities at Revmore.

➪ We read your résumé with interest; your experience is impressive.

⇨ We are always pleased to receive résumés such as yours that show so much rich experience in the oil industry.

⇨ Thank you for the opportunity to read your résumé and evaluate your credentials. Your work history seems impressive and widespread in the industry.

⇨ From reviewing your résumé, we see that you have had an excellent employment history. Thank you for letting us know of your interest in working for Babcox.

⇨ Thank you for your letter and your résumé detailing your work history and credentials.

⇨ We appreciate your letting us know of your availability for employment at Wilmax Associates.

⇨ We appreciate your time in preparing such a comprehensive résumé for our review at Futuro Services.

State that you have no job opening at the present time. If you plan to keep the résumé on file or refer the applicant to someone else, say so. You will also build goodwill by suggesting another company or contact as a possible employer or source of leads.

⇨ We, unfortunately, have no openings. With your permission, however, I'd like to pass along your letter and résumé to our headquarters office, just in case they have an opening of which I'm unaware. If so, they'll contact you directly.

⇨ We regret that we have no openings at the present. May we keep your résumé on file for the future?

⇨ Occasionally we have unanticipated openings that might be appropriate for your skills. Should that be the case, we will pass your résumé along to others in the organization who might want to talk with you further.

⇨ We will keep your résumé in our active file for one year. If we have openings within that time frame, you can be assured that we will again review the information you sent.

⇨ Although we have no openings in the sales area, we suggest that you contact our Minneapolis office to see what their needs are there.

⇨ Unfortunately, we have nothing available at the moment. In case an opening does materialize, I'll have my office contact you immediately to talk further.

⇨ We have no vacancies in line with your qualifications and expectations; however, we suggest that you may want to consider nonprofit organizations in the area.

⇨ Although we have no needs in the areas you mention, please feel free to write each of our district offices about their employment plans.

⇨ Although we don't foresee any vacancies for which your skills would be appropriate, we do encourage you to keep looking in this industry. The needs of some of our fellow service organizations are quite different from ours.

Wish the applicant well in his or her job search.

⇨ We wish you success in your job search.

⇨ Thank you again for writing. Best wishes.

⇨ We hope you find an opening that matches your expectations completely.

⇨ Thank you for letting us know of your interest. We wish you success in your search process.

⇨ Good luck in finding an organization that can give you the career success you deserve.

⇨ We hope you are able to find more suitable employment opportunities elsewhere. Best wishes.

⇨ Thank you for thinking of us in light of your career-change plans. Your résumé indicates that you have much to offer.

⇨ With your achievements and academic record, you should have no trouble in finding employment.

⇨ Best wishes in finding the right job.

⇨ We know you will be successful in finding the job that you want in this region.

⇨ We value the opportunity to review the credentials of such a qualified individual. Best wishes.

⇨ Thank you again for sending us information on yourself. We hope you find a job that offers the opportunities you want for the future.

❖ ❖ ❖

Dear Mr. Toombs:

Thank you for forwarding your résumé to our offices and letting us know of your interest in the accounting area. Although your experience and academic credentials certainly look appropriate for such a position, we have no openings at the current time.

With your permission, we will keep your name in our active file for the next few months, and should we learn of a vacancy in the accounting area, we will again review your information and talk with you further.

Thank you for writing. Your work history is a gold mine—we know you will make an excellent employee with such a breadth of experience.

Sincerely,

❖ ❖ ❖

NONSELECTION OF APPLICANTS—SALARY REQUIREMENTS _____

Guidelines and Alternate Phrasing

Thank the applicant for his or her interest in working for your company, being specific about the time and effort spent in interviewing, travel to your site, and references or other information furnished for your evaluation.

⇨ Thank you for forwarding your résumé to us; we appreciate the opportunity to look at so qualified a candidate for our clinic.

⇨ We want you to know first of all how grateful we are for your willingness to interview with us when such a great distance was involved. Your travel here made it so much easier on all our staff to talk with you firsthand about their expectations for this position.

⇨ Thank you, Marilyn, for visiting with us about the job we have available in Clinton. We also very much appreciate the time you took in supplying us with such a complete portfolio.

⇨ Now that the dust has settled, we as a team have been able to talk more seriously about the position for which you interviewed. We thank you for your patience and interest in coming to work for us.

⇨ Frank, we so much appreciate the time you've spent with us during this past month while we have been outlining plans for the European expansion.

⇨ I wanted to update you on the status of your résumé with our Facilities Management division, and to thank you for bearing with us. As you probably realize, when we fill a position as important as the one we discussed with you, we are very deliberate in our evaluation process.

⇨ Thank you for taking the time to interview with us. We realize that time is one commodity that graduate students have in short supply, and we appreciate the interest you've shown in Wellesey.

⇨ Thank you for talking with us about the management position in Saudi Arabia. Your experience and achievements have such a direct bearing on the position that we have been most anxious to work out all the details.

⇨ Thank you so much for spending the time to go through the lengthy interviewing process with us. In addition to the time here on site, I know you also spent hours on the phone with other of our managers.

⇨ Thank you for the two trips you made to Dallas to talk with us about the sales position. They were time-consuming, and we appreciate the effort.

(Note: See phrases in the previous subject category.)

Comment on the applicant's experience, achievements, or attributes appropriate to the job, and then give the salary issue as your reason for the turndown. State under what conditions, if any, you might reconsider the decision.

⇨ With your telecommunication expertise and your management experience, we certainly wanted to be able to bring you aboard in this position. However, as we discussed among ourselves in evaluating your résumé, budget has always been a thorn in our side here. We find that we just can't come up with the money to meet your salary expectations.

⇨ We were very impressed with your achievements at Belview—the two service awards this past year particularly. But after reevaluating our needs here, we just do not feel that we can justify the salary requirements you outlined for us.

⇨ Although we wish we could hire someone with your pleasant disposition and willingness—even eagerness—to travel, we find that your salary expectations exceed what the job pays.

⇨ Frankly, Belinda, we thought you were perfect for the position, but we can't meet your salary demands.

⇨ Your experience at Barington and your academic ties seemed just the thing to sway our management team here. The problem is the salary range you mentioned.

⇨ Although there is no doubt you are qualified for this job—even over-qualified—we simply can't justify the salary you asked for the skills this job requires.

⇨ Quiet honestly, Bob, you were the best qualified candidate. We just can't pay the $80,000 salary you requested. Perhaps, if we ever reorganized so that this position encompassed both divisions, that salary might be feasible. But we have no such plans at the present.

⇨ We have no doubt that you could handle the job we discussed. Our problem is with the salary—we simply can't meet your requirements.

Wish the applicant well in the job search. If you wish, express regret in not having been able to agree on salary.

⇨ Thank you again for talking with us about your career plans; we regret that we were unable to agree on salary. In any case, best wishes to you.

⇨ We appreciate so much the opportunity to get to know you and regret only that we were unable to make you an offer. Our best wishes as you look elsewhere.

⇨ It was so nice to learn more about your work and plans for the future, and it is with regret that we have to forego the opportunity of a suitable working arrangement. We hope you find exactly what you're looking for.

⇨ Thank you for making the effort to interview with us. I wish we could have found a position for you here. Good luck elsewhere.

⇨ We wish you the best in finding the job you want and deserve.

⇨ We want you to know that we think your qualifications justify the salary requirements you have, and we wish you the best in locating a suitable position immediately.

   (Note: See the previous category.)

❖ ❖ ❖

Dear Mr. Terciametz:

Thank you for taking the time to talk with us about the engineering position in our Montana location. After visiting with you last week, we were impressed with your investment results in the last few years and particularly intrigued with the new investment strategy you overviewed for us.

As we discussed, however, in a beginning fund such as ours, budget decisions aren't changed lightly. We have established what we feel is a reasonable salary for the position and have determined to stay within that range. Although you no doubt could contribute greatly to our efforts here, we regret that we can't meet your salary expectations.

You have our best wishes in your job search as you seek a position with a more seasoned organization than ours. We'll be hoping to hear good things from you in the future.

Sincerely,

❖ ❖ ❖

NONSELECTION OF APPLICANTS—OTHERWISE UNSUITABLE _____

Guidelines and Alternate Phrasing

Thank the applicant for his or her interest in your company.

⇨ Thank you for the opportunity to review your résumé.

⇨ Your application with Wellesey has been routed through various technical departments for consideration by members of our staff. We appreciate your giving us the time to review your experience with our requirements in mind.

⇨ Thank you for completing our job application forms.

⇨ We appreciate your forwarding your résumé to us for consideration.

⇨ We are always pleased to hear from those who have heard favorable reports about our company and seek employment here.

⇨ Thank you for your interest in working for Bellview Clinic.

⇨ We are always flattered to receive résumés.

    (Note: See phrasing in previous categories.)

Focus on the hiring decision you've made, avoiding statements about why the reader was not selected. If you have not selected another candidate, simply state the requirements that you have for the position.

⇨ For this position, we have selected a candidate who has the prerequisite six years experience with our Model 388T computers.

⇨ After careful review of all the résumés we received, we have chosen a candidate who brings exactly the kind of experience and academic credentials we feel this job demands.

⇨ We have completed our review of the résumés and have chosen to interview several candidates who have firsthand design experience in their work history.

⇨ The candidate we selected has had the management experience we deem to be essential in this demanding position.

⇨ With the opportunity to review so many résumés, our choice has been difficult. Nevertheless, we are pleased to say that we have hired a candidate with the in-depth academic background we were hoping to find.

⇨ With such an overwhelming response to our ad, we have taken far too long to review the résumés of the qualified people interested in this position.

After much work, we are pleased to say that we have selected an individual whose career achievements in the sales industry have been outstanding.

⇨ After a lengthy process of reviewing résumés and interviewing applicants, we have narrowed our consideration to two and will be making a final decision about them within the next few days.

⇨ We have now filled the position you referred to in your letter. The individual who accepted the position has the difficult-to-find experience on the equipment we have here at Fairview.

⇨ We've now made our selection for the position. The candidate we chose has the in-depth experience, the travel flexibility, and the disposition we think this job entails.

⇨ We will be reviewing the résumés we received within the next two weeks and plan to schedule interviews with those applicants who have a masters degree and the prerequisite experience for this position. Should we want to talk with you further, you will receive a call within the next few weeks.

⇨ We are continually reassessing our needs for mailing-list brokers and will certainly keep your past relationship with our company in mind as we hire additional help.

⇨ At this time, we have selected candidates for the positions that were advertised and offers are being made to those candidates. Unfortunately, we had many more qualified candidates than positions.

⇨ It's always so difficult to choose from a field of highly motivated applicants who can contribute to the growth of our organization. However, we have finally narrowed our choice among several individuals, to whom we will be making offers shortly.

Wish the applicant well in his or her job search.

⇨ Please accept our wish for your success in the industry.

⇨ Good luck in your future endeavors.

⇨ We wish you success in finding an interesting and challenging position in your field.

⇨ We hope you have no difficulty at all in finding a position that interests you.

⇨ We want you to know that you have our best wishes for success with your career plans.

(Note: See phrasing in previous categories.)

❖ ❖ ❖

Dear Willis:

Thank you for giving us the opportunity to consider you for our training position. The résumé and curriculum samples you left with us were especially helpful in our interviewing process.

We have been very deliberate in our selection and have taken longer to fill the vacancy than we originally anticipated. After careful thought, however, we have chosen someone who has the specific combination of background, experience, and disposition we thought essential for the position. Such decisions are always difficult but rewarding, both to the individual and to us.

With your permission, we would like to keep your résumé on file for one year. Occasionally, unanticipated vacancies occur, and we want to consider you for any such openings.

Your experience is certainly valuable, and we wish you success in finding a position that suits your needs and expectations. Thank you again for your interest in Baker Consolidated.

Sincerely,

❖ ❖ ❖

POLICY AND BENEFIT STATEMENTS/EXPLANATIONS _____

Guidelines and Alternate Phrasing

Give a general overview of the policy or benefit, pointing out any major changes in the existing situation. Focus on key benefits in the policy and the positive reason for changes.

⇨ This policy should help us assist you in . . .

⇨ This change has become necessary for increased accuracy in reporting your travel expenses . . .

⇨ We are pleased to tell you that you can directly access information about your retirement benefits. Arrangements have been made with . . .

Provide a way for employees to have their questions answered and their concerns addressed—a hotline, a brochure, a forum meeting, and/or a contact name and number.

⇨ For your convenience, we have set up a hotline to give you immediate help in preparing the necessary paperwork.

⇨ You are invited to an open forum discussion on the issues that I'm sure this change will generate.

⇨ Please feel free to call our corporate headquarters with questions at extension 3345.

⇨ We welcome your questions—your complete understanding is essential to the smooth implementation of this new policy.

⇨ If you have concerns or otherwise feel that your needs have not been addressed in the enclosed packet of information, please call us. We can arrange to have someone visit your location and conduct short, informal sessions to explain the policy.

Thank the readers for their cooperation, making the tone either upbeat or neutral rather than patronizing or antagonistic.

⇨ Thank you for your usual excellent consideration.

⇨ We appreciate your patience in this time of transition.

⇨ As always, your cooperation is essential in handling these details. Thank you.

⇨ Thank you for helping us help you.

⇨ We value your support in this temporary change of plans.

⇨ We seek your patience as we work out the fine print and will let you have other details as they become available.

⇨ We hope this explanation will address most of your concerns.

⇨ We hope this communication will clarify any questions the new policy raises.

❖ ❖ ❖

To All Employees:

Because of our growing concern about the stability of Fortune Life Insurance Company and the rising costs of coverage, we have made arrangements to place our insurance with a new organization, Belton Mutual Benefit. You should benefit two ways from this change: the monthly premiums for the dependents you now carry should be an average of 5 percent lower and the deductibles will be $300 per family rather than the current $500. There will be no requirements for health exams; all who are now covered will be eligible for coverage in this new arrangement.

We will be mailing to each of you a brochure that overviews the program and answers most questions about coverage. But, of course, as with any change, there will be questions about atypical situations. For those questions or situations not addressed in that brochure, please call Helen Dolittle at ext. 3469. She is well-versed in the insurance field and will be happy to talk with you about your unique situation.

Although many organizations around the nation are now asking their employees to share in assuming the cost of health insurance, we are happy to continue to provide this coverage at no cost to you. We care about your peace of mind. Thank you for your continued fine work on behalf of BIV and your cooperation in this changeover.

Sincerely,

❖ ❖ ❖

RECRUITMENT LETTERS

Guidelines and Alternate Phrasing

Mention your recruiting efforts, being as specific as possible about any current openings. If there has been some previous contact, refer to that person, occasion, announcement, or ad.

⇨ Richard Marun gave me your name as an employee facing a possible change in careers because of RTW's downsizing plans. Therefore, I was writing to let you know of our interest in talking with you about the research opportunities at our laboratories.

⇨ We were intrigued by your recent advertisement in the *Wall Street Journal* about your employment goals in the Far East. We have just the position we think you might be interested in—director of communications for our Tokyo office.

⇨ In reviewing the academic records of students who have contacted the USC placement office, we see that your achievements are quite impressive. We're wondering if you may be interested in discussing a programmer\analyst position with our company.

⇨ We saw a recent article in the latest *Training and Development Magazine*, highlighting your work at Rocco. As a result, our vice president has asked me to let you know of our interest in visiting with you about working with us to achieve some of the same results with our engineering staff.

Overview the opportunities with your organization.

    Suggest the next action.

⇨ If you will be in the area in the near future, please call us and we'll see about scheduling time to visit with you further.

⇨ If you're interested in pursuing this opportunity, would you write or phone us.

⇨ Please let us hear from you if you have any inclination toward putting your legal background to use in this position.

⇨ We look forward to hearing from you about your plans upon graduation.

⇨ We look forward to hearing about your career-change plans.

⇨ If we can provide further insights about exactly what type individual we're looking for, give us a call at 345-9902.

⇨ If you should be interested in interviewing for this position, please call Dave Gowers at ext. 345 to schedule a convenient time the week of August 5.

⇨ If this position interests you, please forward a complete résumé to my attention.

⇨ Please write us again, if you will, providing the information I've highlighted here in my letter.

❖ ❖ ❖

Dear Joseph:

I was on campus last week and came across your records in the Placement Office. You have the kind of academic record that impresses us here at National Engineering, and I want to take this opportunity to invite you for an interview when we return for our fall recruiting visit.

We will be back on campus October 12–14 with the SRT team, scheduling our interviews in the Placement Office. If you are interested in discussing employment with us, please phone me (306-222-4468) any time before that date or drop by the Placement Office during Oct. 12–14 and sign up for an appointment time then.

As you may know, our SRT team is a subsidiary of Packard, with primary responsibilities involving security and energy research for various federal agencies. We employ a technical and support staff of about 6,800. As one of only a few nuclear-research laboratories, we have traditionally emphasized engineering research and development, with strong supporting activities in the physical sciences.

In recent years, our mission has expanded to include energy research that compliments our weapons technologies. We now play a major role in the national effort to develop new or improved sources of energy.

If you are interested in pursuing employment opportunities with our organization, we look forward to meeting with you on our next visit to your campus.

Sincerely,

❖ ❖ ❖

REPRIMAND

Guidelines and Alternate Phrasing

Overview the performance or attitude problem.

Document specific details of the situation and its seriousness. Be sure to be specific about exactly what attitude, action, or decision needs to be corrected.

Make any positive comments you can about past performance, attitudes, or contributions, and show confidence that the situation can improve.

⇨ You have always given your cooperation in similar situations, and we know we can count on you again to solve this problem.

⇨ We appreciate your willingness to work toward a remedy of this situation.

⇨ You have performed in a completely satisfactory way up to this point; we hope you will have no difficulty with this recent assignment.

⇨ May we count on your support in correcting the problem?

⇨ You have been conscientious about your jobs on other occasions, and we want to assume you have that same attitude about improving this situation.

⇨ You have been punctual with your orders until these last few weeks; we are eager to return to that appropriate order-processing condition.

⇨ We hope you will decide to improve the situation.

⇨ We hope you will decide to give us your cooperation in this matter.

On any subsequent warnings that you find necessary, refer to past repri-mands and give notice of the next action if the situation does not improve.

⇨ This is our second notice, and we hope our last before the situation turns around. A third warning will be immediate cause for dismissal.

⇨ If I discover this situation again, we will be forced to terminate your employment.

⇨ We hope these notices are sufficient to change the situation. If the disagreements continue, we will have no choice but to terminate the employment of all those involved.

⇨ Should this problem recur, we will have to ask for your resignation.

⇨ The decision is yours. We need to see a 20 percent increase in your output or we will have to let you go.

⇨ You will receive no further warnings about this performance. Our next action will be to terminate your employment here.

⇨ This memo is our second warning about the unacceptable actions. Any recurrence will mean immediate dismissal.

❖ ❖ ❖

TO: Harold Springer

RE: Kitchen Requirements Planning

On August 9, you and I had a discussion about the need for you to schedule your workday each Friday so that you could prepare the food and supplies requisitions for the executives' club kitchen for the upcoming week. Then you were to secure the items from the warehouse and store them in the kitchen or walk-in freezer for easy access during meal-preparation hours. To date, you have not been performing these duties as I outlined them for you.

This failure creates a serious problem in maintaining control over warehouse access and inventory. When the food and supplies are not handy on a daily basis, other employees feel free to enter the warehouse for these items without recording them on our inventory sheets. When this is the case, we cannot possibly maintain the proper inventory to keep the club operating efficiently or economically. Single items purchased on a last-minute basis are much too expensive.

In the future, you are to schedule, receive, and store all warehouse requirements for the coming week: for normal dining operations, for the cocktail hours, and for special functions booked by the caterer.

If you have problems with these procedures or want to suggest alternative arrangements, please discuss the situation with Helen Dickerson or me immediately. Otherwise, I will assume you are going to begin to complete these tasks as detailed. We are eager to remedy the associated problems and want to count on your cooperation.

❖ ❖ ❖

REQUEST FOR RAISE/PROMOTION/TRANSFER

Guidelines and Alternate Phrasing

State your reasons, then ask for the raise, promotion, or transfer. Elaborate on why you think the request is appropriate, emphasizing your qualifications, accomplishments, assumed responsibilities, and goals in light of the decisionmaker's standards for evaluation. Try to quantify past results—sales increases, new accounts serviced, increased productivity, reduction in costs, new employees trained and supervised, new skills acquired, and so forth.

⇨ I want to take this opportunity to outline some of my past accomplishments here at Fairfield and to suggest expanded responsibilities for this next year.

⇨ I want to review my contributions in the current job and to inform you of my interest in transferring to a new position in our Ohio division.

⇨ This past year has afforded me the opportunity to increase my territory with 42 new accounts, resulting in a total sales volume increase of 160 percent. In light of this extra effort, I want to suggest a salary increase for this coming year.

If you have knowledge of the market, you may want to suggest a specific amount—at least as a point for negotiations.

⇨ I think that an increase of $3,000 would signify your appreciation of these contributions.

⇨ May I suggest an increase of 15 percent for next year?

⇨ From my random survey of other corporations in the industry, a salary of $50,000 is not at all out of line for these responsibilities.

⇨ With an increase of, say, ten percent, I could be more positive about working the extra hours this project will entail.

Emphasize the symbolic meaning of the promotion or raise rather than your need for the money.

⇨ This increase will confirm to me that you value my past contributions here at Metcalf.

⇨ This promotion will support the comments that I've received from other staff working with me on the project.

⇨ This salary increase would solidify in my mind the future opportunities for advancement with Huffco.

⇨ This transfer, with the accompanying raise, will confirm your commitment to groom me for advancement within the company, as we have discussed on previous occasions.

⇨ The extra money will be useful, of course, but beyond that, I would look upon the raise as your expression of intentions about my future here at United.

Mention anyone you have trained as a replacement to minimize the decisionmaker's hesitancy about a disruption in the current operations.

⇨ Alice Whitaker has been involved in the Hellman project from start to finish and is fully capable of completing it.

⇨ I've trained Harriet Brownstone in all the duties of this job, and she is eager to assume this responsibility should you give the promotions your approval.

⇨ With as little as two to three weeks' notice, I can fully train my replacement.

❖ ❖ ❖

Dear Mr. Seidmantz:

As a media specialist for the past two years with our Hargrove offices, I've found opportunity to contribute in new ways to our field groups.

As you will remember, I was hired simply to write press releases and respond to inquiries from the media and the public about environmental issues. During these two years, I've written over 500 press releases and answered innumerable inquiries in a fashion that has, in my opinion, created a favorable impression for Hargrove.

But in addition to these assigned responsibilities, I've assumed the role of scriptwriter and producer for our training department. To address the need to get adequate explanation of employment benefits to the field quickly, I've developed three videos now in use. All of these have received very positive comments from our staff managers, who've experienced a reduction of approximately 50 percent in new-employee training time because of these videos.

In light of these additional responsibilities and achievements, I'd like to suggest a change in title (Media and Training Specialist) and an increase of $4,000 in annual compensation. I see no need at the present time to hire additional staff to assist me in the media area.

Your approval of this arrangement will confirm to me Hargrove's appreciation of the employee's willingness "to find a need and fill it." I'm thrilled to be given such opportunities for growth and am confident that these new training efforts are contributing directly to our productivity in the field.

Sincerely,

❖ ❖ ❖

OFFER OF RAISE/PROMOTION/TRANSFER _____

Guidelines and Alternate Phrasing

Announce the good news immediately. Clarify any details about dates, amounts, locations, and reporting lines.

⇨ We are pleased to approve your request for a merit increase of $3,000, effective with the May pay period.

⇨ Thank you for bringing your most recent contributions to my attention. After talking with several of our other divisional managers to determine the "norm," I agree that your past performance has been exemplary. Therefore, I'm happy to be able to say that we plan to increase your monthly salary by $450, effective immediately.

⇨ Jason, I am happy to say that I've been given approval to go ahead with your promotion to . . .

⇨ We have the go-ahead on your transfer. Effective Monday, May 6, you will assume the role of . . .

Be clear about any trial period in the new role, mentioning your criteria for evaluation.

⇨ Of course, we will want to review your performance after the first six months to see that the new projects are indeed contributing significantly to our operations. Specifically, we will be looking at . . .

⇨ After the first three months, you and I can review how you think the new job supports or frustrates our efforts in the field. To be completely satisfied with this new trial arrangement, I will want to see a 20 percent increase in . . .

Elaborate with a commendation of past performance.

⇨ Your past work in the Bilton research has indeed been valuable in our total efforts.

⇨ Your ability to exceed quota by such a large percentage for the past twelve months has been outstanding.

⇨ Your attitude, your flexibility, and your timing have been excellent on past projects.

Show your pleasure in giving the raise or promotion. Avoid a begrudging tone.

⇨ We are thrilled to place you in this new role.

⇨ We are eager to keep you happy with Belco.

⇨ We are pleased to be able to reward your efforts in this way.

⇨ We are always willing to pay for such excellent performance.

⇨ This increase is a positive step for both you and us. We value your contributions.

⇨ We look forward to your long and rewarding career here at Fullerbrook.

⇨ This promotion is one you deserve. Thank you for your commitment to a job well done.

❖ ❖ ❖

Dear Brenda:

We are pleased to say that we have decided to ask you to assume the position of director in our Orlando office, with the accompanying salary increase of $12,000 annually.

Your past work has confirmed in our minds your ability to put customer needs above that of internal workings and changes in staffing. Specifically, your ability to land the Monroe contract has allowed us to increase our billings by more than eight percent during the last few months alone. And the possibilities with that arrangement are limited only by our creativity as managers.

We appreciate your ability to identify new markets and your determination to forge into them with confidence. This promotion and increase, we hope, will confirm to you our plans for your continued advancement in the company. You have our solid support with your new responsibilities.

Sincerely,

❖ ❖ ❖

DISAPPROVAL OF RAISE/PROMOTION/TRANSFER

Guidelines and Alternate Phrasing

Begin by acknowledging the request and thanking the employee for any past contributions, suggestions, or interest in new responsibilities.

⇨ Thank you for offering to help us out in the Detroit area. From all appearances, we need something to happen there fast.

⇨ I appreciate your writing to let us know of your interest in transferring to our new location at the end of the summer.

⇨ We received your letter outlining the ways you would like to contribute to our success here at Glamore and Associates.

⇨ Thank you for being so candid with your expectations about your future responsibilities here at Bryan-Westin.

⇨ Thank you for forwarding your résumé and information packet with the summary of your accomplishments here.

⇨ We are always pleased to receive new ideas from employees for ways to grow—even if that might involve a complete restructuring as you outlined.

State your reasons for disapproving the raise, promotion, or transfer. If your reasons are deficiencies in the employee's past performance or lack of skills, identify those positively, focusing on ways to improve performance or acquire the necessary skills.

⇨ The rumors you've probably heard are true. We simply are being forced to freeze our salaries at the current level.

⇨ The review committee has already decided that they would like to bring someone in from the outside to get a new perspective on our expansion efforts.

⇨ We believe that we need someone in that position who can travel extensively at a moment's notice.

⇨ We have decided that transfers to the new office should first be offered to our qualified employees with at least ten years' service here.

⇨ I've identified one particular area that we need to work on in the next few months: problem-solving with customers.

⇨ I have decided that the promotion would be inappropriate primarily for one reason—the increased customer contact necessary in that position. There have been some past problems with difficult customers, and I'd like us to work on further improvement in that regard.

⇨ While your telephone skills are certainly adequate, I think organization would be a problem with the increased coordination required for scheduling. Why don't we spend some concentrated time on improving your organizational skills?

Offer an alternative way to meet the employee's needs, if possible. Mention under what conditions you may review your decision.

⇨ If you would like to try your hand in some of these new areas, please feel free to do that on a project-by-project basis. If that arrangement works out well, it may be possible for us to then reevaluate the move you mentioned in your letter.

⇨ Possibly by expanding the job you're now in, we can give you opportunities to . . .

⇨ If your concern is the opportunity to learn more about . . ., we certainly can arrange for some cross-training hours in that office.

⇨ If you feel that solo projects with less supervision would suit you better, we could consider dividing Lisa's responsibilities to allow you the opportunity to . . .

Express appreciation for the reader's strengths and past contributions.

⇨ We certainly have been impressed with your past performance.

⇨ We appreciate your dependability and conscientiousness about the everyday tasks that keep us operating smoothly.

⇨ We appreciate your loyalty.

⇨ We appreciate your willingness to learn new things and contribute in any way we need you.

⇨ We value your eagerness to learn and grow in the job.

⇨ We appreciate your fine support in the Accounting area.

⇨ We are pleased to have you working with us here at Capital Associates.

⇨ Thank you for your contributions to our past growth.

⇨ Thank you for sharing your technical expertise with us.

⇨ We appreciate your new ideas and your willingness to discuss them with us.

⇨ We have the same objectives in mind—satisfied employees and profitability. Thank you for helping us achieve both.

⇨ Thank you for your outstanding work in coordinating our workshops.

⇨ We are so pleased to know of your commitment to our success here. We want to work toward helping you grow into the jobs you feel are in line with your interests.

⇨ We continue to be very pleased with the excellent service you're giving our customers. Thank you for that effort.

❖ ❖ ❖

Dear Flo:

Thank you for writing to let us know of your interest in assuming the position of regional sales director. Should I assume the frustration involved in landing the new Hico account generated that itch to move? Seriously, we appreciate the difficulty of that account and your fine effort in closing the sale.

We are hesitant, I'm afraid, to put you in the newly created regional sales director position for several reasons. The position, as we envision it, will require extensive managerial skills because of the scattered sales force, the demands of a brand new market, and the difficulties we've had in finding distributors in the region. Although you've certainly been an excellent sales rep for us, we believe that we need someone with several years' management experience in this new spot.

If you are interested in assuming a managerial role, I'd suggest that you let your immediate supervisor know that and then avail yourself of our in-house management training programs. We think it's essential that all our managers complete the Victor Profile program. After you've acquired this additional training and find that you're still interested in a supervisory position, bring that to our attention again.

We appreciate the outstanding sales record you continue to build here at Glaydon.

Sincerely,

❖ ❖ ❖

THANK YOU FOR THE INTERVIEW _____

Guidelines and Alternate Phrasing

Express your appreciation for the interview and reconfirm your interest in working for the company.

⇨ I so much appreciate the opportunity you gave me yesterday to meet with you and your staff in such an informal setting.

⇨ Thank you for taking the time to talk with me one on one about the sales and marketing position.

⇨ After talking with you yesterday, I'm even more excited about the possibility of working with you as an auditor.

⇨ Thanks so much for your time in reviewing your needs and the job responsibilities as a media consultant.

⇨ I was so pleased with the opportunity yesterday to discuss with you the management responsibilities and opportunities available in your Detroit branch.

⇨ Our discussions yesterday were so enlightening. I had no idea that you were currently investigating so many new product ideas—that makes me even more eager to work with you at Harbro.

Summarize the key contributions you think you can bring to the company, basing your remarks on the job requirements mentioned in the interview and on problems you think you can solve in the position.

⇨ After hearing of your predicament with the scattered management team, I've given more thought to another possible approach. Perhaps you could . . . I think my experience with . . . would have a direct bearing on that outcome.

⇨ My six years' experience in computer technical support areas certainly has prepared me to address the two continuing problems you mentioned. . . .

⇨ Your mention of the company's plans to increase PR activities in the local community sound particularly interesting to me because of my long-time media contacts. I would be most eager to explore placement of articles with these key people, who could certainly position Forrester in the limelight.

Close with your eagerness for their positive decision.

⇨ I have every confidence that I can contribute to your growth.

⇨ Let me know if we should talk further. I think the possibilities for our association are almost endless.

⇨ I'll look forward to hearing your decision about the copywriting job.

⇨ I do want to go to work for you to see what I can do in turning the sales situation around. I'll be eager to hear what you decide.

⇨ Thank you once again for talking with me about the position. I'll be expecting to hear from you shortly.

⇨ I am happy to know you will be making the decision soon. I'll be eager to get a call from you.

⇨ I'll appreciate your giving me a call when you've made a decision about this position.

⇨ Thanks again for outlining the challenges to me—I'm ready to go to work.

❖ ❖ ❖

Dear Mr. Barnhart:

Thank you for the opportunity to talk with you personally yesterday about the position of technical editor. Your company sounds as though it has a superior strategy for putting together technical proposals to meet client needs. I do appreciate the time you spent in overviewing the entire process from engineer surveys to final copy.

My experience in working with over fifty engineers in the past two years has given me broad experience in combining technical accuracy and principles of good writing. Since our discussion about the current lack of "people skills" in the editing process, I'm even more eager to bring a sense of cooperation to the job and a willingness to work with your engineers on subsequent drafts until we have a winning proposal in hand.

I'm looking forward to your decision about having me go to work with you to increase your winning proposal ratio.

Sincerely,

❖ ❖ ❖

FAREWELLS ≣≣≣≣≣≣≣≣≣≣≣≣≣≣≣≣≣≣≣≣≣

When someone leaves the office for greener pastures, a farewell letter expresses sentiment that possibly has gone unsaid to that point. If the working relationship has been a good one, such letters recall good times and express heartfelt thanks for the opportunities of working together.

All too often, however, the case is that the one leaving has experienced difficulty on the job, strained relationships, or serious personal setbacks that make a career change in order. Under such circumstances, you want to combine genuineness with sensitivity and concern with encouragement.

Farewells should be bittersweet.

FROM EMPLOYEE LEAVING

Guidelines and Alternate Phrasing

State the fact that you are leaving your present position.

⇨ Jack, I wanted you to know that I will soon be leaving Upjohn here to assume a new position at the Kansas City site.

⇨ I am currently planning to begin a new position as director of admissions at the University of Alabama.

⇨ I've had a change of career plans—effective May 1, I will be impersonating a sales rep. What do you think of my chances for success? Seriously, I wanted to say goodbye to you and . . .

⇨ On August 1, I will be leaving Midtone Services to assume a new job at Skydivers, Inc., in Miami.

Mention who will be taking over your responsibilities if the reader will need to continue the relationship with your employer. For example, a vendor may want to know who the new contact within the company will be.

⇨ Jack Gordon will be your new contact for further orders.

⇨ In the future, you should call Lisa Smith to coordinate the workshops for your organizations.

⇨ I'll be replaced by Mike Treadwell, who will very capably service your account when you have needs or questions.

Express your appreciation for the association, being specific about the benefit or value either to you personally or to the company.

⇨ I've valued tremendously my association with Wellington and the growth opportunities here.

⇨ I've appreciated so much the opportunity to work with each of you in the manufacturing and production areas.

⇨ I've appreciated working with you on the various projects that have produced such fine results for both of us.

⇨ The company has certainly invested heavily in my training, and for that I'm especially grateful.

⇨ The hours have been long, but the work has been so satisfying.

⇨ You have contributed significantly to my skills and my philosophy of management.

⇨ Your contributions have been invaluable to my sales success.

⇨ Our discussions over the years have been so helpful to me in charting the waters of design and production on many new product lines.

Mention any plans to stay in touch.

⇨ I'll drop in on you from time to time.

⇨ Let's have lunch after I've gotten in with both feet—I'll be able to present you with a case study for analysis and advice.

⇨ Keep me on your mailing list for the newsletter.

⇨ Call me whenever you're in my area so that we can have lunch.

⇨ What schedule can we arrange for updates? I want to keep up with what happens in your life.

⇨ Keep me posted on the happenings in your life, and I'll do the same. I'll save a free evening at the next ICB convention.

⇨ Don't forget to keep me posted on your own comings and goings.

⇨ I'll be in touch with Margaret in my new job; she'll be sure to keep me updated on what's happening in your life.

⇨ I'll plan to keep my eye out for your name in the trade journals.

⇨ My ears will perk up for news of you around industry gatherings.

❖ ❖ ❖

Dear Kathryn:

As you may or may not have heard, I will be leaving Herrington-Dale on September 1 to begin my own consulting business. That experience may be a dream-come-true or a nightmare—depending on my success or failure.

Whichever way things turn out, I didn't want to leave without telling you of your contributions to my career. The training offered here has been exceptional, and with diligence you have mapped out the formal training programs beneficial to me and managed to see that I got into each one. Additionally, just observing your management style has been an excellent on-the-job case study of course principles. You've kept the work challenging, the stimulants rewarding, and the interactions pleasant. Thank you for providing this working environment that has nurtured my inclination to start and manage my own company.

I'm sure I'll be phoning you from time to time for advice as I consult with clients who demand and deserve as much as clients here at Herrington-Dale.

Sincerely,

❖ ❖ ❖

TO EMPLOYEE LEAVING

Guidelines and Alternate Phrasing

Express your appreciation for the relationship.

⇨ I'm so sorry to hear that you're leaving Vivian International—your going is a big loss to us.

⇨ I hope you realize that you're making quite a few people unhappy with your recent decision to leave us. How can we get the job done without you?

⇨ Over the years our relationship has meant so much to me—I hate to hear that you're leaving.

⇨ I fear the rumors are true—that you're leaving. That's upsetting to so many of us who've grown to depend on you in so many ways.

⇨ Dean, I didn't want to let this moment go by without writing to say how much I have enjoyed both our personal and working relationship.

⇨ Fred Harwell tells me that you recently left Vivian International. I was so sorry to hear that, because I did appreciate our working connections there.

⇨ I want to take this opportunity to say how much we will miss you.

Identify and elaborate on specifics. Mention either personal attributes and talents that you value as an individual or career achievements and contributions to the company. An informal, light touch is usually appropriate on such occasions.

⇨ I feel like pushing the panic-button every time I think of your being gone. Who will handle our irate customers?

⇨ You were instrumental in my getting the last promotion. I will not forget that and my debt to you.

⇨ You have always been so understanding of my family situation and the need for me to be off work from time to time to care for the boys.

⇨ Your sales results have always been a motivating factor in my own career.

⇨ Your warnings and advice have kept me out of immeasurable trouble on the two Monroe accounts.

⇨ You're a talented designer, who has taken us a long way in product development.

⇨ As an excellent manager, you have taught us the value of teamwork and team spirit.

⇨ You have been an inspiration in seeing projects through to completion—especially the tough ones.

⇨ I've watched your time management and organizational skills with awe.

⇨ I have the utmost respect for your ability to identify potential problems and turn them into sales opportunities within already large accounts.

Wish the individual well with future plans, and keep in mind that the employee may be leaving under less-than-desirable conditions.

⇨ Have an exciting, eventful life, and we'll see you again along the way!

⇨ Please let us know of your successes at TMT Services; I know there will be many.

⇨ Keep taking the steps in the direction you want to go, and life will get you there with first-class passage.

⇨ Best of everything as you go to your new job.

⇨ Tell Hargrove Associates that they're getting a real winner—in case they didn't figure that out in the interview. Much success.

⇨ I wish you well in whatever you decide to do when you arrive in Denver. I'm confident your possibilities will be many.

⇨ I want to wish you the best as you assume your new duties.

⇨ We'll be eagerly looking for your name in those press releases from your new company.

⇨ We have every confidence that your future is going to be a bright one wherever you decide to accept a position.

⇨ You have our blessing here at Upjohn in your new leadership role.

⇨ We're expecting to hear good things from you in the future. Keep up the outstanding record.

⇨ It's evident you've worked long and hard for this promotion. Our best wishes for your continued success.

⇨ We're going to hide and watch you go right to the top.

⇨ You deserve every success the future holds.

❖ ❖ ❖

Dear Holden,

So far, I think I've missed every opportunity to say goodbye to you personally—the dinner last evening and the departmental get-together. I didn't, however, want to let the occasion of your leaving pass by without expressing to you how much I've valued our working relationship over the years.

My earliest recollection of your coming to my rescue was the Folger account. Do you remember the days you spent on the phone in my behalf just trying to get their buyer to talk to the "new kid on the block"? Since those days, you've been an excellent pace-setter for the accounts we've managed. Aside from that role, I've appreciated your advice about career decisions and even about family. Jody and the boys remember well your helping to arrange our travel overseas on the Hitton project.

I wish you the best as you assume the leadership role at TRM Services. They're getting a master manager and an all-around nice guy. Let's stay in touch.

Cordially,

❖ ❖ ❖

HOLIDAY GREETINGS

Holidays bring time for reflection and resolve—reflection on accomplishments of the past year and resolve for improving working relationships and performance in the new year. Letters at this season should encompass both perspectives.

Also, you will want to add a warm personal touch. If you believe that your biggest asset in business is people, then this season presents the occasion to make your employees feel special. How do you do that? By including specifics on the projects worked on, by extending greetings and concern to their friends and family, and by commenting on the special attitudes and personality traits that make them special as individuals and as a team.

HOLIDAY GREETINGS

Guidelines and Alternate Phrasing

Commend team achievements during the past year, or simply recall your pleasant work together.

⇨ This year has enriched our friendships and expanded our organizational horizons.

⇨ This year has been an exceptional one. Together we've conquered projects, overtaken deadlines, and charted success after success.

⇨ As the year comes to a close, I want to commend you on all you've accomplished during the past months—the Lamb project, the European expansion, the "derby."

⇨ Before we usher in the new year, I want to express my appreciation for what you've accomplished in the current one. My hat's off to you.

⇨ Are holidays a time for thank yous? They are, if you have a staff as productive and successful as you've been this past year.

⇨ You've accomplished great things this year—it's certainly time for a celebration even if Christmas hadn't been so appropriately placed on the calendar.

⇨ The red circle around December 25 marks a special day for families—at home and at work. As a work family, you've been caring, supportive, and resourceful this past year.

Give details about any plans to get together for a group celebration.

⇨ Let's get a jump on the season and celebrate early at the Westin, Friday, December 20. Please join us.

⇨ Can you join us to share warm wishes on Wednesday, December 18, in the east lobby?

⇨ We invite you to join us in the lobby at 3:00 P.M. on December 22 to share sentiments of the season.

Mention modestly any gift you're sending along.

⇨ Please accept these money-saving coupons as a small gift of appreciation for your business.

⇨ We hope the enclosed *Waypole Journal* gives you a sense of the industry feelings about the political and economic climate. Let us know if 11 more issues don't find their way to your door.

⇨ The basket that will be arriving contains lively "spirits"—the spirit of holiday happiness and good health. Drink up.

⇨ The enclosed bag of nuts is in lieu of a bag of gold—the price being about equal these days.

⇨ Do you think you can find a use for one more desk calendar? This one is special because it marks the anniversary of our first year's service to you.

Express warm wishes appropriate to the season.

⇨ May your Christmas be a special time of joy and love.

⇨ We want to extend the season's best to those whose friendship and goodwill we so deeply appreciate.

⇨ We wish for you and your family a joyous season.

⇨ Our best for the holiday season and the new year to come. May it bring you health, happiness, and success along the way. Enjoy your holiday rest and relaxation with family members; they are the reason for our year-long work.

⇨ We hope the season is everything you want it to be.

⇨ Give our best to your family and your staff.

⇨ May you have a relaxing and warm celebration with your families and return to us ready to greet the new year with gusto.

⇨ Enjoy yourselves with family and friends.

⇨ Enjoy every minute of rest, relaxation, and family hugs.

⇨ Trim the tree, eat those cookies, and wrap those packages all with one thing in mind: You've worked hard and you deserve to enjoy the season with family and friends.

⇨ May God bless you in this special holiday season, and keep you through the new year.

⇨ We hope the coming year brings you bouquets of good fortune.

⇨ We wish for you a bright, five-pointed star: safety, sales, service, satisfaction, and success.

❖ ❖ ❖

To Baxter Employees:

Pardon the paper—I'd prefer to be handwriting each of you a Christmas note on personal stationery if time would allow. But try not to let this formal letter detract from the heartfelt thanks I feel toward each of you. With your help we have accomplished a great deal, and earned compliments from clients and customers on the results.

Most especially in this holiday time when our thoughts turn to family and friends, I want to express my gratitude for the team spirit among you—your genuine caring for each other's well-being and your willingness to be supportive in times of spiritual, emotional, and physical need.

For each of you and your families, I wish a special season filled with love, friendship, and contentment.

Sincerely,

❖ ❖ ❖

❖ ❖ ❖

Dear Friends of Baxter, Inc.:

We so much appreciate your business throughout the year—we hope you're as pleased with our efforts and successes. Your staff has been so helpful and courteous that doing business with you has been a real pleasure.

You have our very best wishes for the holiday season. The enclosed clock will tell you when it's time to relax and enjoy family and friends. Though Christmas is frequently full of surprises, we wouldn't be a bit surprised if you have the best year ever in 19—.

Cordially,

❖ ❖ ❖

INVITATIONS

Growth in business implies activities such as open-house occasions for clients and customers, sports events, and holiday parties for employees' families. Invitations to these events should create the image you intend to project as a company and foreshadow the excitement you hope the event itself will generate.

These invitations may be as informal as a handwritten flier or as formal as engraved stationery. On these occasions, the medium may be even more important than the message. You'll want to give attention to the stationery, the timing, and the tone of your invitation.

OPEN HOUSE

Guidelines and Alternate Phrasing

Extend the invitation, including date, time, place, and purpose.

⇨ We want to invite you to an open house at our new location, 47298 Westway Drive.

⇨ As our supplier, we want to invite you to join us for an open house at our 8792 Barrymore branch office.

⇨ You are important to us—your business, your opinions, your needs. Would you be our guest at a May 20 open house (34899 Riverway Two), where our researchers and engineers can mix and mingle with you and other customers and talk about your ideas and needs?

Give details on the schedule and any planned activities.

⇨ We have planned a guided tour of the grounds at 2:00 P.M.

⇨ Bob Pretone will be giving a 30-minute briefing on new equipment under development. His briefing will be repeated three times during the afternoon (2:15, 4:00; 4:45) to allow all our guests to hear about our plans to meet their future needs.

⇨ We'll have our latest models available for your hands-on experience in . . .

⇨ Our sales representatives will be available to answer your questions about . . .

⇨ An informal time of tea and cakes will be followed by a briefing on . . .

State whether another representative (associate, spouse, or another guest) is invited to attend if the reader cannot be present.

⇨ If you can't attend yourself, load a colleague's pockets with business cards and send him or her along in your place.

⇨ Bring a guest or two to enjoy the informal networking.

⇨ We are asking that only company CEOs attend in order to allow time to share concerns at the highest level of the organization.

Ask for a response to a designated person by a certain date; if no response is necessary, say so.

⇨ Please RSVP to Steve Whitaker by noon on December 10.

⇨ Please let us know if you'll be able to join us for this sharing time. We need your response by March 23 (Margaret Jones, ext. 4782) to make sure we have plenty of briefing packets for all our guests.

⇨ No need to let us know if you'll be dropping by. If you have the time, we have food, facilities, and fun.

❖ ❖ ❖

Dear Mr. Metevrieves:

We are hosting an open house on May 6 for members of the NTSA. If you can join us on July 8 from 3:00 to 5:00 P.M., we think you'll find ample opportunity to discuss common strategies and problems among your colleagues in the industry.

The entire time will be unstructured. During the prerequisite refreshments time, we think all of you will enjoy a chance to put names with faces, exchange business cards, and share leads (and possibly even a few head-aches!).

Looking forward to having you and about 100 of your friends join us.

Cordially,

❖ ❖ ❖

SPECIAL COMPANY EVENT

Guidelines and Alternate Phrasing

Show your enthusiasm about the event. Avoid a business-as-usual tone.

Extend the invitation, including date, time, and place.

⇨ We would like to invite you to . . .

⇨ Please be our guest . . .

⇨ We are eagerly awaiting your answer—would you be able to join us at . . .

⇨ You are cordially invited to . . .

⇨ May we count on you to join us . . .

⇨ You are the center of our attention. As such, we want to you to show up next . . .

Include all the necessary details: the appropriate attire, any fee, an expected gift, and so forth.

⇨ Please feel free to come casually dressed.

⇨ This black-tie event will include . . .

⇨ Regular business attire will be the order of the day.

⇨ The complimentary meal will be provided by . . .

⇨ A small admission charge of $35 will cover the price of dinner, two drinks, and games for the children.

Mention the purpose of the event: a farewell, an award, an appreciation dinner, opportunities for networking among customers, or such.

⇨ Our purpose in gathering is to allow you the opportunity to meet with other subcontractors who may want to share their experience and mutual leads.

⇨ This dinner will give us a chance to express our appreciation to Joe Barnes as he leaves Tulsa.

⇨ This resort holiday allows us to express to you, our client, how much we appreciate your business month after month.

State whether another representative (associate, spouse, or another guest) is invited to attend if the reader cannot be present.

⇨ Please feel free to send a colleague if you yourself can't attend.

⇨ We are limiting this event to one guest from each department.

⇨ If you cannot attend, please ask a colleague who you think can share your views on the subject.

⇨ We hope that all CEOs from the invited organizations can attend personally because we feel that other designated representatives would not have the insights we hope to garner at this event.

Ask for a response to a designated person by a certain date; if no response is necessary, say so.

⇨ Please call Linda Laughton by May 9 to reserve your table.

⇨ Please let Madge Mayfield know by May 9 if you plan to attend.

⇨ We must have your answer by May 9 to make all the necessary arrangements.

⇨ We would appreciate an RSVP to Dana Letterman at ext. 2895. But if your schedule is unpredictable and at the last moment you find time to drop by, please come ahead and don't worry about the RSVP.

❖ ❖ ❖

Dear Ms. Fitzmeyer:

We are having a reunion, and we want you to come! We'll all gather on Friday, April 5, at the Dunnway Center at 11:30 A.M. to hear Dr. Clarence Carver, past president of the center, as featured speaker.

Then we invite you to stay for an informal barbecue lunch and network with fellow staffers and alumni who share the same vision and purpose. Just as this center has been important in molding your past, the reunion and fundraiser can now guide and shape today's students for their successful career and the world's future.

The $25 ticket price buys a delicious lunch, two hours' worth of story-swapping, and endless possibilities for new friends. Quite a bargain to our way of thinking.

We look forward to seeing you. Please complete the enclosed response form and return it to us by May 31.

Cordially,

❖ ❖ ❖

❖ ❖ ❖

Dear Mr. Waterhouse:

We are pleased to invite you and your guest to join us, along with other customers, for an unforgettable dinner cruise on June 6 at the national convention in San Francisco.

Imagine this: Our limousine driver will call for you at 5:30 P.M. at your hotel lobby. After being chauffeured from your hotel to the marina, you will board the 120-foot yacht, Princess Daisy, and sail away on our sunset dinner cruise while enjoying your favorite drink and listening to a live band, the Barrett Beach Boys. You will feast until your heart's content at our buffet of smoked salmon and then dance or just relax as you watch the sun slip past the horizon. When we dock at 10:30 P.M., you will be chauffeured back to your hotel.

We hope you'll be able to join us for this special evening so that we can express to you our appreciation for the confidence you've shown in us by buying our products and services this year. Would you please phone coordinator Lila Williams at 806-389-0091 to let us know if you can sail with us.

Sincerely,

P.S. Dress is casual.

❖ ❖ ❖

MEETINGS

If we can believe what various research studies report, employees spend an enormous amount of time associated with meetings—announcing, inviting, declining, canceling, confirming, attending, recording, and following up. Obviously, such correspondence can become so routine and monotonous that much of it goes unread.

A general rule-of-thumb is to make the key details—what, when, where, who, why—easily accessible to the skimming reader. Informative headings and eye-catching layout help the reader spot the necessary information in a glance. Make your meeting communication a "must read."

ANNOUNCING AGENDA

Guidelines and Alternate Phrasing

Announce the scheduled meeting, giving day, date, time, place, and purpose.

⇨ The next and final planning meeting for the Oktoberfest will be at 10:00 A.M. Monday, August 21, in the Post Conference Room.

⇨ Plan to join us for the next monthly Horizons meeting: 12399 Silvan Avenue, Suite 299, 4:00 P.M. on Tuesday, August 22. We'll be discussing how . . .

⇨ You are asked to attend the next monthly managers meeting (Tuesday, August 9, 9:00 A.M., conference room C) to give your input on the . . .

Ask for a confirmation of attendance. When key people cannot attend, the meeting is often nonproductive. With such negative responses, consider postponing and/or canceling the meeting.

⇨ Please call to confirm that you will attend.

⇨ Attendance is required.

⇨ If you cannot attend, let me know as soon as possible so that we may reschedule the meeting, if necessary, to have a majority present.

⇨ Let me know if you will be attending personally or if you plan to send a colleague in your place.

⇨ If you cannot attend, please designate someone from your staff to attend.

⇨ All interested parties are invited to attend.

⇨ We do not need a confirmation of your attendance, but we hope to see you there.

⇨ We need a completed registration form in order for you to attend the meeting.

Include the complete meeting agenda and even the time allotted to each subject, if possible. This time notation allows those who may not be interested in all aspects of the meeting to attend only for the time their topic is under discussion. Be as specific as possible in stating each agenda item so that attendees know specifically what their purpose is (To receive information? To report information? To discuss? To come to a decision?). If the meeting has a structure different from the routine, explain that.

Tell attendees what preparation they should make or what they should bring to the meeting.

⇨ Please come to the meeting prepared to brief us on . . .

⇨ Please have the July sales figure with you at the meeting.

⇨ We ask that you review the enclosed report before the meeting.

⇨ You'll need to have read the operator manual before you report to the class.

⇨ Please make every effort to talk with several sales managers from your district to gather their opinions about this issue.

Be clear about whether meeting attendance is required or optional.

❖ ❖ ❖

SUBJECT: New Format for Quality-Control Meetings

The next quality-control meeting will be held Friday, March 5, at 1:00 P.M. in the conference room off the atrium. The "news" is that the quality-control meeting will be heading in a new direction. Instead of an open forum, the meeting will concentrate on one quality-control issue/problem.

For this month, the topic is out-of-season inventory. Those supervisors and managers whose departments are responsible for ordering and processing should attend.

The agenda will follow this basic structure:

- issues and trends
- identifying tracking tools
- brainstorming of solutions
- developing an action plan

For future meetings, you will receive notification of the topic on the Tuesday before the next session so that you will know if representation from your area is appropriate. Please call by March 4 to let us know who from your area will attend.

❖ ❖ ❖

TO:

Who: Everyone on the Contracts staff

What: A meeting

When: Monday, April 3, 3:00 P.M.

Where: Room 2929

Why: 1) To correct contract terminology
       2) To review legal issues
       3) To resolve all identified open issues not addressed
          in the standard contract

Please call Debbie Winter by April 1 at 806-444-3396 to confirm your attendance. Since a meeting without all managers present would be counterproductive, we will reschedule the contract review should anyone be unable to attend. (In that event, we would let you know the new meeting date, place, and time by no later than the close of business April 1.)

We would also like for you to review the attached contract prior to our meeting. At the conclusion of our meeting, I will seek agreement to submit the contract for approval by our General Counsel.

Jack Forman and I will be meeting this week to discuss the financial issues of the compensation to user-designers. This should give us data useful in completing our own contract review.

❖ ❖ ❖

❖ ❖ ❖

TO:

We request your attendance at a special Arcon meeting scheduled for Tuesday, January 14, 10:00 A.M. to 3:00 P.M., in Building G, Room 30. William Blackley will be present to discuss the following:

- Procedures and guidelines concerning the new accounting processes (one-hour briefing)
- Overview plan for scheduling (five minutes)
- Suggested approaches (two-hour discussion) (lunch catered)
- Format models for basic departmental reports (45 minutes, information only)

For those individuals who will be unable to attend this meeting, please call Sharon Gargden (ext. 223) so that she can make arrangements to forward a copy of the review comments and handouts to you.

❖ ❖ ❖

Dear Parents:

Please join us on September 8 at 7:30 P.M. in the auditorium at Belview High to begin to make our school a school without drugs.

We are all aware that drugs threaten the lives of our children, destroy family ties, and disrupt the educational process. Your concern as parents is shared by educators throughout the state. It is time for us to join forces to address the drug problem.

By uniting parents, community members, educators, and law enforcement officials, we hope to send a strong message to those who use or sell drugs to our students: We will not tolerate illegal drugs on our campus.

Help us help your kids. Please attend this meeting to share your ideas and learn how you can put others' ideas into action.

Sincerely,

❖ ❖ ❖

CONFIRMING ATTENDANCE _____

Guidelines and Alternate Phrasing

State that you will be attending.

⇨ I'm pleased to say that I will be able to attend the May 4 accounting review meeting.

⇨ Thanks for your invitation; I'll be happy to attend the August 6 New Customer Orientation.

⇨ Yes, I'll be at the August 6 meeting in Plano.

Confirm any vague details such as location, time, travel arrangements and so forth.

State your intentions to complete any preparation for the meeting.

⇨ I have phoned all my area supervisors to get their input and will be prepared to summarize their comments to the group.

⇨ Yes, I plan to bring with me the Fullerton report.

⇨ By the meeting time, I will have available all figures from our local region and will bring five copies of all the reports you mentioned.

⇨ I noted the reading assignment and intend to complete that before arriving.

Suggest any other agenda items, if appropriate.

⇨ Is the agenda still open? If so, I'd like to add time for a discussion about . . .

⇨ There's one other thing that I'd like to add to the agenda: . . .

⇨ May I suggest two other topics for our meeting? One is for decision and one is for discussion only. . . .

❖ ❖ ❖

Dear Mr. Haverty:

I'm pleased to say that I have been able to rearrange my schedule so as to be able to attend the Rockford branch meeting on August 1. Laura Reed, our secretary here, has made all my travel arrangements, including hotel. I'll be coming in the evening before the meeting and will give you a call upon arrival about 8:00 P.M.

The models have been shipped directly to the hotel. I'll be bringing the building plans with me, as you requested.

May I suggest that one other item be added to our meeting agenda? A five-minute overview of the committee's objectives in their building design would be helpful to those of us who have not been involved from the beginning.

I'm planning on a productive two days with you!

Cordially,

❖ ❖ ❖

DECLINING ATTENDANCE

Guidelines and Alternate Phrasing

State that you will not be attending, giving your reason. To give no reason at all makes your decision sound arbitrary.

⇨ I will be unable to attend the May 6 meeting due to a scheduling conflict; I'll be attending the IAVF convention in Orlando.

⇨ I regret that I won't be able to participate in the May 12 conference; I'm scheduled for some minor surgery that week.

⇨ After reviewing the agenda you enclosed for your April 6 meeting, I'm afraid that I don't find enough issues that relate to our particular situation to make the travel worthwhile.

⇨ After talking further with our managers about the proposal, I've decided that attending your May 1 demonstration would be premature in our current situation.

⇨ I'm afraid that your invitation to the March 11 seminar has been misdirected; Ralph MacGregor would likely be more interested in attending than I would. My work primarily entails . . .

⇨ I regret to say that I won't be available on May 30 to attend the review meeting. I've scheduled several appointments already for that day—appointments that I must keep.

⇨ Thanks for letting me know of the transaction-review meeting on August 9; I'm afraid, however, I'll have to let the opportunity pass. I'm up to my eyeballs in paperwork after having returned from a four-week trip.

Tell the reader how you plan to be informed about the outcome of the meeting: an associate, meeting minutes, review reports, and so forth.

⇨ I'll plan to phone Marty Pewter after your meeting to get the details.

⇨ I'll be sure to get a copy of the meeting minutes.

⇨ Frank Smith will give me a review of the suggestions gathered during the meeting.

Wish the meeting planner success with the meeting.

⇨ I hope the meeting will be all you expect.

⇨ Here's to a productive two days.

⇨ With such advance planning, the meeting's certain to go well.

⇨ The meeting attendees list looks impressive. I'm certain your conclusions and recommendations will be sound.

⇨ Have a good meeting!

⇨ A meeting of the minds—sounds like a great idea. Good luck.

⇨ I'm looking forward to hearing any suggestions from the meeting.

❖ ❖ ❖

Dear Mr. McKinney:

I'm sorry to say that I will be unable to attend your October 9 Roundtable. I'd like to say the reason is that I'll be sunning in the Mediterranean, but the truth is that I'm simply two weeks behind in a major project and cannot afford the time away from the office.

I have asked Matt Johnson to attend in my place, to share our latest concerns with you, and to bring me back all the suggestions he can garner from the meeting. Matt has been most intimately involved in the work and can no doubt contribute to your meeting, probably far more adequately that I.

The agenda sounds full of challenge. My best in turning up some answers to all our concerns.

Sincerely,

❖ ❖ ❖

CANCELING/POSTPONING

Guidelines and Alternate Phrasing

State the cancellation, giving a specific reason.

⇨ We regret to say that because enrollment has been insufficient for the May 10 ETC seminar, we are being forced to cancel it.

⇨ Dr. Harvard, our keynote speaker scheduled for the May 9 Kansas City meeting, has canceled because of unexpected surgery. Finding a replacement of his caliber at such a late date would be highly unlikely. Therefore, we have decided to postpone the meeting until Dr. Harvard can be with us.

⇨ The March 16 meeting in Seattle for senior staffers has been canceled. Obviously, we must have inadvertently selected a date that creates traveling difficulties for many people in the field.

Return any fees for registration and so forth.

⇨ Your refund check will be mailed in two weeks.

⇨ Your full $45 will be returned immediately.

⇨ I've enclosed your $40 check for the dinner reservations.

Apologize for the inconvenience of the cancellation.

⇨ I know you spent time in planning your attendance, and I regret the inconvenience.

⇨ I always regret having to cancel anything at the last minute because of the inconvenience we cause you, our customers.

⇨ Please accept my apologies for the postponement. Your attendance, I'm sure, involved some wasted planning time.

⇨ I apologize for having to ask you to change your plans. That's always irritating and inconvenient. I just hope the day can be used now to even better benefit.

End with a positive note. You may want to announce or suggest ways you can accomplish some or all of the meeting objectives under the conditions stated.

⇨ We are enclosing a videotape of the same meeting conducted at other regions. Most of the ideas should be applicable to your own situation.

⇨ The enclosed report should give you some insights to the issues involved.

⇨ After schedules become less hectic, we will try to plan a similar meeting in early spring.

⇨ On a more positive note, at least you'll have one less plane to catch!

⇨ Think of it this way: You have one more day in the office to catch up that week.

⇨ We do think such a meeting would have far-reaching results, and we plan to reschedule as soon as feasible.

⇨ Perhaps at a later date, we will reschedule and can once again ask you to visit our facilities.

❖ ❖ ❖

Dear Ms. O'Shea:

Much to our regret, the San Marcos meeting on May 9 has been canceled. Because of a miscommunication with the assistant director at the San Marcos site, we recently discovered that the center would permit only 15 attendees from any one region. That limitation, of course, made the chartered bus trip economically unfeasible.

We know this cancellation has caused some inconvenience in clearing your calendars, and we regret the misunderstanding.

In lieu of our firsthand observation, we have arranged to purchase video-tapes of the presentations and the facilities. Those tapes will be mailed to each office by the end of the month. We hope the tapes will give you some of the information you need for working with the clientele there.

Sincerely,

❖ ❖ ❖

INVITING SPEAKER

Guidelines and Alternate Phrasing

Invite the person to speak, giving the date, time, place, and purpose of the event.

⇨ We think you're an outstanding teacher, educator, and trainer. And because we look for the best, we are inviting you to speak to our Forum Club on the evening of October 6 at the Hyatt Regency in Wakesville. Our monthly meetings center on . . .

⇨ Would you consider giving our group a brief overview of your company's products and services in an upcoming staff meeting? If so, any of our next three meeting dates are open: March 12, April 9, and May 4.

⇨ We want to extend to you an invitation to speak to our group of sales reps when they convene in Atlanta, August 16, 1:00 to 5:00 p.m., for their new-product orientation. Your keynote address will set the tone for . . .

Add appropriate details about the event and the audience to help the speaker tailor his or her comments to the occasion. The more specific you are in your invitation, the more pleased you'll be with the presentation.

⇨ Most registrants will be first-time attendees.

⇨ Your listeners will have had from five to ten years' experience in the industry.

⇨ The audience will be an unusual mix: 70 percent will be males in their mid-to-late twenties, and 30 percent will be females in their retirement years.

⇨ The audience will have heard previous presentations on . . . and, therefore, will be more interested in the . . . aspects of the subject.

⇨ We are more interested in how-to's than theories.

⇨ I've enclosed programs from the last two years so that you can get an idea of the caliber of speaker and the cutting-edge presentations we've had in the past.

⇨ Our focus this year will be quite different from previous years in that this year we hope to give attendees help with . . .

Mention any fee or honorarium, and explain how the speaker should handle any related expenses such as for travel, audio-visual equipment, or handout reproduction.

⇨ We encourage you to use handouts and will pay up to $200 for the printing of our materials.

⇨ If you want us to print any session materials, we must have your originals by May 9. After that date, we ask that you pay your own reproduction costs.

⇨ We will, of course, reimburse your travel expenses.

⇨ Would it be possible for your company to pick up the cost of your travel?

⇨ We will pay your fee of $4,500 for the keynote address.

⇨ Our honorarium is $1,000 for the day's briefing.

⇨ We can offer an honorarium of $400 for the presentation.

⇨ We understand that your fee will be $7,500, plus expenses.

Include any expectations about a paper or abstract in the conference proceedings, if the meeting is a formal one associated with a convention.

⇨ We encourage you to submit an abstract of your comments for inclusion in our Conference Proceedings manual.

⇨ As part of your participation in the program, you will be expected to submit a paper outlining your key ideas for those unable to attend your session.

⇨ If you can help us with a written abstract of your speech, the members always appreciate such back-on-the-job reference materials. And, of course, such a paper keeps your name and work in front of the audience.

Ask for a reply by a certain date, keeping in mind that you must select another speaker if the response is negative.

⇨ We need your answer by May 4.

⇨ We're hoping for your positive reply by May 4.

⇨ Would you please let us know by May 4 if you can address our group?

⇨ By May 4, we will have to have all our speakers confirmed. If you immediately find you're available, it would be most helpful if you could send us your answer even before that date.

Show eagerness about having the speaker accept your invitation.

⇨ We've seen a tremendous interest from the members in your topic.

⇨ Your title and subject have raised quite a few eyebrows; we're eager to hear the elaboration.

⇨ We're expecting great things.

⇨ I hope the next phone call will be yours, telling me you've decided to accept our invitation.

⇨ All of us are anxiously waiting to get your views on . . .

⇨ Your comments are always so succinct yet so provocative; we are eager to hear you.

⇨ We are eager to hear your innovative solutions to the industry's worsening situation.

⇨ We know your talk will both entertain and inspire us.

⇨ We know your presentation will enlighten as well as motivate us.

❖ ❖ ❖

Dear Ms. Grant:

We've heard that you're an outstanding motivational speaker, both because you've "been there," and because your technical expertise matches your enthusiasm. That's why we want to extend to you an invitation to make a 20-minute presentation at our upcoming ICGGB meeting, May 3–7, in Las Vegas. Your presentation would be part of a panel response to the topic "Making the Media a Repeat Customer."

To give you a little more detail about our audience: We are a national service organization of approximately 700 local chapters, providing public relations services to nonprofit organizations. We serve the very large and the very small agencies—from those who employ thousands to those who employ only two. In order to acquaint you with our organizations and some of the current issues faced by our members, I am enclosing a fact sheet and the latest issues of our trade magazines.

Because our member organizations are nonprofit and because, consequently, we try to present our programs at a minimal cost, we cannot offer you an honorarium. In the past, we also have asked panelists to arrange for their employer to pay expenses. If your company will not agree to do that, we can reimburse for limited travel expenses ($300) and handout reproduction ($50).

We hope the no-pay predicament we always find ourselves in will not deter your participation. The networking opportunities have certainly been a bonus to the presenters in past years, and we think that will be the case again for you at this conference.

As you probably understand, the logistics of putting together such a meeting take time. Would you please let us know by January 4 if you can participate on our panel?

We would be so pleased to add your name to our distinguished guest list.

Sincerely,

❖ ❖ ❖

CONFIRMING SPEAKER

Guidelines and Alternate Phrasing

Thank the reader for agreeing to speak at the meeting.

⇨ On behalf of the NACE program committee, I am so pleased that you have agreed to speak to our group on August 9 about . . .

⇨ Thank you for so promptly accepting our invitation to speak to us on August 9.

⇨ We are thrilled that you have agreed to be with us on August 9 to share your ideas on . . .

Confirm all the details of the program: the logistics of the meeting, the fee or expense reimbursement, the audience makeup, and the program objectives.

⇨ We will have a limo driver meet you at the gate.

⇨ You will be guest of honor at the luncheon to precede your afternoon workshop.

⇨ Of course, you are also invited to join us for cocktails before the evening's program and your speech.

⇨ Please keep in mind that the lighting will be poor for any audio-visuals you might normally use.

⇨ With such a large group, you'll probably be unable to provide an opportunity for questions from the audience.

⇨ Please allow the last ten minutes of your presentation time to answer questions from the group.

⇨ We have reserved a room for you (guaranteed for late arrival) at the convention hotel on the night before your presentation.

⇨ We will have two assistants on hand to help you set up the demonstration.

⇨ We will arrange to have the hotel bill us directly for your room and meals.

⇨ Enclosed is a map of the area, showing where you may park your car and where the actual meeting rooms are located.

Show your confidence in the speaker's success at the upcoming meeting.

⇨ We know we can count on you for a quality program.

⇨ You are sure to be a sensational success.

⇨ Your remarks will be the highlight of the evening.

⇨ Your comments will be just the motivation we need at this critical time.

⇨ Your words will be welcome indeed.

⇨ Your words, I'm sure, will be appropriate and well-grounded in years of experience.

⇨ Our audience will love you.

⇨ Our audience will be most interactive and supportive.

⇨ Our audiences always rave about such practical help as you plan to give.

⇨ Your speech outline looks intriguing. We can hardly wait.

⇨ Your words will not fall on deaf ears.

⇨ Your words will no doubt spur us to action in the coming months.

   (Note: See phrasing in the previous category.)

❖ ❖ ❖

Dear Mr. Sprinter:

I am so pleased to confirm your participation in our upcoming November 12–14 conference at the Marriott Waverly, Fullerton, California (23499 Hosea Boulevard, 303-449-2897). We expect 300–350 registrants to attend your session.

The complete program brochure should be available for me to forward to you in late August. But in the meantime, let me give you a few preliminary details: You will be one of ten speakers over the three-day period, all focusing on the theme of ""Quality Investments for Long-Term Growth."

You will be responsible for preparing camera-ready materials for the participant manuals. We will be responsible for reproducing, binding, and shipping the manuals to the workshop site. You will need to send me your camera-ready materials to arrive no later than September 1.

For your presentation, we will provide an honorarium of $500, plus reimburse you for travel, meals, and lodging expenses associated with your presentation. Upon completion of the workshop, simply send us your invoice for expenses, along with your receipts. You should receive a check within two weeks.

I'll be calling you later to discuss your A/V equipment needs and the room setup, along with any promotional materials we need such as biographical data and a press kit.

Our members are eagerly looking forward to hearing your suggestions and advice on how to ensure a sound financial future in this depressed economy! We think you'll also profit from the exposure to our member firms, and we encourage you to follow up with them about their individual needs at the various locations around the nation.

Sincerely,

❖ ❖ ❖

SOLICITING DETAILS ABOUT THE AUDIENCE _____

Guidelines and Alternate Phrasing

State your purpose.

⇨ I want to make sure I'm meeting the specific needs of your audience. Would you help me by answering a few questions? . . .

⇨ Audience needs and expectations vary, so I want to make sure my comments are appropriate. Your answers to the following questions will help me focus my efforts.

⇨ I'm wondering about my aim. That is, I want to shoot my comments straight to the heart with your group. For example, will you answer the following: . . .

Ask your questions as specifically as possible.

  Make response easy.

⇨ I've enclosed a two-page questionnaire for you to complete. Simply circle the appropriate numbers.

⇨ Simply jot your notes in the margin.

⇨ You may want to review these questions, think about your answers, and then phone me with your responses.

⇨ Will you direct me to two or three other members of your group who might answer the following questions for me?

❖ ❖ ❖

Dear Barbara:

I'm looking forward to speaking to your group on April 14. Would you help me make my comments as appropriate as possible by giving me a profile of the group members?

Simply jot your answers to the following questions in the margins of this letter. Or, if you prefer, you can call me at 379-7796.

- What is the male/female mix?
- What is the age range?
- What is their socio-economic level?
- What is their education level?
- Describe their technical background with regard to . . .
- Is attendance required or by choice?
- What is their attitude about my subject?
- What is your objective for the meeting?
- Are they used to audience participation activities?
- Should I allow time for questions and answers?

Thanks for your help in making sure I'm on target with your audience.

Sincerely,

❖ ❖ ❖

THANK YOU FOR THE OPPORTUNITY TO SPEAK _____

Guidelines and Alternate Phrasing

Thank the reader for the opportunity to speak.

⇨ Your soapbox was solid and lofty: thank you so much for letting me climb on it last week to share a few "words of wisdom."

⇨ I appreciate so much the opportunity you gave me to address your group last Monday.

⇨ Thank you for letting me share my ideas with the Forum group last week.

⇨ Thank you for the opportunity to conduct the sales seminar for your group.

⇨ Thank you for your confidence in having me address your group of engineers last week.

⇨ What confidence you showed in asking me to be a part of last week's panel before your managers! I thank you for the opportunity.

⇨ Thank you for letting me do what I do best—talk. Your group made marvelous listeners!

Give your assessment of how the meeting went, showing modesty about your contribution.

⇨ The group seemed genuinely interested in hearing how . . .

⇨ The audience members were so good about responding to all my shenanigans.

⇨ The audience asked some tough questions. I like that because it allows me to . . .

⇨ They were so willing to participate in all the activities I'd planned for them.

⇨ The synergy of the group was fantastic; their potential to work together to achieve . . . will be unlimited.

⇨ Although I'm sure there were some who disagreed with my theories, the majority expressed a great deal of support.

⇨ Although some of the group already seemed well-versed in the subject, I hope they, too, picked up a few ideas about specific uses for . . .

⇨ The group certainly kept me on my toes with their questions.

⇨ From reading the faces of the audience members, I think they were most receptive to the changes I suggested.

Remind the meeting planner of any promises about referrals or other follow-up publicity efforts.

⇨ The mailing list you offered to send will be quite helpful to me in making follow-up materials available to your group.

⇨ I'll be looking forward to getting some calls from the audience members about presenting this information at your local branches.

⇨ Thank you for your offer to phone Jack Dunaway about the possibility of facilitating such a meeting with his group. That certainly will give the ideas wider exposure.

⇨ I've enclosed a photo and print materials for the follow-up story you mentioned writing for your in-house newsletter.

Ask for a testimonial letter if you want to seek other speaking opportunities.

⇨ Would you mind dropping me a note about the presentation? As you may know, speakers live by word of mouth.

⇨ I'll appreciate it if you can write a letter mentioning your own and the group's reaction to the briefing. I'd like to have some record to pass along to my supervisor, who is in the process of determining whether such briefings are really worthwhile.

⇨ May I ask a favor? Would you drop me a short note giving your reflections on the meeting? Do you think the group will find the ideas helpful? How specifically will they profit from the information? These comments would be helpful for other managers trying to decide whether their teams would benefit from such a seminar.

⇨ Would you please write me a letter about the audience's reception to my ideas? No, I'm not planning to sit around and pat myself on the back. Rather, I want to have something in the file for other managers who might be considering a workshop similar to the one I presented for you.

❖ ❖ ❖

Dear Kenny:

Thank you for the opportunity to speak to your group this week about relationship selling. I always look at such meetings as a learning experience for myself when I leave with so many true stories that underscore the validity of the concepts presented.

The group members seemed very receptive to the ideas. They asked some particularly thought-provoking questions that make me think they plan to use the information right away to their benefit. After you yourself have had time to talk with others in the group, I'd also appreciate a note summing up their reactions to the ideas and the meeting. This feedback gives me invaluable direction for any follow-up sessions at other branches.

For those in the group who left their business cards with me, I'll be mailing further information. If you have later inquiries, please direct them to my office.

All in all, I was thrilled about the potential of your group to change the way our industry does business.

Sincerely,

❖ ❖ ❖

THANK YOU TO SPEAKER

(Note: See "Commendations.")

PUBLIC RELATIONS/ISSUES ≣≣≣≣≣≣

Public opinion sways to different drummers—those who communicate their message persuasively and clearly. On some such occasions, we take every opportunity to step into the limelight with our actions and urgings; we write editors and legislators. On other occasions, such as during a crisis, we want to avoid the spotlight until we have our house once again in order.

We've all heard it said that the squeaky wheel gets greased. The same holds true for those individuals and companies that can most effectively articulate their needs and desires to government officials and the general public. Expressing an opinion on a social issue, a legislative matter, or a current event is both a responsibility and a privilege not to be taken lightly.

RESPONSE TO CRISIS

Guidelines and Alternate Phrasing

Acknowledge the crisis situation.

⇨ We do find ourselves in the middle of a temporary crisis.

⇨ ... has reached crisis proportions, and we must immediately take the situation in hand before the crisis overwhelms us.

⇨ Our pipes did burst and there has been a leak—that much is undisputed.

Give behind-the-scenes actions, as well as any publicized actions, you are taking to minimize dangers or damages.

Show genuine concern for all those affected by the situation. You can always express concern, whether or not you accept responsibility for the situation.

⇨ We are primarily concerned with the safety of our customers and employees. Company profitability always takes on less significance in a crisis such as this.

⇨ We trust that this strong action conveys how serious we are about the situation.

⇨ We hope you will agree that we have acted responsibly in light of the testing done to date.

⇨ As the facts from our study become available, you can be assured that we will interpret them, with safety being utmost in our minds.

⇨ Our biggest concern is the future safety of our employees, customers, and the public.

⇨ Although we fail to see how the situation could have been avoided, we do want to express our vital interest in seeing that employees and customers do not have to endure such hardship again.

Calm employees with your promise to keep them informed of details as they become available.

⇨ We will let you know about future actions as details become available.

⇨ As soon as we know anything more, we'll pass on the information to you.

⇨ You are concerned about every detail and rightly so; we pledge to keep you informed every step of the way.

⇨ We will be monitoring the situation 24 hours a day and will release all the details to you, the public, as soon as we have them ourselves.

⇨ I personally plan to stay in touch by phone every hour and will go on TV with any new developments.

Avoid saying the situation will never recur.

❖ ❖ ❖

Dear:

I've been at Eastern for three months now. Since my arrival I've been impressed by the consistent commitment to service from the people here. We're producing a first-rate product and running a good, on-time airline. Those of you who fly us regularly know first-hand what I'm talking about.

In recent days you have undoubtedly read or heard news accounts about the indictment of nine Eastern employees on charges of falsifying repair records and failing to maintain aircraft. I want to address this in detail because it is a serious issue and because you deserve an explanation.

At the outset I want to make one point clear—the allegations concern events that occurred almost two years ago at a maintenance facility that has been closed for a year. The investigation has nothing to do with our operations or maintenance practices today.

In every respect, today Eastern is running a safe, efficient and courteous airline. Eastern may have its share of problems, but operating a safe airline is *NOT* one of them. This airline has undergone a rigorous inspection by the FAA, a rigorous inspection by the Department of Defense, as well as our internal audit. In every case, Eastern has passed these inspections in good order. And the FAA continues to be a vigilant observer and enforcer of regulations on the Eastern property to an extent unprecedented in American aviation history.

When the U.S. Attorney advised me that the company and certain management personnel would be subject to criminal indictments, I asked our attorneys to enter into discussions with the U.S. Attorney to try to put this investigation and these matters to rest.

We were prepared to acknowledge to the U.S. Attorney in the form of a guilty plea that improper maintenance practices occurred during the pre-strike period up until March of 1989. Where wrongdoing was found by our own and a separate FAA investigation, employees were terminated or reassigned and penalties were levied by the FAA.

These discussions ended, and the indictments were handed down, because the company simply could not agree to the U.S. Attorney's demand for a guilty plea to a conspiracy charge, which in our judgment would have called into question our present superior maintenance program and all employees and managers involved in that program.

I want to sincerely thank you for your support, past and present. Our product is improving and people are responding. And nothing is going to stand in the way of this progress. We have enjoyed serving you in the past, and we hope that we can count on your continued support in the coming months.

Sincerely,

Martin R. Shugrue
Trustee

Reprinted with permission by courtesy of Eastern Air Lines.

❖ ❖ ❖

LETTER TO THE EDITOR _____

Guidelines and Alternate Phrasing

State your position—either agreement or disagreement on an issue—or point out an error in the media information.

⇨ I wholeheartedly agree with your position on . . .

⇨ I, too, become disturbed by reports that say . . .

⇨ Your editorial statement on . . . is extremely premature.

⇨ I disagree most definitely with. . .

⇨ In an August 6 article entitled "Candid Shots," you printed very dated statistics on our company with regard to . . .

Give the correct information in the case of error. If you are offering a different position on an issue, state your reasons and cite sources of any statistics.

Request a retraction, if necessary, for erroneous information.

⇨ We demand a retraction in your next issue.

⇨ In an upcoming issue, please give the correct source of that statistic and explain the conditions under which the survey was done.

⇨ We expect an immediate decision about retracting your claim.

⇨ In the next issue of your journal, we ask that you include our company among the other vendors listed as offering this service.

⇨ We demand that you correct this impression immediately with a statement to the effect that . . .

Thank the editor for his or her efforts in informing the community when you agree with the editorial position.

⇨ Thank you for your vitally important contributions on the issue.

⇨ We appreciate your service to the community.

⇨ We appreciate seeing such provocative opinions carried in your paper.

⇨ Your efforts may save a life. Thank you.

⇨ We appreciate your using your media spotlight so responsibly.

⇨ Thank you for your concern as evidenced by your article on this disturbing trend.

⇨ Thank you for putting the safety of the community above your own profit.

⇨ Thank you for expressing the issues so succinctly and poignantly.

⇨ You have done us all a great service today with this editorial.

⇨ You have treated the situation responsibly and with sensitivity. We commend you.

❖ ❖ ❖

Dear Editor:

In your March 1 issue of *NTR*, you stated that our organization has been losing money ever since we launched our new product line, Mixus, and that we were on the brink of bankruptcy. The truth of the matter is that we have shown a profit in six out of the past eight quarters. In no way has the Mixus line been our downfall, as you imply. Our revenue for this product has been just slightly under our projections during this period of product introduction to our customers.

As you are aware, such implications of impending bankruptcy directly affect our relationships with suppliers and distributors. We insist that you immediately print a statement that corrects this misinformation.

Yours truly,

❖ ❖ ❖

Dear Editor:

Your stand on the literacy problem here in our community is commendable. With the necessary sensitivity, the feature focused on the everyday problems facing the illiterate citizen and then hit the rest of us hard with statistics that cannot be ignored.

For years, we've waited for "somebody else" to do it—to fund the projects that we know can make a difference in the local workforce. The Literacy One-Plus-One program provides an innovative strategy to involve people in volunteer work that can literally change the way we do business here in Edenburgh and improve life for all our citizens.

Thank you for using your strong voice to highlight this program and to appeal for the appropriate funding.

Sincerely,

❖ ❖ ❖

LETTER TO LEGISLATORS _____

Guidelines and Alternate Phrasing

Address only one subject in the letter. A letter that mentions everything that has gone wrong in the country will dilute your effectiveness on the key issue under scrutiny.

Identify the issue by a legislative bill number or the name that's widely publicized for the issue/bill.

State your position and ask your representative to either support or reject this legislation.

⇨ I disagree with this legislative action and urge you to vote against it.

⇨ I support this position to . . . and encourage you to lend your support also.

⇨ I agree with the need to . . . and would like to see you take a stronger stand by co-sponsoring a bill to . . .

⇨ When the bill comes up for a vote, I encourage you to reject it in its entirety.

⇨ I disagree with the basic premise of the legislation and suggest that you form a study committee to discover and report the true statistics with regard to . . .

Include information that will add to your credibility and identify your voice as one that stands out above the crowds and can influence others. For example, are you an active voter? A frequent campaign worker or contributor? An executive in a large corporation? A writer?

⇨ As a frequent campaign worker, I will wholeheartedly support any representative who believes that . . .

⇨ Enclosed is a recent copy of an article I published in our industry trade magazine on this subject. This information should give you an appreciation for the dramatic difference this spending will mean in the industry.

⇨ As I am going about the country doing radio and television interviews, I'm frequently asked questions about . . .

⇨ As spokesman for the national American Society of Training and Development, I wanted to let you know how our organization and its 28,000 members feel about . . .

Ask for a reply if you want to know how the representative stands on the issue.

⇨ Would you let us know how you plan to vote on this matter?

⇨ Will you clarify your activities on this committee?

⇨ I'll appreciate your response about what action you plan to take on this important issue.

⇨ Would you please release a statement to the press about your position on this legislative action?

⇨ Would you please voice to the national media your opposition to this deadly weapon and its destruction?

⇨ Your constituents want to know how you plan to vote on this issue. Would you please make some statement?

❖ ❖ ❖

Dear Representative Massey:

As a long-term campaign supporter and frequent contributor, I am appalled by the recent legislative (HR3980) push to give members of Congress, federal judges, and high-level managers a salary increase. At a time when we are trying to balance the budget—and having little success—the 40 percent increase strikes me as ludicrous.

We believe that congressional pay raises should be contingent on actions to reduce the federal deficit. As chief executive officer of my corporation, I believe that pay raises for my employees should be based on employee performance. The same should be true of government; Americans have a right to expect the same criterion—performance—for their elected representatives. Our chronic budget deficits are clear indication that Congress is not doing its job in this regard.

I urge you to vote against this pay increase. Would you please release a statement to the press about where you stand on this issue? Our 8,500 employees want to see if Congress works under the same rules and premises of performance as private-sector employees do.

Respectfully yours,

❖ ❖ ❖

SUGGESTION FOR INTERVIEW

Guidelines and Alternate Phrasing

Grab attention with a startling statistic, pithy quote, intriguing question, or provocative statement.

Suggest the interview and possible topics of discussion.

⇨ Sam Levett is an expert in . . . and can make himself available for an interview on August 9 or 10.

⇨ I'm enclosing some further information on the new product line, along with a biography of the principal engineer involved. If you would like to interview Sam, please call 349-009-3879.

⇨ Your readers would most certainly be interested in how they can..., and Sam Levett is just the kind of guy who can inspire them to action. He will be doing interviews in your city on August 10 and would be glad to set something up with you.

Emphasize the interviewee's credentials.

⇨ As an engineer with 23 years' experience for the company, . . .

⇨ John has been on the President's Task Force for the past two years . . .

⇨ Having published frequently in trade journals, Myron now has put his information into book form and has sold the rights to Prentice Hall.

⇨ You'll find Myron a particularly knowledgeable consultant with a wide range of expertise to draw from in fielding questions. His corporate clients such as IBM, Exxon, and Procter and Gamble . . .

Include a contact name and number.

⇨ If you're interested in pursuing this subject, please call . . .

⇨ If you think your audience could profit from hearing about ..., Dan James (312-688-9998) will be happy to schedule an interview.

⇨ To discuss this idea further, please phone . . .

⇨ If you need a guest who can motivate your audience to ..., then call Dan James at 312-688-9998 to arrange a convenient interview time.

❖ ❖ ❖

Dear Mr. Jamieson:

"I can't get anything done at the office; I'm going home to work." When employees utter that sentiment, it's time for a change. Last year, 18.3 million people ran their businesses from home, a 23 per cent increase over the previous year. The IRS reports that one in three businesses registered in the last two years has been home-based. The typical home worker is a 41-year-old male college graduate, married with children, making $40,000 annually.

Over 200 major corporations in the U.S. now have pilot projects allowing their employees to work at home at least part of the day or week.

Myron Jones, director of Human Resources, at Fountain Corporation has just completed a study among these 200 corporations on productivity increases. Myron will be available for interviews the week of August 5 and would be willing to share with your readers some other fascinating survey results such as:

- why current flextime policies miss the mark
- why large companies fear small businesses
- how husbands and wives can blend business and family under the same roof

Myron's studies have taken him into corporate offices around the world, where he has met with heads of major corporations to get their feedback on such at-home arrangements. He also has published widely in trade journals in the human resource field.

If you'd be interested in interviewing Myron about supervising work-at-home employees and the productivity increases associated with this phenomenon, please call Margaret Hayden (315-378-9873).

Sincerely,

❖ ❖ ❖

THANK YOU FOR INTERVIEW _____

Guidelines and Alternate Phrasing

Express appreciation for the time and effort the reporter made in giving you air time.

⇨ Thank you for the August 6 opportunity to share with your listeners how they can . . .

⇨ I appreciate your taking the time to interview me and prepare a feature story on the issue of . . .

⇨ Your questions proved quite out of the ordinary in our August 2 interview. They were a welcome change to the mundane issues that usually come out of such a discussion. I appreciate your thorough preparation on the subject.

Summarize modestly your contribution to the publication, radio, or TV audience.

⇨ I hope your readers now will have a better idea about how to . . .

⇨ As a result of the interview, the public now can put a name and an agency with their funds.

⇨ At the least, your audience now will be aware of all the available avenues to accomplish their tasks of . . .

⇨ The key message your audience should benefit from is that . . .

Remind the reporter to direct inquiries to you and provide details about where you can be reached.

⇨ If your listeners call you for more information, please refer them to my office.

⇨ Should you receive inquiries about ..., let your readers know that they can call us direct at 680-8890.

⇨ We'll have staff on duty all weekend to handle calls from your viewers who may need help with . . .

❖ ❖ ❖

Dear Ted:

Thank you for the August 6 interview on work-at-home arrangements offered to employees by major corporations. No doubt, you had read several pieces on that growing trend because you asked such intriguing questions. I hope my answers were equally on target.

Also for those would-be entrepreneurs, the article might spur them into early retirement and a brand new career. I do think that decision will be easier after they face the realities we covered in the interview.

Should you have any inquiries about the research or our organization, please refer them to Merry Ringer at 1-800-898-9876, and we will follow up.

Sincerely,

❖ ❖ ❖

PERMISSION TO USE QUOTED OR COPYRIGHTED MATERIALS

Guidelines and Alternate Phrasing

State who you are and your purpose for writing.

⇨ As an author working on an article for *World Oil,* I need permission . . .

⇨ Ralph Smith, CEO of Dublin Associates, will be addressing the ASTD convention on May 9 and in his speech wants to use a story about your company. I'm writing to make sure all the facts are correct and to ask permission to use the following anecdote:

⇨ In an upcoming issue of our in-house newsletter, we want to use the four principles of leadership that appeared in an article entitled "Walking the High Wire" in your November 9 issue of *Working Woman.* Would you grant permission for us to use these four principles as an outline for our own article?

Request permission for the specific material. You'll need to give the full title of the publication, page number, and line. For some materials such as original stories or anecdotes, it's best to enclose a copy of the information you are asking for permission to use.

Explain the exact use of the material.

⇨ This material is for our own limited use for approximately 30 training classes each year.

⇨ This material will be used in a speech and then included in a paper for the ARVE's Conference Proceedings.

⇨ We want to use this material in a book to be published by Prentice Hall in 19—.

⇨ We plan to print these words on the back of a laminated memory-aid card for all our secretaries.

Include wording for the permission line you intend to use.

⇨ We will credit you as our source.

⇨ If this is agreeable to you, we will include the line: "Reprinted with permission of . . ."

⇨ We will include the line: "Used by permission of . . ."

⇨ The line "Reprinted by courtesy of ..." will accompany the information.

Make response easy. Include a self-addressed envelope, a permission form, a copy of the information to be quoted, or a simple approval line at the bottom of your own letter.

    Thank the reader for granting permission.

⇨ Thank you for granting rights for this limited use.

⇨ Thank you for granting permission to use this material.

⇨ We appreciate your help in letting us use this material.

⇨ This information will be of vital importance to our readers; we appreciate your granting us the right to reprint.

⇨ Thank you for this courtesy in allowing us to reprint this information.

⇨ We appreciate the courtesy in permitting us this use of your material.

❖ ❖ ❖

Publications Department

Ladies or Gentlemen:

Subject: Copyright Issue—Requesting Permission to Quote

I am preparing a training manual for our safety course and would like to include some information that appeared in your in-house newsletter, *Think Smart.*

I'm referring to an anecdote involving chemical sprays that appeared in your July 6 issue:

> Author: Gerald Blum
> Title: "Chemical Sprays and Safety"
> Volume 7, Issue 3
> From page three, column two, line 12, beginning with the words
>   "Forest fires result . . .
> To page four, column one, line two, ending with the words . . .
>   "in our lifetime."

If you will permit this limited use of the material, please sign below and return a copy for my files. So that you can see the context in which the anecdote will appear, I've enclosed a copy of the appropriate training manual chapter. And, of course, we will print a credit line "Courtesy of Dell-Howell Corporation" with the material.

If you do not own the copyright on this material and have taken it from another source, would you please let me know whom to contact about getting this permission to quote.

Thank you for your help with our safety manual.

Sincerely,

Agreed to and accepted by:

_____

Signature   Title   Date

❖ ❖ ❖

REFERENCES

Given a choice as customers, we like to do business with those we know. The same is true as employers; we like to hire those we know. And because we can't always find qualified employees among our own family and friends, we rely on the next best thing—friends, family, and colleagues of those whose opinions we respect. Thus, the reference letter has become a fact of corporate life.

When requesting such letters on your own behalf, be sure to seek out opinions from those in positions of authority who know you well and who also can communicate persuasively about your credentials and personality.

If you find yourself in the unfortunate circumstance of being asked to supply a reference for an unsuitable employee, you will do better simply to verify facts of employment such as dates, salary, and job title. On the other hand, when agreeing to give references for other dedicated employees, consider it a privilege and an opportunity to comment as specifically as you can. The more specific, the more valuable your reference.

REQUESTING FROM SUPERVISOR/COLLEAGUE

Guidelines and Alternate Phrasing

State your request and the reason.

⇨ Would you do me the favor of supplying a reference?

⇨ May I ask a favor? I need a reference letter covering the period I worked for your organization (May 19— to September 19—).

⇨ I'm considering an engineering position with Dalton Services and need a reference letter about my work with your organization.

⇨ Dalton Services, an engineering firm in Atlanta, is considering me for an accounting position, and I'm writing to ask you for a letter of reference.

Recall the dates of previous employment so the reader can immediately check past records.

Overview the new job responsibilities so the reader can comment appropriately about experience, skills, or personal qualities that would make you (or the individual you're inquiring about) successful. The more specific you can be in your request, the more appropriately the recipient can focus on the job in question.

⇨ The job will require the ability to get along well with people and an even temperament in handling dissatisfied customers.

⇨ The job will require travel and flexibility in week-to-week scheduling.

⇨ Attention to detail and punctuality, as you can imagine, will be extremely important in such a job.

⇨ Tenacity and determination are key ingredients for the successful person who accepts this position.

⇨ Extensive knowledge of desktop-publishing packages is a real plus in the job.

⇨ As with many jobs, sound judgment and the ability to make quick decisions will be qualities uppermost in the prospective employer's mind when filling this position.

⇨ Communication skills, both verbal and written, will be of utmost importance in this particular assignment.

⇨ My extensive experience in sales will certainly come in handy as a springboard for this managerial job.

⇨ Although this may sound trite, the prospective employer is looking for someone who really cares about doing a good job—who cares as much as if the business were his or her own to run.

⇨ Extensive computer experience is a must in the new job, along with the natural curiosity that spurs one to continue to look for ways to improve the current program or process.

Express appreciation for the help.

⇨ Thank you so much for your help in this way.

⇨ I appreciate your time in doing this favor.

⇨ I appreciate so much your help in securing this position.

⇨ I realize that drafting a letter is time-consuming. And I do thank you for your help, when there's absolutely nothing in it for you.

⇨ Thank you for helping me land this new assignment.

⇨ This job will mean a great deal to me. Thank you for helping with this reference.

⇨ My thanks for writing on my behalf.

⇨ Thank you for your comments; they will be highly beneficial as we try to match the position with the most suitable candidate.

⇨ I appreciate your honesty in helping us determine how successful and happy Bob would be in this job.

❖ ❖ ❖

Dear Mr. Davenport:

I'm currently seeking employment with Bledson Healthcare Services and need a letter of reference from you. If you recall, while employed by your firm, I worked on long-term assignments with elderly patients (Ms. Elma Scott and Mr. Todd Forenzon) from March 19— to April of 19—.

This new job will require experience and temperament quite similar to that which I had with your organization. I'll be administrator for all nursing services provided to home-bound patients. As administrator, I'll need to evaluate what the individual can do for himself or herself and what kind of services the situation warrants. Then, I'll match nurse to patient according to personalities. The job will require interaction with the public (family members and those of the medical community) and extensive knowledge about government-assisted medical aid and all the administrative paperwork required by law. Finally, the job requires someone who can work alone with very little supervision because Bledson's headquarters are in Atlanta.

If you can comment on my experience in getting along with both patients and family members, my self-motivation, and my attention to the detail and the technicalities of the medical and legal fields, that should give my prospective employer great insight into how successful I might be in this new job. Thank you for taking the time to prepare this reference. The job means a great deal to me.

Sincerely,

❖ ❖ ❖

SUPPLYING FOR SUITABLE EMPLOYEE _____

Guidelines and Alternate Phrasing

Recommend the person immediately.

⇨ I am pleased to offer you my highest recommendation for Bill Eaton.

⇨ For approximately 22 months I've had the privilege of working beside Bill Eaton, and I can heartily recommend him to you.

⇨ Without reservation, I highly recommend Bill Eaton to you for any engineering position.

⇨ I'm thrilled to be asked to write this recommendation for Bill Eaton.

⇨ As Bill Eaton's immediate supervisor for the past six years, I can offer only the highest recommendation for his experience, his skill, and his personal integrity.

Detail the individual's association with your organization—length of employment, skills displayed on the job, personal attributes that will contribute to his or her success.

⇨ Bill's loyalty and integrity have been above reproach.

⇨ Bill's commitment to helping people has been in the highest tradition of the social work profession.

⇨ Bill's willingness to work long hours and his ability to manage time extremely well allowed him to run the department almost single-handedly.

⇨ Bill proved to be a capable engineer and was able to diagnose and solve mechanical problems with ease.

⇨ Bill was career-motivated and self-motivated in achieving the goals he set for himself as well as those we set for him.

⇨ Bill was loyal to the company and his superiors.

⇨ Bill has a gentle but persuasive management style that motivates employees, but he can be firm and straightforward in difficult employee situations.

⇨ Bill understands budgeting and can live with the budget guidelines set for him.

⇨ Bill communicates well—he was very effective with both customers and with new employees who looked to him for training.

⇨ Bill was very gracious in accepting different shifts when such scheduling became necessary.

⇨ Bill's technical skill and judgment are thorough and sound.

Verify the reason for the termination.

⇨ Bill resigned his position as a manager, giving appropriate notice and leaving us with a trained replacement.

⇨ Bill left his employment here to accompany his wife to a new job.

⇨ Bill left his employment here to accept a position with Highland Corporation.

⇨ Bill's employment here terminated as part of a major staffing reduction of almost 40 percent.

Close with a summary of your opinion of how the new employee will work out in the position.

⇨ Bill will make a valuable contribution to your organization.

⇨ If past performance is any indication of future success, Bill will be a superb employee in your organization.

⇨ Bill will succeed anywhere he chooses to work.

⇨ Bill has been and will continue to be a valuable employee—the kind that keeps customers and clients coming back.

⇨ In my opinion, you will be lucky indeed if Bill chooses to accept a position with your company.

⇨ Bill will be an asset wherever he is hired.

⇨ Bill has my highest regard both personally and professionally.

⇨ Bill should prove to be an excellent manager with your organization.

⇨ Given Bill's outstanding record here, we would not hesitate to rehire him. You will have made an excellent decision, should you offer him a position with your firm.

❖ ❖ ❖

Dear Mr. Weldon:

I am pleased to write to you concerning Dianna Frazier's work history here at Fornsbury and Associates. From March 19— to June 19— she did a splendid job as administrative assistant to me, owner of the firm, and to our vice president.

To be honest, I'd have to say she was more than an assistant. In many cases, she managed the entire office of 23 professionals and kept us all free to deal with clients while she took on the problems of day-to-day operations. Specifically, she coordinated travel arrangements for 12 to 15 of us, selected and purchased office equipment, maintained our inventory of manuals and videos, prepared financial reports, and supervised a staff of 3 clerical support people. Dianna required very little direction in these duties and no day-to-day supervision, because she approached the job as if she were the owner and as if every problem-client signed her paycheck.

Dianna resigned her position here to move to Miami to care for her elderly parents. However, if she ever returned to the area, we would be most eager to have her rejoin us.

I highly recommend Dianna to you and know, without a doubt, that she will handle any administrative assistant or office manager position with great success.

Sincerely,

❖ ❖ ❖

SUPPLYING FOR UNSUITABLE EMPLOYEE

Guidelines and Alternate Phrasing

Acknowledge the individual's employment, giving position titles and dates of service.

⇨ As a system engineer, Alissa Klein worked under my supervision for two years, until August 19—.

⇨ Alissa Klein held the position of account executive with our corporation for two years, until October 4, 19—.

⇨ Under the supervision of Moss Summers, Alissa Klein served as account representative to Grayson Corporation. She held that position for two years, and then was promoted to a sales position within our regional office, where she worked for the remaining two years of her four-year tenure here.

Verify the reasons for the employee's termination.

⇨ Alissa left this position to accompany her husband to San Francisco.

⇨ Alissa left this position to reevaluate her career goals and plans.

➡ Alissa left this position to do freelance work.

➡ Alissa left this position to establish her own consulting firm.

➡ Alissa stated health reasons in her letter of resignation.

➡ A difficult personal situation at home was the reason Alissa gave for leaving this position.

➡ Alissa left this position to find employment in the computer area.

➡ Alissa's employment was terminated as part of a staff reduction here at Belcher Associates.

State any weaknesses without malice, being mindful of legal difficulties.

➡ Alissa's attendance record did not meet our standards of regularity.

➡ Alissa's duties were not always performed with the extra attention to detail required in such a position. Perhaps that would not be the case in another situation.

➡ Alissa could not be as flexible as necessary in working the weekend hours our operations required.

➡ Alissa's written communication skills were not satisfactory in the position she held here. In a situation where writing was not part of the job assignment, Alissa possibly would do quite well.

❖ ❖ ❖

Dear Mr. Slaughterbaugh:

Alissa Klein was employed as an auditor by Hearst Corporation for four years, from June 19— to August 19—. After the first six months, she received a promotion and an appropriate salary increase. During the last 3½ years, she received annual cost-of-living increases.

Ms. Klein left our company to move back to New York and seek employment there.

Sincerely,

❖ ❖ ❖

REFERRALS

Just as employers want to hire people they already know, customers like to do business with people they know. When that isn't possible, they do the next best thing: they ask people they know for referrals.

In a situation where you yourself cannot help the prospective customer or client, take the opportunity to do a favor for two people: the client and the one who ultimately receives that client's business.

Such favors almost always come full circle—even months or years down the line. Therefore, you will want to actively seek opportunities to link buyers with sellers. Buyers remember the effort to put their interests above your own and often become even more determined to do business with you on later occasions.

REQUESTING

Guidelines and Alternate Phrasing

Recall your past association with the reader, such as a mutual friend or attendance at a convention.

⇨ Gerald Hines mentioned to me last week that you might know of ....

⇨ After leaving Snyder's summer employment program over two years ago, I've found plenty of opportunity to use the skills learned as an apprentice there. You were kind enough to let me observe you in your job for two weeks, and as I result I've carved out a sales position of my own here at Ibco.

⇨ I enjoyed our short airplane chat last week on the way to Los Angeles.

State briefly the products or services you provide to what clientele.

Thank the reader for any referral he or she may have occasion to give, and include any mutual benefit that you foresee.

⇨ Do you ever run across anyone in need of placement services? If so, I'll appreciate your giving them my name.

⇨ As I see it, you and I sell complementary products to the same customer. Seems to me that whichever of us gets to the customer first should suggest the next logical step in the set-up process. Can you envision a way that we could construct a mutually beneficial referral arrangement?

⇨ I'll thank you for mentioning my name to any interested prospects.

⇨ Thank you for passing on any of my information to interested colleagues.

⇨ I'll appreciate any name-dropping you can do.

⇨ Do you think it would be to our mutual benefit to set up a formal arrangement for commission referrals?

⇨ I'll appreciate it if you can pass my name along to anyone who might be interested in this service, and I'll do the same for you.

⇨ I'd like to work out a mutually beneficial arrangement for referrals. Do you have suggestions?

⇨ I'll appreciate your referring to me anyone who needs such services.

❖ ❖ ❖

Dear Ms. Kai:

I enjoyed visiting with you at the trade show last week in Baltimore. Opportunities to relax around the dinner table certainly provide a more civilized way to get to know colleagues than on that jammed expo floor! Your work with the court systems sounds fascinating.

Although I didn't get to go into much detail about our consulting services, I wanted you to know that our clientele resembles your own. We provide sales training to small organizations of approximately 50 employees or fewer. We go much beyond the usual rah-rah motivational meetings to help individual reps design and achieve personal sales goals, providing the training they need in a one-on-one setting. Our methods may involve only recommending certain audiotape programs for self-study or consulting with individuals on a three- or four-day proposal project.

I will appreciate any referrals to individuals or small corporations you think may be interested in such one-on-one sales training. Certainly, I'll keep my eyes open for opportunity to refer any investment business your way. Let's plan to stay in contact—at least at the next IACB convention, if not before.

Sincerely,

❖ ❖ ❖

OFFERING

Guidelines and Alternate Phrasing

Mention the referral immediately, stating why you yourself can no longer provide the service or product.

⇨ We are no longer in the hardware business. But I would like to refer you to another organization that excels in this area....

⇨ May I offer a suggestion for your next drilling job? I want to let you know of ...

⇨ We no longer carry the Nexus product line you mentioned in your recent order, but we are pleased to refer you to Belton, Inc., who recently became a Nexus distributor in an exclusive arrangement.

⇨ I would like to make you aware of a new firm in your locale that offers janitorial services much superior to what you or I have had to settle for in the past.

⇨ Thank you for thinking of us with your recent order for plumbing supplies and fixtures, but we no longer sell those products. We suggest that you contact Belton, Inc., for the custom work you described in your letter.

Elaborate on the referral specifically.

State your expectation that the referral will be of mutual benefit.

⇨ I think you two will enjoy working together.

⇨ I think you'll find Mary a delightful person to work with.

⇨ We think you'll be pleased with the quality of work Gemco produces.

⇨ Gemco performs to the highest expectations; I don't think you'll be disappointed in any project they tackle for you.

⇨ Gemco has a reputation to be envied in the industry; I don't think you'll go wrong with them.

⇨ With your rigid criteria and Gemco's screening, I think you'll be very satisfied with the results on any project you undertake together.

⇨ The results on any Gemco project should be exceptional.

⇨ We think both your organizations rank with the best in the industry; you should complement each other.

⇨ If you do decide to give them a call, I think you'll be very pleased with the way they'll work with you.

⇨ I think you'll be more than pleased with any project you decide to undertake with them.

⇨ We have the highest regard for both of your organizations; any working relationship between you should be mutually satisfying.

❖ ❖ ❖

Dear Ms. Morrison:

Thank you for your vote of confidence in writing us about the kind of candidate you want to hire in your Dallas sales office. However, we've changed our focus in the past two years since last working with you and no longer place employees below the executive vice presidential level. I do want to recommend a placement firm in your local area that handles job openings for middle management positions: Merrill and Merrill (504) 784-3489.

This firm has done exceptionally well in the past two years, successfully placing several managers at Dowell Corporation and at Boeing Gardner. Their screening process is rigorous, especially for any position requiring technical experience in the physical sciences. I suggest calling Michelle Shong there at 778-9862 to overview your needs; it could be that the company already has someone in its data base that would be appropriate for you.

I think you'll appreciate their discrete way of working and the caliber of candidates they send you to interview. Let me know if something there works out for you.

Sincerely,

❖ ❖ ❖

RESIGNATION

Whether resigning to accept a more rewarding position or to leave the workforce altogether, your official letter of resignation may follow you for years. You will want to take care that it expresses gratitude for what you have gained through the work association, as well as a positive attitude about your future.

And if you are the recipient of an employee's resignation, your expression of gratitude for what that individual has contributed will keep a positive association intact. Resignations provide opportunity to reflect on the benefit of every association and wish the individual well.

OFFERING

Guidelines and Alternate Phrasing

Offer your resignation from a specific position on a specific effective date.

⇨ Effective May 1, I will assume the position of marketing manager at Universal Builders in Omaha. Therefore, I'm offering my resignation here, effective April 30.

⇨ Please accept my resignation as systems programmer, effective May 13.

⇨ I've recently decided to leave my position as auditor with Utco. My last day here will be April 30, although I do have some flexibility in that effective date should the situation warrant my staying on a few weeks longer.

⇨ I offer my resignation as executive director of United Philco, effective March 1, 19—.

Give your reason for leaving. If you're resigning on a positive note, you may mention a new position you're assuming or some other valid reason for terminating employment. If you're leaving under negative circumstances that you don't want as part of your permanent file, you may couch your reason in vague, general terms.

⇨ I must offer my resignation because I cannot sign the new non-compete agreement extended as part of our current contract negotiations.

⇨ I will be assuming a position more in line with my graduate studies and current interests.

⇨ This new position will offer me the opportunity to travel overseas, an adventure I've looked forward to for sometime now.

⇨ I want to pursue a hobby that, with a little more attention, may turn into a full-time career.

⇨ As you may know from our past discussions, I've kept my eyes open for something that would offer me the chance to do a little more research, and I think this new position will provide such opportunity.

⇨ This new position, while somewhat less challenging, will require fewer hours and allow more time for me to care for my elderly parents.

⇨ The long drive between office and home has just become too frustrating; I've decided to seek employment closer to where I live.

⇨ For sometime now, I've been longing for a position with a little more challenge and a greater variety of duties. I believe this new position will give me the chance to "try my wings" along new paths.

⇨ I constantly need new stimulation on the job, and to be quite frank, I need a chance to learn new things, to win new clients, to solve new problems.

⇨ Routine work has never been one of my strong points; I thrive on change. And from the new job description, that will be the order of the day.

⇨ This new position will allow me the chance to interact more frequently with customers and vendors.

⇨ I prefer working on a single project that allows me full control from start to finish. This new position allows just that kind of total quality control that I think is necessary in smooth operations. I want to pursue other interest in retail sales.

⇨ I plan to look for an investment opportunity that will allow me to own and manage my own business.

Mention anyone you've trained to replace you, if appropriate, and any unfinished projects in progress.

⇨ I've trained Cheryl Anderson in all my daily job duties.

⇨ I have every confidence that Cheryl Anderson can handle my job.

⇨ I would have no qualms in leaving my job in the capable hands of Cheryl Anderson, at least until you've made a thorough search outside the organization.

⇨ Cheryl Anderson is fully capable of assuming my position, should you decide to promote from within the organization.

⇨ Pending projects include the Jefferson case and the Blythe will.

⇨ Unfinished projects that will need your attention include ...; Cheryl Anderson is familiar with all the details of these ongoing efforts.

Express your appreciation for the job, citing either experience, training, skill development, or relationships with those customers or co-workers. On the other hand, if leaving on a negative note, you may omit any further reference to the current position. But do avoid a negative tone that may work against you in landing later jobs.

⇨ I've appreciated all my dealings with Neilsen and Neilsen.

⇨ Thank you for the personal and professional growth I've enjoyed here at Neilsen and Neilsen.

⇨ The job here has been richly rewarding.

⇨ The experience I've gained here has been invaluable in preparing me to assume a larger role in managing a similar organization.

⇨ The close personal friendships, as well as the professional liaisons, have been a meaningful part of my work life here.

⇨ My work here has given me rich experience in management and in life.

⇨ I have the utmost respect for the high ethical standards this organization has maintained with me as a employee as well as with its customers.

⇨ The associations here have been gratifying and meaningful for me.

⇨ The friendships and professional relationships with colleagues in the industry have contributed to a well-rounded, enjoyable tenure here at Neilsen and Neilsen.

⇨ My training has been exceptional, my relationships deeply meaningful, and my work very rewarding. Thank you for the opportunities here.

❖ ❖ ❖

Dear Charles:

Effective October 1, I will assume the position of director of Human Resources for Avco, Inc., in Baton Rouge. Therefore, please accept my resignation as benefits and compensation coordinator of the Human Resources Department within Pilburgh Associates, effective September 30.

The decision was a difficult one for me because I have enjoyed so much my working relationships here. The job description has given me great latitude in assisting other coordinators within the Human Resource area, and as a result, I've gained skills in several related fields. These cross-training opportunities have been invaluable. And in a much more formal, classroom setting, I've been able to take advantage of classes in management, inter-personal skills, writing, and oral presentations. All of this training has been a worthwhile effort for both Pilburgh and me.

As I go to the new position, I'll do so with the utmost respect for the management examples and philosophies learned here and with gratitude for the personal attention to my career growth.

Thank you for the rewarding experience I've enjoyed during my seven years' association with the organization.

Sincerely,

❖ ❖ ❖

Dear Mr. Salinas:

I offer my resignation as marketing director, to become effective July 15. After a few weeks of vacation, I'll assume similar duties with Dutton-Harvan, Inc., here in the city.

As you and I have discussed the past few months, the marketing budget has been cut so drastically as to curtail most of the activities that I consider essential to launch a new product line. Consequently, I cannot in good conscience continue in a position where I feel my best creative efforts are limited to only point-of-sale displays and trade-journal adver-tising. I do hope you'll understand my internal struggle to do the kind of job that a new-product launch requires and still stay within such a limited budget.

May I suggest that Allen Hartman assume my position? Allen and I have worked closely on many projects, and I've had the opportunity to admire his creative problem-solving skills with temperamental clients, as well as his supervisory skills.

I do want to thank you for the experience I've gained here, particularly in the successful introduction to the market of our 389 laptop. Likewise, I have the utmost respect for the creative talents and commitment to excellence of all those I've worked with in the marketing area. My best wishes as the company continues to reposition itself amidst the current financial difficulties.

Sincerely,

❖ ❖ ❖

Dear Mr. Weimeyer:

Please accept my resignation as hospital administrator, effective April 1. I have decided to pursue other career opportunities nearer my family in the Kansas City area.

Sincerely,

❖ ❖ ❖

ACCEPTING

Guidelines and Alternate Phrasing

State your regrets that the employee is leaving.

⇨ With regret, we accept your resignation.

⇨ I'm deeply disappointed. We had hoped that you'd "signed on" with us for life. That indeed would have been our good fortune.

⇨ We will miss you very much as you leave to assume your position at Hydril. You've been a model employee here.

⇨ With disappointment, I read my morning's mail and your letter of resignation. We will find it difficult to replace you.

⇨ Two weeks will certainly be inadequate to find a replacement of your caliber. Two months or two years would be more appropriate. But accept your resignation, I guess we must.

⇨ We accept your resignation as marketing manager with much distress. You've made an excellent leader and motivator, one that will be difficult to replace.

⇨ Your sales record with us has been outstanding. We regret very much your decision to leave us at the end of the month.

Thank the employee for his or her contributions. The more specific your comments, the more sincere the letter will sound.

Offer any alternatives to effective dates for termination.

⇨ Since you're not assuming a new position right away, would it be feasible for you to work one month longer than you've originally stated in your letter?

⇨ Is there any way at all you could delay your move for another two weeks?

⇨ If you've not made a definite commitment as to a starting date with the new employer, would you consider working with us until the end of the month?

Give your best wishes to the employee on his or her future plans.

⇨ We trust everything will work out as you have planned.

⇨ We hope you find the future inviting and satisfying.

⇨ We wish you great success with your career plans.

⇨ We wish you the very best as you assume the parent role full-time for the next few years.

⇨ I admire your courage in making this career change. I have great confidence in your ability to make things work.

⇨ We hope your future is a bright one wherever you go.

⇨ Your future plans sound challenging and exciting; we wish you great success in working them to a successful end.

⇨ We hope you and your family will be very happy as you relocate to the Bay area.

⇨ If you ever need an excellent reference, call on us. Best of everything as you go.

⇨ Your children are very lucky to have your sacrifice and commitment to their well-being.

⇨ Your parents, I'm sure, are very grateful for your move to live near them and help meet their needs at this time of their life.

⇨ Godspeed as you go.

⇨ Godspeed as you work your new plans. You deserve success in whatever job you pursue.

⇨ Your future sounds full and rewarding. We hope you will be very happy in the new position.

❖ ❖ ❖

Dear Byron:

We accept your resignation as chief accountant, but we do so with great reluctance.

Finding a replacement for you will be extremely difficult. If we considered your accounting duties alone, possibly the task would not seem so arduous. But you've done so much more for our company than perform accounting functions for our clients; you've built relationships. And believe me, there's a big difference.

Specifically, I think of the way you've handled Scullenberger through its restructuring and Bolton, Inc., through the massive layoffs and the related tax posturing. Their confidence in the way you personally handled their tax questions and offered advice at every juncture is the reason both clients are still with us. Thank you for making such a conscientious effort to "be there" whenever they've called.

I do have one last favor. Would you consider working two weeks longer than the effective date stated in your resignation letter? As you know, with Richard out of the country, we will be delayed in even beginning our search for a replacement.

We wish you the very best as you go to work for Unity Life; you're the kind of employee who will make a success out of every assignment. We hope the new job affords you all the growth opportunities you deserve.

Sincerely,

❖ ❖ ❖

SOLICITATIONS

What a different place our world would be if it weren't for those who care enough about their environment, their fellow human beings, and their country to give money and to volunteer time for charitable and civic projects.

Related to that involvement are many behind-the-scenes communications: letters soliciting funding or volunteers, letters requesting honorary use of a celebrity's name, letters presenting both positive and negative answers, and thank-yous to those contributing money or time. An appropriate tone—motivational, yet factual—may mean the difference between failure and success.

SEEKING

Guidelines and Alternate Phrasing

Use an attention-getting opening appropriate to your cause.

⇨ Would you help us improve our schools so that your children get the education they will need to make their way in the world?

⇨ Does it disturb you that ...?

⇨ Are you one of the group who thinks somebody ought to do something about ...?

⇨ These statistics don't lie: ...

⇨ Within the next two months you will be hearing an announcement that.... And here's what you can do to help: ...

Elaborate on your organization and be specific about what you want from the reader.

⇨ We need your contribution immediately.

⇨ We ask that you appoint two volunteers from your organization to join our committee...

⇨ We want to add your company's name to our list of contributors of $1,000, a list that will be going out with our letter to ask for ...

⇨ Can you send us something, anything today—$100? $25? $10?

Support your request with testimonials from prominent people who have endorsed your cause or even with comments from the "average" recipient of the money or services you're soliciting. In other words, make the reader hear firsthand the good that can come from the donation.

⇨ Our cause is a worthy one, as any of the people in our shelters will share. One 22-year-old woman commented to us recently, "......"

⇨ Many of our finest citizens have been personally involved, from our mayor to the president of our local chapter of ...

⇨ If these victims could talk with you one-on-one, they would share what a critical difference this mission made in their turnaround....

Mention your hopes for a specific amount (of money or time) from each contributor if you have a certain goal and are trying to raise the money from a limited number of large corporations or wealthy individuals. When that's not the case, let the reader know that any amount or donated time will be welcome.

⇨ We want to limit our sponsorship to about 20 corporations. If you would like to be one of these twenty, we need $10,000 toward the construction of ...

⇨ With our membership of over 12,000 individuals, if we receive just $10 from each member, we could meet our goal to ...

⇨ Someone has suggested that we should make this effort an entirely local one—something that we as a community do for "our own." To make that a reality, we'll need approximately $1,000 from each organization.

⇨ With our active membership, we could provide 24-hour coverage of the hotlines if each individual could contribute four hours per month.

Be specific about what effort will be involved in any honorary use of the reader's name for your cause.

⇨ As chairman, we'd ask you to attend our celebration banquet to give the closing remarks to thank contributors.

⇨ As a member of this advisory board, we would ask that you accept calls from committee members on two or three issues per month. Your total investment of time would be no more than one to two hours a month in giving your opinions on the issues before the board.

⇨ We hope you'll contribute to the project as you see fit, but more than any monetary contribution, we simply want to add your name to the list of advisors for this project.

⇨ Before we send out any letter with your name and photo, it will be sent to you for your full approval.

Express appreciation for the contribution in a summary statement of the benefit.

⇨ Thank you for helping with this important research.

⇨ We appreciate your considering our request for help in providing shelter for these homeless victims of abuse.

⇨ Thank you for your foresightedness in contributing to this project, one that will put us on the tourists' agenda for future vacations.

⇨ We appreciate your sensitivity in contributing to this seldom-mentioned, behind-the-scenes effort in our community.

⇨ How can we thank you for your help? We hope your own satisfaction will come in knowing that you've fed and clothed a hungry, cold child today.

⇨ On behalf of those your money will help, we appreciate your caring concern.

⇨ Your contribution will make a lasting difference in educating our young people here in Britely. We thank you on their behalf.

⇨ Your money—and, most of all, your time—are a constant reminder that there are those who care.

⇨ The citizens of Dunsburg will enjoy and appreciate your contribution for years to come.

⇨ With pride, you can point out to your children and your children's children how citizens of Hillsboro value every human life.

⇨ Thank you for underwriting our efforts to beautify the city. Citizens for years to come will receive pleasure from your efforts.

⇨ Your money can save a life.

⇨ Your help with these data may just be the impetus our institution and our governmental agencies need to take action.

Research Help

❖ ❖ ❖

Dear Human Resource Director:

We at Samson University are evaluating our programs to determine if we are providing the skills needed by the workforce in your industry. The results of this important study can help you with training, retraining, and other organizational development tasks. Additionally, knowing more about your specific needs will enable us to:

- minimize your initial training costs for new employees
- reduce your upgrading and retraining costs
- train a ready pool of individuals within your specific hiring area

We are requesting a list of all the job titles and job descriptions for your company's workforce. The data will be analyzed to determine if our training programs are providing the skills needed for the positions listed in our immediate community. The information collected will be kept strictly confidential and will be used for educational research purposes only.

Your providing us with this research data can mean significant dollar savings to you over the years in helping us train now the individuals you will hire tomorrow.

Sincerely,

❖ ❖ ❖

Funding for Charitable/Civic Project

❖ ❖ ❖

Dear Mr. Keystone:

As you know, in July Houston will host the 16th Annual Economic Summit to be attended by the leaders of the world's seven leading industrial democracies. With the changes that are sweeping the world today, the importance of the Summit cannot be overstated. We are writing to ask that your company join with others in the corporate community in contributing toward the success of this momentous event.

At the Summit, President Bush will welcome to Houston the leaders of the democratic world: Margaret Thatcher (United Kingdom), Francois Mitterand (France), Helmut Kohl (West Germany), Brian Mulroney (Canada), Toshiki Kaifu (Japan), Giulio Andreotti (Italy) and Jacques Delors (Commission of European Communities). These leaders will discuss and take action on critical global economic and security issues. Thousands of foreign diplomats and journalists will also be here, and the world's attention will be sharply focused on our city.

The Houston Economic Summit Host Committee has been formed to help prepare for the Summit and to ensure that we take full advantage of Houston's time in the international spotlight. Civic, social and entertainment events are being planned for Summit participants and a number of companies have already stepped forward with financial support for these important activities.

A total of $2.5–3.0 million will be needed to underwrite Houston's Summit role. To date $1.2 million has been pledged or already paid by Houston companies, including Exxon, Shell and Conoco, which have each committed $250,000. In addition, $150,000 each has been pledged or already paid by Pennzoil, Tenneco and Enron. We hope that Booher Consultants will join with these other corporate leaders by pledging $10,000.

All contributions and donations to the Houston Economic Summit Host Committee may be deductible under the Internal Revenue Code to the extent allowed by law as an ordinary and necessary expense of conducting a trade or business. However, such contributions and donations are not deductible as a charitable contribution. The Houston Economic Summit Host Committee has been determined to be exempt from federal income tax under section 501(c)(6) of the Internal Revenue Code. Please consult your tax advisor regarding the deductions, if any, allowable under the law in connection with your contributions and donations.

This is a once-in-a-generation opportunity for Houston to shine in the eyes of the world's most powerful leaders and the international media. We hope that you will be able to participate, and we very much appreciate your consideration of this request.

Sincerely,

Kenneth L. Lay   George W. Strake, Jr.

Reprinted with permission by courtesy of Houston Host Committee, Economic Summit of Industrialized Nations.

❖ ❖ ❖

Volunteer Time

❖ ❖ ❖

Dear Friend:

AIDS continues to ravish many of our citizens and touch all our lives in significant ways. In our city alone, someone is diagnosed with AIDS about every ten hours; someone in the city dies from the disease every 14 hours. These statistics shock us. But do they shock us into caring? Into easing the burden for those suffering and for their families?

Our AIDS Foundation, Inc., continues to make education and social services its priority. Informed citizens run less risk of contracting the disease. That's why our Mayor Wright and city council representatives Cecil Seaman and Greg Barber have given of their personal time in this volunteer educational effort.

We are asking that you volunteer a day or a week of your time to hand out tens of thousands of brochures to schools, churches, clinics, and other community groups. We also need volunteers to speak on a variety of civic occasions about the disease and its prevention. Our hotline, which responds to more than 3,000 inquiries every month, needs volunteer coverage. Volunteers also help victims and their families get Social Security benefits and avail themselves of the temporary shelters and food pantries stocked by other concerned citizens.

To keep this ray of sunshine in a dark, diseased corner of the world, we need people like you who care. With your help, there is more hope than ever before. Please call 304-889-7632 to volunteer your time—a few hours a week or a day or two a month. You personally can make a difference in an individual's life.

And if you can't volunteer your time, would you consider making a donation so that we can hire the help we need? Any amount ($500, $100, $50, $25) will be welcome. (You may use the enclosed envelope.) Just care.

Sincerely,

❖ ❖ ❖

Honorary Use of Name

❖ ❖ ❖

Dear Mr. Davenport:

I am writing to ask you to do something that will require very little time and no money on your part—but it will pay big dividends in the lives of young cancer patients here at St. Agnes Children's Research Hospital. Would you allow us to use your name as the honorary chairman of our fund-raising drive for cancer research?

When I first opened this hospital in 1955, the survival rate for our children was 6 percent. Today, we save more than 60 percent, and many are completely recovering from diseases once thought to be incurable. Still, we can't accept losing 40 percent of our children to such dreaded diseases. You may have recently seen the KHRV cable TV program about the Stringer family. Last October, they lost their four-year-old girl to leukemia. Now, their 18-month-old son has been diagnosed with the same disease. At St. Agnes, these children and others get the best possible care while they're fighting for their lives. And our doctors become more optimistic with each advance in our knowledge about the diseases.

On the average, the first year for a child's treatment costs about $35,000. Each year after that costs about $20,000. Our fund-raising effort to the general public will help us defray the high costs that no family alone can bear. Our research costs, of course, are ongoing. You no doubt have heard of the work Drs. Forest Ledman and Charlotte Simpson are doing with the link between refined sugar and abnormal cell generation.

Specifically for this campaign, we'd like to use your photo and name as honorary chairman for our fund-raiser on the appeal letter (enclosed for your review). Someone of your community stature will certainly lend the necessary credibility for our efforts. That's the entirety of your involvement.

Would you please write or phone us (320-499-5789) to say yes? Your support can literally make the difference between life and death for someone's precious child.

Sincerely,

❖ ❖ ❖

NEGATIVE RESPONSE _____

Guidelines and Alternate Phrasing

Use a neutral opening, stating that you have considered the request for money or other participation. Agree, if possible, that the cause is worthwhile.

⇨ We have received your letter about expansion at the children's home; your plans sound exciting and will obviously afford the needed room to house more abuse victims.

⇨ Thank you for letting us know of your needs for funding further research.

⇨ The museum project you contacted us about sounds wonderfully educational.

⇨ We thank you for contacting us again this year about the Ravenhurst Foundation's efforts toward literacy.

⇨ The work you are doing with the Boy Scouts sounds both fascinating and educational.

⇨ The project you described in your letter about the renovation of downtown sounds plausible and encouraging.

⇨ We have reviewed your letter about the funds needed to underwrite summer camp tuition for underprivileged children. Camp can certainly build character in young people and teach them valuable lessons about life and work.

⇨ We thank you for writing us about the opportunity to contribute to the Maxim Foundation for Social Research.

Begin with your reason, and then state your decision not to contribute.

⇨ We've found that our own funds for worthwhile causes such as yours have had to be directed to helping some of our own employee families through this difficult economic time.

⇨ As you can probably imagine, we receive hundreds of requests for funds each year, and as much as we'd like to, we simply cannot respond to all of them.

⇨ Our committee for earmarking our charitable contributions has directed our funds toward different organizations this year.

⇨ Our policy is to contribute 5 percent of our profits to charitable contributions, and we have already reached that point earlier in our fiscal year.

⇨ We don't mean to offend you and your noble intentions, but our organization simply does not agree with the tenets of your organization and its programs.

⇨ We wish we could feel more positively toward your fund-raising efforts, but I'm afraid we disagree with the organization's philosophies and basic interests. Therefore, we must decline to underwrite this current effort.

⇨ As a private organization, we try to let our key employees select the organizations and causes that are nearest to their own experiences and needs. Thus, we have decided to contribute our available fund to the Heart Fund and to the Spoocher Halfway House.

⇨ In our organization we have a policy to match every employee's personal donation with one of our own to the same organization. Therefore, the list of those who receive our contributions is determined by the wishes of our employees individually in their personal giving.

⇨ We wish we could contribute to your cause, but we simply don't have funds available this year to do so.

Express your good wishes for the organization and the successful fund-raising/volunteer campaign if you agree with the cause.

⇨ We wish you the best in your efforts.

⇨ We hope you meet your goal; your cause is entirely worthwhile.

⇨ You have our best wishes for raising the funds to meet this literacy need.

⇨ We wish you success in soliciting the volunteers who can help you meet this great need.

⇨ We appreciate all you're doing on behalf of the community, and we wish you success in this most recent undertaking.

⇨ Your organization meets a great need in the community; we wish you success in your fund-raising efforts.

⇨ Your organization can make a big difference in the lives of the needy; we wish you success in this effort.

⇨ You have our thoughts and prayers in your efforts.

⇨ We wish you success in gaining the support you need for this cause.

⇨ Your plan sounds feasible and sound. We wish you success with it.

(Note: See the alternate phrasing in the following category.)

❖ ❖ ❖

Dear Mr. Cantelloni:

We have received your letter about the scholarship funds now being established at ACL University. With the high cost of education nowadays, such scholarships can really make a difference in a young person's direction and later contribution to society.

As you may know, our organization established a committee several years ago to consider and evaluate each request we receive for donations and personal involvement. Our policy is to contribute 3 percent of our gross sales each year to charitable causes such as yours. This year the committee has decided to contribute our funds to other organizations and their programs. We certainly wish that we had unlimited funds to donate to the many needs we see around us. But just like the family budget, ours has its limitations also. Perhaps in other years we can be more positive in our response.

Thank you for letting us know of your efforts toward the scholarship funds, and we wish you every success in meeting your goal to help deserving students further their studies. Education truly demands our attention in corporate America.

Sincerely,

❖ ❖ ❖

POSITIVE RESPONSE

Guidelines and Alternate Phrasing

Comment favorably on the organization and the cause.

⇨ The name of your organization is certainly on the lips of anyone who has followed the plight of the homeless in our community.

⇨ Because of agency efforts like yours, we as citizens can be proud of our community.

⇨ You've done an admirable job through the years of providing relief for local disaster victims.

⇨ Morris Chapman, one of our employees, speaks very highly of your efforts toward the prevention of drug abuse. Upon his suggestion, we are enclosing ...

⇨ We are pleased to know that your organization is directing its attention toward the need for better mental health care in our community.

⇨ Thank you for contacting us about the opportunity to help in the restoration of such a rich cultural site as the Nateson Building.

⇨ We appreciate your efforts on behalf of our own employees and the community at large. Through your work, many suffering people will find comfort and immediate help.

⇨ We appreciate the attention your organization is focusing on literacy. The plans you describe in your letter will be a welcome relief to many who have difficulty functioning in our complex world.

⇨ We appreciate the fine work you've been doing in our community—for the friends and families of our employees and our corporate neighbors.

⇨ Your cause is a worthy one that deserves attention from all corporations interested in an educated workforce for the future.

State what amount you are pledging or forwarding. If you're contributing time, be specific about the hours you can volunteer on what days of the week or month.

⇨ We are enclosing our check for $500 in support of your cause.

⇨ We are pleased to present to you our $1,000 check for underwriting your efforts with the hospices in the region.

⇨ Our check for $1,000 will, we hope, help you in supplying the necessary
⇨ medical equipment.

⇨ We hope you can use our contribution of $1,000 (enclosed) to alleviate the suffering of some individual with this dread disease.

⇨ We are pledging our donation of $1,000 to fund the restoration project.

⇨ For your expansion plans, you can count on our support in the amount of $1000. We've gladly signed the enclosed pledge card.

⇨ I will be happy to donate a halfday (four or five hours) on the third Saturday of each month.

⇨ I can volunteer to work the hotline in the early morning hours any time between 5 A.M. and 7 A.M. Tuesdays.

⇨ I will be happy to help serve on the project committee with the duties you outlined in your letter.

Wish the organization success with the campaign for funds or volunteers.

⇨ We wish you every success in meeting your goal of $1 million.

⇨ We commend your efforts and wish you success in raising the funds.

⇨ We appreciate your organization and the fine work you as staff do there. God grant you success in this most recent effort.

⇨ Thank you for your commitment to eradicate drugs from our schools.

⇨ Thank you for caring about the plight of our homeless citizens. We wish you success.

⇨ We wish you success in getting the dollars and donated time you need to carry on this important work.

⇨ Your efforts deserve our support—both monetary and otherwise. Thank you for your successes.

⇨ We appreciate your work toward this goal. May you be successful in all you attempt for this worthwhile cause.

⇨ For all your efforts on behalf of the homeless, we thank you. And we wish you success in this current fund-raising project.

(Note: See the alternate phrasing in the previous category.)

❖ ❖ ❖

Gentlemen or Ladies:

Your efforts to raise scholarship funds to help young people interested in the social sciences reflect a growing awareness that not all the world's problems can be solved through scientific or mathematical formulas.

We are happy to enclose our check for $2,000 to the scholarship fund. Thank you for giving us the opportunity to contribute to this educational effort and the long-term mental and spiritual health of our community. We commend your foresightedness and work.

Sincerely,

❖ ❖ ❖

THANK YOU FOR SUCCESSFUL CAMPAIGN

Guidelines and Alternate Phrasing

Commend the organizations and/or individuals on their efforts, giving an overview of the success of the campaign.

⇨ We want to commend your efforts to ...

⇨ You should be very proud. Together, you have just given over $92,000 to ...

⇨ You are a caring group. To date, your donations have just topped $92,000 to the ...

⇨ Thanks to your efforts, the Natshu Foundation has just raised over $92,000 to begin construction on ...

⇨ You have responded in an overwhelming way. Thanks to your efforts, we now have the funds to ...

⇨ You have been so generous with your time. During the past six weeks, you as members have contributed more than 1,600 hours on behalf of ...

⇨ How can we express our appreciation for your efforts? In case you haven't heard the final tally, you as a group have just contributed $92,000.

⇨ You have made a tremendous difference in our future here at the University. As a result of your generosity during this year's annual fund drive, we have received more than $92,000 to fund our research, attract scholarship students, and ...

⇨ You have shown your concern in a most tangible way. We have received $92,000 to date toward the restoration of the Nateson Building, and we are ready to begin work immediately.

Elaborate on specific benefits of the effort or on at least one future use of the donation.

Thank the reader for his or her support.

⇨ Thank you for your generosity of spirit and your contributions.

⇨ We appreciate your support of this worthwhile project. Our community will be a better place because you gave.

⇨ We thank you sincerely for your gifts. The money has made possible so much more than what any one organization could do alone.

⇨ Your support has made the difference in several individuals' future.

⇨ Thank you for your sensitivity to a need and your generosity in meeting that need.

⇨ Thank you for caring and giving.

⇨ Your willingness to support these efforts will be long-remembered by the community.

⇨ On behalf of generations to come, I thank you for your help in seeing this project to fruition.

⇨ We appreciate your interest and your open hands. The generosity of people like you make things happen.

⇨ Our community is a better place because you gave of your time and your love.

⇨ We appreciate your support in seeing this project to its ultimate goal—a new hope for the suffering.

⇨ Thank you for being a part of the good that one community can do when its people pull together.

⇨ We've reached our common goal—better schools for a more educated workforce. We thank you for the role you played in this effort.

⇨ We appreciate your assuming responsibility for leadership and voluntary participation in this project. You and your colleagues have done something of which you can be very proud.

⇨ We commend you on the wisdom, foresight, and generosity your contribution represents.

❖ ❖ ❖

Dear Members,

Our fund-raising and tutoring efforts at Boys Country have been an overwhelming success. During the past four months, you have contributed $120,000 and donated over 1,240 hours of volunteer time in helping the students master this semester's studies.

With the $120,000, the 8,000 square-foot dormitory that houses from 22 to 26 boys can be renovated and expanded to include eight other badly needed bedrooms and a large recreational game room. The directors also plan to buy two personal computers for the boys' use in their school work and as part of their own learning and entertainment.

And we don't have to tell you what the hours spent in personal tutoring meant to the boys' attitudes about school work and to their own self-esteem. Ten of you spent two hours two evenings a week during the entire semester working one-on-one with these children. As a result, 12 of the 14 boys saw a drastic improvement in their grades. No less important than their academic achievement, their improved attitudes about themselves and their abilities can be attributed to knowing someone cares about them individually.

On behalf of Boys Country, thank you for expressing your concern for those less fortunate in such a memorable way. Your efforts will bear results in the lives of these boys for years to come. We hope that brings you great personal satisfaction.

Sincerely,

❖ ❖ ❖

TERMINATIONS

Announcements of terminations and layoffs present one of the biggest challenges managers face. To shield themselves from their own emotional pain in delivering bad news, writers sometimes cloak the message in vague generalities that make such letters seem cold and impersonal.

On the other hand, recipients of such a letter need to feel that the organization recognizes the serious personal implications of such decisions and cares about them as individuals. That's the challenge in writing such letters—the appropriate balance between *impersonal* decisions based on economics and job performance and *personal* concern.

Future public relations toward the company depend on such letters.

LAYOFFS

Guidelines and Alternate Phrasing

Begin with a summary of the situation and reasons, and then announce the layoff.

⇨ Whitney Mitchell's merger with Bromson, Inc., has initiated many staffing changes as we have tried to eliminate duplicate services during the past three months. Your position is one of those now being affected by the changes. Effective May 1, your division will be laid off under the provisions of our workforce-reduction policy.

⇨ The reality of our business is that we must continually evaluate our needs from all regions of the country. Market demands constantly change. While we have a surplus of technicians in one geographic location, we have a shortage in another. Your area now has the surplus, and we regret that your position will be eliminated on May 1.

⇨ You are a member of a work division that has been determined surplus. In order to help reduce this surplus, the company is eliminating your current position and asking you to accept voluntary early retirement benefits.

⇨ Recently, our company lost its contract with Metcalf Corporation, and as a result, we regret to say that your employment must be terminated.

⇨ Certainly, we've all watched media reports of the current recession and how it has affected jobs in our local area. The fact is that now the recession has spread to our industry and our own corporation. We regret that your own plant will close its doors, effective May 1, and your employment with Hemlay Corporation will be terminated as part of this plant-closing action.

Show concern for the effect of the layoff on the individuals involved and the larger community. You may want to elaborate on other alternatives, such as early retirement options, that you considered in lieu of the layoff.

⇨ As you recall, we have tried to reduce our staffing costs by offering two early-retirement options. But the present layoff has become necessary because we did not have sufficient numbers of volunteers who elected to leave the company under the early-retirement plan. We want to make every effort to help you find suitable employment elsewhere.

⇨ We regret that this action has become necessary, but we must also consider what's best for our shareholders and the future of all our employees and company operations.

⇨ Your individual efforts have assisted us in reaching organizational goals through the years, and our only regret is that we could not reach our cost-reduction goals without this layoff action.

⇨ Such reductions are always most difficult on those employees terminated, and then also on the community as a whole. We as a community have always rallied around our large corporations as leaders in civic projects that have improved the quality of life for all citizens. Belt-tightening is painful for all of us involved.

Mention any available help the organization can provide such as outplacement services, referrals, continuation of benefits for a limited time, and so forth.

⇨ We can continue to provide you with an office and telephone for job-hunting purposes during the next 30 days.

⇨ We have arranged with Borden Consulting to provide outplacement services.

⇨ We have circulated a list of names and job titles to our subsidiaries to determine if they have openings where they could use employees being terminated in our area. We encourage you also to make your own inquiries about such unexpected openings in other parts of the company.

⇨ You will still have available for the next 30 days the company car for your personal use.

⇨ All your health insurance coverage will still be in force during this transition time. The insurance company will contact you directly to ...

⇨ You, of course, are entitled to unemployment compensation under the regulations and policies of the State.

End with an expression of appreciation and concern for their future well-being.

⇨ Thank you for your past achievements with us; we wish you well in your future job.

⇨ Whatever career plans you may have, we wish you the best.

⇨ Whatever you ultimately decide about transfers or termination, I want to wish you the best with your plans.

⇨ We have every confidence in your future with another company.

⇨ We wish you the best in finding a job that affords you many opportunities for advancement.

⇨ Thank you for your work here. We know you will find a job you enjoy elsewhere.

⇨ We have appreciated your patience, support, and cooperation during this difficult time.

⇨ I would like to thank you for your loyalty and to express our best wishes for a bright and rewarding future.

⇨ Thank you for your fine work here. Please accept our best wishes for your future employment elsewhere.

❖ ❖ ❖

Dear Bryan:

As you know, the company has been struggling with the rising costs of production and the falling prices caused by overseas competition. In our efforts to cut overhead and remain profitable, we have streamlined our staff operations at headquarters and your position is being eliminated, effective October 15.

Rather than finish any pending projects here, your primary concern now should be locating another position within one of our subsidiaries or with another corporation. Please feel free to make use of any contacts or referrals here to search for the job you want.

You will be given four weeks pay in lieu of advance notice, and your insurance will continue under the provisions of COBRA. The insurance company will contact you directly about payments and the filing of claims. We encourage you also to take advantage of our outplacement services here if you are unable to make arrangements for a transfer within Transton. We have people who can help you with preparation of your résumé, with aptitude testing, and with referrals for interviews.

You've been a valuable member of our headquarters team, and we regret that the economic downturn has made this workforce reduction necessary. We extend to you our best wishes and have every confidence that you will find a position that brings you personal satisfaction and allows you to use your talents effectively.

Sincerely,

❖ ❖ ❖

UNSUITABLE EMPLOYEE

Guidelines and Alternate Phrasing

Begin by summarizing the employee's history with the organization and state the reason for dismissal. Be clear, factual, and objective about the reasons because your documentation may be used later in legal proceedings. If you do not include all the reasons for termination in a letter to the employee, do include a full explanation in your files.

Tell the employee that your company will release only job titles, salary, and date of employment to prospective employers if it is your company's policy to withhold other details about performance and reasons for termination.

⇨ Let me assure you that the reason for termination will not be disclosed to future employers.

⇨ It is our company policy to withhold all details of your employment here except to verify job title and dates of employment.

⇨ The reason for your termination will be held in confidence inside our organization, so you need have no fear of prospective employers seeing our records.

⇨ We will not disclose details of your termination with any prospective employer.

⇨ We can assure you that your termination is a confidential, personal matter, and the reason for our decision will not be discussed outside our organization.

Avoid a hostile tone; instead show concern for the employee's future well-being.

⇨ We wish you success in your future work.

⇨ We trust you'll find a satisfying job elsewhere.

⇨ We hope you find work that more closely matches your desires.

⇨ We wish you the best in finding work where you can fully use your skills.

⇨ I wish you the best in locating another job that you enjoy.

⇨ Best of luck in finding a position more in line with your interests.

⇨ We hope you'll find other employment soon. We wish you success in finding other employment that meets your expectations.

⇨ We hope you find suitable employment immediately and are happy in that situation.

⇨ We wish you the best in finding another situation that allows you the freedom and flexibility you want.

❖   ❖   ❖

Dear Mr. Teitlebaum:

On two previous occasions we have discussed the seriousness of losing your composure when dealing with customers, even those customers who may be angry and discourteous themselves. Customer satisfaction, particularly resolutions to problems with customer orders, has been a top priority with our company; in fact, good customer relations are the keys to our future business. Therefore, because of your explosive temper and abusive language in dealing with customers, we are being forced to terminate your employment, effective immediately.

We are providing two weeks salary in lieu of advance notice.

You can rest assured, however, that it is our company policy not to release any details about your job performance here or the reason for termination. If prospective employers ask, we will release only name, job title, dates of employment, and salary at the time of termination.

Your have our best wishes in finding suitable employment elsewhere.

Sincerely,

❖   ❖   ❖

THANK YOUS (BUSINESS)

If *pleases* motivate, *thank-you's* reward. You'll want to express your gratitude to bosses and colleagues on many occasions: for referrals, bonuses, awards, donations, gifts, hospitality, service to the community.

Certainly, too, customers want to hear your thanks for their confidence in your products and services, as well as for their loyalty and referrals over the years. Organizations that depend on repeat business know the value of frequently expressing that appreciation and never taking loyal customers for granted. The following letters will help you express your gratitude simply and sincerely.

FOR ARRANGING BENEFICIAL MEETING/CONFERENCE

Guidelines and Alternate Phrasing

Thank the reader for taking the initiative in setting up the meeting and handling any details.

⇨ I appreciate your interest in my work with Hightower Associates and your help in arranging for us to meet at last.

⇨ Thank you for arranging the details of our most profitable meeting to date with Hightower Associates.

⇨ How insightful of you to arrange for me to meet with the representatives from Hightower Associates.

State the positive benefit to you or the others involved. Avoid mentioning any difficulties that would detract from the overall positive results.

⇨ We were able to overcome the initial obstacles in any such purchase.

⇨ We immediately were attracted by each other's direct style of communication. You were especially perceptive to note that would be the case and arrange a meeting between us.

⇨ As a result of the meeting, we were able to put aside our concerns about ... and focus on ...

⇨ In such a relaxed atmosphere away from the routine, we had ample time to discuss our differences with regard to ...

Offer to return the favor when possible. At the least, express your gratitude for the reader's consideration.

⇨ I'll be watching for my chance to do you a similar favor.

⇨ May I return the favor?

⇨ I'll be eager to return the favor for you.

⇨ I'll look for opportunities where I can be equally helpful to you.

⇨ In what way may I help you now?

⇨ If another such meeting is in order where I have the contacts to return the favor, you can be sure I'll do so.

❖ ❖ ❖

Dear Karen:

The dinner meeting last evening turned out to be such a great way to talk with Dr. Blair in an informal setting without interruptions. I so much appreciate your taking the initiative to call her and arrange the details.

As a result of the meeting, I think we both communicated the obstacles facing us on the joint project and the reservations we had about the conflict of interest. Thank you for being instrumental in our working out these details and preparing the way for contract negotiations to begin.

I'll keep my eyes open for opportunities to return the favor.

Sincerely,

❖ ❖ ❖

Dear Randy:

Just a note to say thank you so much for making my life easier today. I appreciate your willingness to change the date of my August 28 meeting so that I could avoid the tension involved with such a tight travel schedule.

As I explained on the phone, I received a call from a major client who set up a meeting with all their senior executives and "requested" that I attend to explain our programs on that same day (August 28). Although I was able to schedule a flight to return to St. Louis at 5:15 P.M., the timing would have been too close for my comfort—and I'm sure yours as mediator in these negotiations. Thanks to you, I can now both meet with my client and negotiate for funds on behalf of MRWT.

I know that volunteer work in a professional organization can sometimes be a thankless job, so here's a sincere "thanks" from a fellow member who means it!

Cordially,

❖ ❖ ❖

FOR AWARD OR BONUS

Guidelines and Alternate Phrasing

Thank the reader for the award or bonus.

⇨ I appreciate your honoring me with this award.

⇨ What a way to recognize a hard year's work! I'm thrilled.

⇨ Thank you so much for recognizing my contributions this year with your Monroe Award.

⇨ I'm so pleased that you've selected me as recipient of this year's Monroe Award.

⇨ This award makes my work ever so much more enjoyable and challenging.

⇨ I appreciate so much your thoughtfulness in designating me for this award.

⇨ This award is certainly an honor. I do appreciate the recognition.

Compliment the organization for providing such recognition and opportunities to excel.

⇨ Our organization provides so many opportunities for growth and service that it's difficult not to excel in something.

⇨ Your organization is one I've come to depend on for leadership and up-to-the-minute information about our industry.

⇨ Our company, I think, once again proves itself mindful of the need to compete for excellence. This award is just one way they let us as employees share in their success.

⇨ I appreciate the farsightedness of our organization's leadership in establishing such awards to encourage excellence.

⇨ The award distinguishes our company as one with a real commitment to helping its employees reach their highest potential.

⇨ I appreciate the opportunity to work in a setting where people care about quality and commitment.

⇨ I recognize the good fortune I have to work in an organization that recognizes and rewards excellence in its employees.

⇨ The organization has provided the freedom, time, and financial support to complete this work.

⇨ Our leadership is to be commended for encouraging employees to give their best by making such opportunities and recognition available.

Keep a modest tone.

⇨ Although I don't feel deserving, I'm appreciative just the same.

⇨ I don't feel as though my contributions have been any greater than those of others; nevertheless, I thank you for this recognition.

⇨ You're a great group of people to recognize me for this work.

⇨ I'm still mystified about how I was selected, but I do appreciate the honor.

⇨ With so many as deserving or more so than I, I don't understand why I was chosen for this honor. But I am thrilled.

⇨ You are so gracious to recognize my work in this way.

⇨ So many of you have contributed to my personal and professional growth that I feel as though I should accept the award on behalf of all of us.

❖ ❖ ❖

Fellow NATD Members:

Thank you so much for honoring me with the Member of the Year award. The leadership of our local chapter provides so many opportunities to serve the community and our professional industry group that it was not difficult at all to get involved in several projects. I consider the time well spent and a contribution to my own personal and professional growth.

I'm appreciative of your recognizing my work in this way and of having the opportunity to interact with such a group of dedicated colleagues.

Sincerely,

❖ ❖ ❖

FOR DONATION

Guidelines and Alternate Phrasing

Thank the individual or organization for the donation.

⇨ We appreciate your help so much—your donation of $500 arrived today.

⇨ Thank you for responding so generously to our appeal for help with the restoration of the Haven Center.

⇨ We are so encouraged by your positive response to the Kellogg Foundation, the $500 check.

⇨ A great big "thank you" for your donation of $500 toward the ATV scholarship fund.

⇨ We were so pleased to receive your check for $500 to help us provide shelter for the needy in our local community.

Be specific in mentioning at least one way the money or gift will be used. Or, you may prefer to summarize the overall result of the donation and what the money represents.

⇨ To us, your response was the encouragement our staff needed to carry on the struggle to keep the Center's doors open.

⇨ Your donation represents to us the kindness and caring that run deep in our community where our own citizens' needs are concerned.

⇨ The money you sent will mean the difference in some young person's life-long dependency on others and his or her self-sufficiency in the future.

⇨ Your gift means that our workforce will be better educated to meet the challenges of the next decade.

⇨ Your giving will help us buy new equipment and continue our research toward finding a cure for this dreaded disease.

❖ ❖ ❖

Dear Mr. Hazelwood:

Your check for $2,500 arrived today. We appreciate so much your contributing to our fund for establishing a training center to focus on the literacy needs in our local community.

Thanks to companies such as yours, families can now raise their standard of living as fathers and mothers learn to read and thus become qualified to handle more rewarding jobs. Children can hear their parents read them a bedtime story for the first time. Grandparents can complete their health-insurance claims and read a map to travel across the city.

We hope it gives you great personal satisfaction to know that with this donation you've helped to give many people a fresh start toward their life's goals and dreams. Thank you.

Sincerely,

❖ ❖ ❖

Dear Ms. Seitz:

Thank you for your recent contribution of furniture and tools to our mission. This contribution will help us improve the quality of life for persons who are handicapped and disadvantaged in our community. Specifically, the donations translate into training and work opportunities for several individuals you may or may not chance to meet. The feelings of independence and self-worth that come with both are something we all need and value.

We thank you for your partnership in this important ministry.

Sincerely,

❖ ❖ ❖

FOR GIFT

Guidelines and Alternate Phrasing

Thank the reader for the gift.

⇨ Thank you for the nice ...

⇨ I so much appreciate your thoughtfulness in sending the ...

⇨ What a nice surprise with today's mail; your _____ came and with it, your kind note.

⇨ Your painting was delivered today. How thoughtful for you to remember our move to the new office!

Elaborate specifically on how you will use the gift or the value or significance of the gift to you. Your specific comments assure the the reader that you will enjoy this special gift.

⇨ Every time I use the _____, I'll remember your thoughtfulness and trouble in sending it.

⇨ Your gift makes me feel so welcome among the group. I appreciate your including me.

⇨ Your thoughtfulness in sending the _____ underscores the kind of atmosphere we have in the office—that among friends rather than mere co-workers.

⇨ I know you must have taken hours to find just the exact color to match the pieces I already have.

⇨ I know you must have spent hours searching for just the right addition to my collection.

⇨ The _____ should create just the right image with clients!

⇨ I'll use the _____ ever so much in my travels.

⇨ This _____ should make my job so much easier.

⇨ This _____ represents quite a few calories, I'm sure, and I'll enjoy each and every one.

⇨ This _____ is an intriguing idea. I'm fascinated with it.

⇨ This _____ will afford hours of enjoyment over the coming months.

⇨ My family will be delighted with the tickets. On the few occasions we've been able to attend such an event, we've enjoyed ourselves immensely.

❖ ❖ ❖

Dear Elaine:

The luscious fruit basket was waiting in my room when I checked into the hotel last Thursday for the convention. What a nice surprise—especially after the usual airline delays and missed connections. I had a bedtime snack and retired for the night, knowing that someone still thought of nice things to do for other people. I enjoyed the fruit again for breakfast; thanks to your considerateness, I didn't have to worry about going out for breakfast or calling room service and wondering whether the meal would appear on time.

You were so thoughtful; that gesture certainly started my convention week on a warm note.

Cordially,

❖ ❖ ❖

FOR HOSPITALITY AT CONFERENCE/MEETING/VISIT _____

Guidelines and Alternate Phrasing

Recall the occasion or event when the reader showed hospitality.

⇨ You made our week in Atlanta so memorable!

⇨ Thank you so much for your hospitality last week in hosting our operations people in your facilities.

⇨ The tour you and your staff provided during our recent trip to Philadelphia was the highlight of the convention week. What an enjoyable Saturday!

⇨ Thank you so much for agreeing to host our NSA chapter meeting in your facilities, particularly on such short notice and with such class!

Elaborate specifically about what the individual did to show thoughtfulness and make the occasion particularly enjoyable or memorable. How did he or she spend extra time, money, or effort on your behalf?

Mention your eagerness to reciprocate, if appropriate and sincere.

⇨ We will be eager for our turn to show you such a nice time.

⇨ Won't you let us know when you plan to visit our city so that we can reciprocate your hospitality?

⇨ We'll look forward to an opportunity to return your thoughtfulness.

⇨ We'll look forward to a time when the tables are turned and we can show you such a good time.

⇨ Needless to say at this point, we had a wonderful time. When can we host your group in our city?

⇨ We'd love the opportunity to show you our facilities and treat you to a cookout here.

❖ ❖ ❖

Dear Palan:

Thank you so much for our warm reception and your gracious hospitality on our recent Malaysian tour.

Without your advice and constant attention to detail, we would not have enjoyed ourselves nearly so much. Your rapport with the business community was obvious as you were able to provide introductions to all the distributors that we wanted to meet.

But more than the business arrangements, you were so considerate of helping us make the best use of time to see the country and learn more of the Malay culture. Taking us to dinner all three evenings at the most elegant restaurants, I'm sure, took you away from your family. Please express our appreciation to them also for allowing us the extra time to visit with you and your colleagues.

Would you please plan on letting us show you our state when you attend next year's NTS convention here? Thank you again for such an enjoyable, as well as profitable, time with you in your country.

Sincerely,

❖ ❖ ❖

❖ ❖ ❖

Dear Fred:

On behalf of the Froston project team, I want to thank you for the time you took to organize and host our tour of your plant on April 8. The tour and commentary were informative and made valuable use of our limited time. Special thanks are in order for scheduling Mike Wilson to answer questions and for providing our lunch at the plant cafeteria.

The visit helped our co-op trainees to understand that, through education and hard work, opportunities for career success are available to them. Additionally, our students who are studying engineering and computer science found the tour particularly meaningful.

Again, thank you for making our visit a memorable and encouraging experience for all of us. You can be sure that the communities and families of these students will hear of your hospitality.

Sincerely,

❖ ❖ ❖

FOR BUYING

Guidelines and Alternate Phrasing

Thank the customer for the recent purchase or welcome the organization as a client.

⇨ Thank you for your recent order from us.

⇨ We appreciate the confidence you've placed in our organization by opening a new account with us.

⇨ Welcome to Hartford Bank. We are so pleased to have the opportunity to provide banking services to you.

⇨ Thank you for giving us the opportunity to show you what we can do to service a car properly.

⇨ We welcome you as a new client. We've scheduled your first appointment on September 9, as you suggested.

Highlight one or two key benefits of the purchase or the working relationship.
Our store is open when you're ready to shop—be it early morning or late at
night.

⇨ Our capable staff has the proper training to deal with the routine and
the unusual needs that might arise.

⇨ Our convenient locations throughout the area should make it easy for
you to take advantage of ...

⇨ We think our _____ provide the necessary security at the lowest possible
cost.

⇨ Our people are trained to know the appropriate questions to ask and the
pitfalls to avoid in assisting customers with their buying decisions.

⇨ Remember to use our toll-free 800 number when you have any question
at all about service or scheduled maintenance.

⇨ Help with support services is just a telephone call away.

Express your expectation for a mutually beneficial partnership and your
appreciation for customer loyalty.

⇨ We look forward to working with you for years to come.

⇨ We anticipate a mutually beneficial relationship in the marketplace.

⇨ We're eager to win your confidence all over again every time you call us
for advice and service.

⇨ Our two firms have much in common; I'm looking forward to a very
profitable working relationship.

⇨ We will work very hard to deserve your business.

⇨ We will work very hard to deserve the confidence you've placed in our
employees who service your account.

⇨ You deserve the best, and we aim to give it.

⇨ Our aim is to provide the high quality service you deserve.

⇨ We appreciate your willingness to let us show you what we can do. We
don't intend to disappoint you.

⇨ We appreciate the opportunity to provide this service to you. You won't
be disappointed.

⇨ We thank you for the chance to "join hands" on this project. We think
you're going to be very pleased.

⇨ We appreciate your ongoing business and loyalty through the years.

⇨ Customers like you keep us in business. We continue to appreciate your
loyalty.

⇨ You seem like family by now. Your loyalty is so important to us.

⇨ Your business is our business. We appreciate the opportunity to meet your needs in whatever way necessary.

⇨ You and your staff have been more than customers; you are friends. And we appreciate your business.

❖ ❖ ❖

Dear Mr. Davidson:

Thank you for the August 9 purchase of office furniture for your new office suite on Oakgrove Lane. We think the popular designs you chose will be both serviceable and attractive even after years of use by your employees. And we were also pleased to be able to accommodate your move-in date with our delivery service.

We have appreciated your repeat business through the years as we've watched your firm expand to include various offices around the city. So often, businesses fail to get to know their good customers and hear only from those few who are displeased. That's not the case with us. We never want to take your confidence in our furniture and custom design work and your loyalty for granted.

We appreciate your business and plan to keep on meeting your changing needs as you grow. Keep in touch and we'll try to make your wishes our commands.

Sincerely,

❖ ❖ ❖

FOR SERVICE TO COMMUNITY

Guidelines and Alternate Phrasing

Thank the reader for the service to the community.

⇨ Thank you for sharing your time and your expertise with us on the recent Fullerton project.

⇨ You have rendered an invaluable service to the community with your involvement on the Fullerton project.

⇨ Our community has profited greatly from your energy and inspiration surrounding the Fullerton project.

⇨ Your time, money, and emotional energy have been well spent on the Fullerton project.

Be as specific as possible about the individual's contribution. Mention details of the work, the hours spent, the positive result, any personal expense involved or whatever. Avoid being so general as to make this sound like a form letter sent to all participants on a project.

Include your hope that the effort has brought the reader personal benefit and satisfaction.

⇨ I hope you immediately realize the community's goodwill for your efforts.

⇨ Although I'm sure it was not your motivation in the least, we do hope that you experience an immediate increase in your own professional practice because of your generosity on this project.

⇨ We hope you've gained personal satisfaction in watching the enthusiasm of our young people who are recipients of your efforts.

⇨ In some small way, we hope you'll know the lasting benefit you've achieved for the community.

⇨ We hope the results brings you great satisfaction throughout the years.

⇨ We trust the overwhelming response your leadership generated will bring you great personal joy.

⇨ As you see the many ways your service has benefited needy families, we hope you'll remember your efforts with great satisfaction and pride.

⇨ We hope you share great pride with the community for your efforts on this project.

⇨ The goodwill that your efforts have generated is certain to be felt by you and your staff and family in the months to come.

❖ ❖ ❖

Dear Mr. Mikolowitzski:

On behalf of the Town Theatre, I want to express our great appreciation for your efforts and those of your staff in making available the Pistone Recreation Center for our productions during our own building renovations.

I know that your generosity in making the center available to us was not without personal expense to your own organization. The utility bills increased because of our rehearsal and production time, as well as the expense of janitorial work.

As a very small token of our appreciation, we are enclosing ten lifetime complimentary memberships for distribution to your senior executives or anyone within your organization especially involved in arranging our temporary use of the building.

In addition to enjoying the theatre's production, we hope that you also gain personal satisfaction not only in helping to minimize our own renovation difficulties, but in providing a way for the entire citizenship to continue to enjoy the arts. Thank you. We trust the community will remember over the years your generosity of spirit.

Sincerely,

❖ ❖ ❖

FOR SPEAKING

Guidelines and Alternate Phrasing

Express your appreciation for the presentation in a general summary statement.

⇨ It's really encouraging to have individuals come forward who are willing to contribute their knowledge and experiences toward the professional development of others. Your presentation was no exception; we so much appreciate your expertise.

⇨ Thank you for taking the time last Friday to share your insights on new trends in the electronics field.

⇨ We appreciate your speaking to us last week about investment trends among the top corporations in the nation.

⇨ You did an excellent job last Thursday when you addressed our group on the pitfalls of drug testing in the workplace.

⇨ Your presentation was, in a word, outstanding.

⇨ Our group was so pleased to have you speak last week on the drilling rigs of the future.

⇨ What an impression you made on our group members last week as you talked about the need for personal career planning within the large organization.

⇨ What an impact your presentation will have for years to come on our group of trainers as they "go out into the world" to revitalize our organization with new ideas.

⇨ You did an exceptionally fine job last week in stirring our members to action.

Elaborate by adding several specific details about the presentation that were particularly beneficial, memorable, or personally useful to you.

⇨ Your information and examples are certain to make an impact on the organizations represented at the meeting.

⇨ You made the difference in my attitude about the value of the entire convention. I came to realize that ...

⇨ Your multimedia presentation certainly added the pizzazz our audience needed after four days of convention.

⇨ Your story about . . . really made your point about quality memorable and real.

⇨ Your case studies gave us the necessary hands-on practice in applying the theory. Application is what's usually most necessary and most often missing from other presentations of this nature.

⇨ Your statistics should wake up all of us to the need for some immediate changes.

⇨ Your stories about _____ Princeton, Inc., were all too real.

⇨ Your anecdotes about customer service touched a nerve with our group. We're all painfully aware of the improvements we need to make in this regard.

⇨ We certainly appreciated your humor—a delightful surprise on such a serious topic.

⇨ You took what could have been a dry subject and made it so entertaining, as well as informative.

⇨ The assistants you brought along to help with the demonstrations were an excellent idea; they left you free to mingle with the audience before and after the presentation.

⇨ You amazed us with the manner in which you responded to such high-pressure questions with such charm and graciousness.

⇨ Your energy level was contagious. You had people participating in your activities who have been sitting on the sidelines for years.

⇨ Your answers to the questions asked were straightforward and honest; we couldn't have asked for more.

⇨ Your true expertise was certainly apparent as you fielded the audience's questions with such ease and simplicity.

⇨ Your explanations were easily understood, even for the layperson in the audience.

⇨ You cut through the usual jargon, buzzwords, and weasel words, and spoke to the real issues with accuracy and honesty.

⇨ Your smile and your entire demeanor disarmed the audience and gave them opportunity and encouragement to ask the questions that were really on their mind.

⇨ You were honest and you were direct—both qualities that we always appreciate in organizational spokespersons.

⇨ The pace was exactly appropriate for our group—fast enough to keep even the most knowledgeable interested, but slow enough so as not to lose the average user. Your extensive knowledge of the subject was even more apparent during the question-answer time.

⇨ You put the group at ease from the very beginning, and they loved you for making them feel special and understood.

⇨ I heard several audience members rehashing your points at the break— always an excellent sign that the speaker has made his ideas memorable and useful.

⇨ The feedback we received from the audience was wonderful; they felt your presentation was exactly on target for their needs.

⇨ Several audience members commented that you obviously knew their organization and their team members well, and that says to us meeting planners that you took the time to customize for our group.

⇨ You presented a picture of our work here that was alarming in its urgency, but not offensive to us personally.

⇨ You included just the right mix of theory with how-to's and practice.

Mention any intentions you have to pass on a referral or to publicize his or her excellent job. For professional speakers, publicity and referrals mean additional business. To colleagues, the praise may mean career recognition internally.

⇨ I assume you won't mind if I tell everyone I see to sign up for your next session.

⇨ I've passed your name and address on to our home office staff, along with my recommendation that they contact you about presenting the ideas at a national meeting.

⇨ Your name will be on the tip of my tongue every time the subject of quality control comes up around here.

⇨ I plan to include a feature story highlighting your work in our next in-house newsletter.

⇨ We've decided to run a short excerpt on your presentation in our convention paper.

⇨ I'm personally planning to call several managers in the eastern region to let them know of your availability and expertise on this subject.

⇨ I've written your manager a note about the presentation, because I think she should be aware of the service you're doing for our branches by providing this information.

⇨ I'm placing your card in my card file so I can have it handy whenever I hear of a colleague facing these same problems.

⇨ My professional organization certainly could use a program of this nature. I'll give your name to our program chairman at our next meeting.

❖ ❖ ❖

Dear Ms. Nixon:

Thank you for taking the time to fly to Sheraton County to share your research work with the educators in our school system. Your ideas on "active learning," creativity, and multimedia interaction fascinated our group. Several members were particularly pleased to hear the positive effects these teaching methods had on the attitude of the children involved in your research groups. We had no idea that business and industry organizations were so heavily involved in research fields so closely related to ours.

Several members of the audience have expressed interest in hearing more about your work and will be recommending to their individual schools that you speak at other locations during their in-service training. You may be receiving calls from the various directors of curriculum throughout the year, and we hope you can speak to us again as your schedule permits.

Should there ever be an occasion for us to return the favor by actively participating in some of your research projects, we would be more than willing to do so. Again, thank you for taking the time to share your work with us in such an enlightening way.

Sincerely,

❖ ❖ ❖

FOR REFERRAL/REFERENCE

Guidelines and Alternate Phrasing

Thank the reader for the referral. Be specific enough to let the reader know you understand and appreciate the time and effort involved—and possibly even the risk of his or her reputation if the referral arrangement doesn't work out.

⇨ Thank you so much for giving our name to Wheaton and Blyble. I understand that you had to phone several times to make contact with the right person—a frustration that we've run into often. We admire your persistence.

⇨ Thank you for your referral to Wheaton and Blyble. They phoned us immediately after they received your letter. Your effort in writing rather than phoning them gave our name "staying power" as they passed the letter through the offices of the executive staff.

⇨ I appreciate your kind words to the Wheaton and Blyble representative last week at the convention. He said that you spent almost half an hour with him explaining our methodologies and successes with your company. Such word-of-mouth is invaluable to us.

⇨ We appreciate so much your bringing up our work in the Kencaid meeting last week. Several members at the dinner phoned as a result of your mention. A referral from someone as respected as you in the industry certainly carries a lot of weight.

⇨ Thanks so much for passing along our name and phone number to Earl Hughes last week on your flight to New York. When Mr. Hughes phoned us later, he mentioned that he had kept you from your paperwork for almost an hour as he pumped you for more information about our consulting work. Thank you so much for giving him such a splendid, detailed explanation.

⇨ Thank you for referring your client, Wheaton and Blyble, to us for their software needs. On such occasions, we realize that your own reputation is at stake in recommending clients to other vendors and we don't take that risk lightly. Thank you for your confidence in us.

Elaborate on your expectations for the outcome of the referral. You want to reassure the reader that his or her effort was worthwhile and appropriate for both parties involved.

⇨ Mr. Hughes seems ready to move forward at this point.

⇨ We expect at least to get an opportunity to quote our prices for their consideration.

⇨ They have assured us that they definitely want to talk further about the possibilities of a long-term partnership.

⇨ We have been able to schedule an appointment with their buyer.

⇨ They've asked us to forward materials for consideration by their management committee.

⇨ Your referral gained us the opportunity to submit a proposal for the project.

⇨ Thanks to your efforts, Mr. Hughes has agreed to meet with us next Friday.

Show your goodwill with an offer to reciprocate in some way.

⇨ I'll be looking for an opportunity to return the favor.

⇨ May I take you to dinner as a small token of my appreciation for the referral? How about Wednesday, August 6?

⇨ You can be sure that when we have opportunity to do so, we will suggest your firm to our clients in need of maintenance work.

⇨ We've made our staff aware of your referral, and they are looking for ways to repay the favor.

⇨ Let me know when I can reciprocate with a referral on your behalf to some of our member organizations.

⇨ I'll look forward to mentioning you and your firm on other occasions.

⇨ We're anxiously awaiting the opportunity to refer your own organization to our colleagues and clients and hope to do so soon.

⇨ We plan to return the favor of a referral whenever an occasion arises.

❖ ❖ ❖

Dear Pete:

Thank you for taking the time to phone Mark Rhodes about products that can help him control his heat-shrinkage problems in the Lafayette plant. I know you're extremely busy and on the road often, and I appreciate your effort to get in touch with him on our behalf.

We were able to schedule an appointment immediately and have already met with him about solving the problem. He seemed quite interested and has asked us to prepare a formal proposal and present it to his management staff in New Orleans next month.

It's only through references for past work and new referrals that we survive in this business, so please accept my gratitude. We hope to provide such excellent service that they will not be taking your name in vain for the referral! Thanks so much.

Cordially,

❖ ❖ ❖

WELCOMES

There's no better time to catch employees or customers in a receptive frame of mind than when they first join your staff or first move to your community.

Letters of welcome should always make the new staff member feel as though you've noted his or her arrival as an important event and that you welcome his or her individual contribution to the organization. Your correspondence will also help the new employee relate to others in the company and feel a part of the team by understanding the corporate culture conveyed.

Likewise with newcomers in the community, your letter often shapes their impression of the neighborhood. Take this opportunity to invite newcomers to do business with you while they're still looking for places that deserve their attention.

TO NEW STAFF

Guidelines and Alternate Phrasing

Show pleasure at the employee's decision to join the firm.

⇨ Jack, we're thrilled that you're casting your lot with us.

⇨ We were so pleased to learn that you had accepted the job offer here.

⇨ We are so pleased to hear you will be joining us shortly in Sarasota.

⇨ Welcome aboard. We can't wait until you get here to help us call the shots.

⇨ We want to welcome you to the Hintze staff; we're eager to have you help us improve our services here.

⇨ We're looking forward to having you join us next month. There are many who've already spoken with you during the times you visited and who are so eager to have you on the team.

⇨ We've been so proud to announce to our clients that you will be joining our staff August 1.

⇨ We've made the right decision in offering you a position here, and you've certainly made the right decision in accepting our challenge. We can hardly wait to have you aboard and working on the challenges that face us in the coming months.

⇨ The other members of our management team and I want to formally welcome you to the organization. We continue to appreciate your past accomplishments elsewhere and are expecting equally good things here.

Elaborate on the challenges and excitement of the new job responsibilities and goals. You may make complimentary remarks about the people in the organization, the organization's past successes, or the abilities and experience of the new employee.

⇨ Our Sarasota location has lagged behind our other divisions for two years now, and we're looking forward to your turning things around there.

⇨ Your smile and energy will be a welcome addition to the front office and customer counter.

⇨ Your enthusiasm and expertise make a package that will be difficult to beat during the upcoming months.

⇨ The quality and productivity issues we discussed with you during the interviewing process are the primary challenges facing us as an organization and you individually in your leadership position. The workers at your site are definitely looking to you for new ideas about reducing wastes and improving the overall efficiency of our operations.

⇨ Your sales quotas will present both a challenge and a sense of great accomplishment as you bring new accounts to the organization.

⇨ Your first concern will be to reduce our delivery time overseas, a major issue in winning repeat business in those markets.

⇨ The new software development programs you'll be designing will have top priority with all our managers, and their successful completion will gain you visibility throughout the organization.

⇨ We're looking forward to hearing your innovative ideas, to seeing your plan for redesign of the facilities, and to following your lead in improving customer service.

Offer any help you think may ease the employee's adjustment to the new community or work environment.

⇨ The people in our Personnel office can provide a plethora of lists—everything from doctors to tennis instructors. Please call them.

⇨ If I can answer questions about the community, such as available medical facilities, child-care centers, or recreational activities, let me know.

⇨ We'd be happy to make a few phone calls on your behalf to see if we can find your two teenage sons summer employment, if they're interested.

⇨ We've enclosed season tickets for you and your wife to the community theatre. We want you to become immediately involved in our social activities here and meet other couples who may share your interests.

⇨ We'll be happy to reimburse the travel expenses for your wife to join you over the next two or three weekends until the family gets moved here permanently.

Be personal and specific in your comments; a welcome-to-the-organization too often sounds like a form letter and loses its impact with vague generalities.

❖ ❖ ❖

Dear Robert:

We are so pleased that you've accepted the position as plant manager for our Harrisburg site. Your past accomplishments and experience at Ravenswood should have whetted your appetite for the tasks and challenges at the new location. Coming in at such an early stage will give you opportunity to hire and shape your staff into a dynamic team that will serve as a model as we expand into other manufacturing operations.

May I suggest that you bring your wife and three sons by the office sometime soon so that we may meet them and welcome them personally? If your wife can't get away from her job in the daytime, I'm always around during the early evening hours. Anyway, our July 4 company picnic looms on the horizon, and I'll certainly get to meet your family then if not before. Changing jobs when a move is involved always becomes a family effort. We want to make the adjustment as easy as possible by letting your wife and boys know that we plan to be an extended family in times of emergency.

We're excited about your potential here and what you can contribute to the organization. Likewise, we hope you'll grow personally and professionally through the years of association. Welcome.

Sincerely,

❖ ❖ ❖

TO POTENTIAL CUSTOMERS/CLIENTS NEW IN THE COMMUNITY _____

Guidelines and Alternate Phrasing

Extend a welcome.

⇨ We want to welcome you to the neighborhood.

⇨ We're thrilled that you've chosen our city to make your new home.

⇨ Welcome to our community. We think you'll agree even after a few weeks that it's a nice place to enjoy life.

⇨ We want to extend to you a warm welcome to the work and family communities here in Jonesboro.

⇨ Have you settled in yet? Pictures on the wall? Drapes hung? Food in the refrigerator? Well, if not, don't worry. Everything can wait but the food in the refrigerator. We want to make your move and your life a little easier. Here's how: ...

⇨ Welcome to our city. Your name keeps popping up on newcomer lists everywhere, and we wanted to make sure you knew we were glad to have you in the community.

⇨ Do you have a moment for us to welcome you to the area and introduce ourselves?

Introduce your product or service and highlight one or two key benefits. Avoid making the letter sound like an ordinary direct-mail sales piece; you want to convey a personal interest and welcome.

Suggest the next step in building a business relationship—perhaps an offer to put the newcomers on your newsletter mailing list, a response card expressing interest in receiving further information, an invitation to attend an informational seminar sponsored by your firm, or a welcome to introduce themselves the next time they're in your store. Mention also any incentive such as a free gift, a discount, or money-off coupons.

⇨ At the risk of adding to your pile of paperwork, we've enclosed complimentary registrations to the next seminar, scheduled for August 6.

⇨ We've taken the liberty of enclosing a flier listing the services we have available. May we suggest that you tack it on your refrigerator to keep it handy for your next trip downtown?

⇨ Bring this letter with you the next time you come into our store, and we'll be happy to discount your total purchase by 15 percent. How's that for a welcome?

⇨ You'll find enclosed a discount coupon worth $10 off your next purchase.

⇨ When you have a few extra moments, drop by and introduce yourself to our staff. Ask for Marilyn Dow, Cindy Crow, or Michael Breadwom, and they'll give you a brief overview of our operation and services available to your family.

⇨ Let us meet you and welcome you personally the next time you're in our building.

⇨ Simply phone us about your intent to open an account here, and we'll write for your family's records.

⇨ Drop by to let us know you want to do business with us, and we'll handle all the paperwork necessary for us to go to work for you.

❖ ❖ ❖

Dear Mr. and Mrs. Denton:

We want to welcome you to the community. You'll find this a supportive place to raise a family and enjoy life: excellent schools, many places of worship, civic events, educational attractions, and many pleasant folks ready to lend a helping hand in times of emergency.

And while I'm listing the nice things about the community, I don't want to leave us out. By "us," I mean Johnson Kelsey Medical and Diagnostic Center located at 1748 N. Grant at Sanford Drive. Of course, the last thing you want to think about during a move is sickness, but it's nice to know we're here when there's a need.

We have a team of physicians, dentists, psychiatrists, and other medical professionals ready to share their expertise to meet your crises. Our diagnostic and emergency-care facilities make use of the latest technology with their state-of-the-art equipment. And for patients who need extended care, we have comfortable accommodations for them and a family member who might want to stay overnight with their loved one.

Please keep our clinic in mind for your routine medical and dental care. We invite you to stop by our information booth in the lobby (or phone 786-3376) to discuss with the receptionist the specialities of our professional team and the other available services.

We are here to keep you and your family happy and healthy.

Cordially,

❖ ❖ ❖

PART II

PERSONAL AND SOCIAL LETTERS

CHARITABLE CONTRIBUTIONS

The opportunities are staggering—opportunities to contribute to civic projects, social agencies, churches or synagogues, universities, or other organizations worthy of our support. Once we've decided where our money can do the most good and we write that all-important check, our accompanying letter should be one of appreciation rather than pride.

In other words, these organizations thrive not only on our dollars but on our devotion to their causes. Are you one of the many who have little time to offer as a volunteer and find money a good substitute for personal involvement? If so, in your letter take the opportunity to commend those who have devoted their lives to the causes you espouse and the work you believe will build a better world.

Guidelines

State that you are making a contribution.

Elaborate on your reasons for contributing (your belief in the worthiness of the organization's cause or a memorial for a loved one).

Request any necessary acknowledgement for tax purposes.

Be modest in tone.

❖ ❖ ❖

Dear Mr. Freidan:

I am enclosing a check for $2,000 to be used in your agency's work among the troubled teens that you house, feed, and counsel. We have from time to time heard of your work through various friends and acquaintances, and Sunday's *Chronicle* carried a superb feature story on the results you are achieving with teens who've made a dramatic turnaround in their lives.

Although we have not taken the time to get personally involved in the lives of these youth, we admire those who do. God bless you as you strive to make a difference in the world.

Sincerely,

P.S. Would you please send an acknowledgement of this gift for our tax records? Thank you.

❖ ❖ ❖

Ladies and Gentlemen:

We read with interest your intention to begin a memorial fund for the T.H. Woo family upon the tragic loss of their home and business. Enclosed is our check for $200 for this fund. Although we did not know them personally, we admire their longing for freedom and their foresight in coming to this country to educate their children and make a new life for themselves.

Please express our best wishes to them as they rebuild their home in the midst of American friends.

Sincerely,

❖ ❖ ❖

COLLEGE

Letters written to enter an undergraduate or advanced degree program, to request consideration for a scholarship, or to discuss the transfer of credit hours from one institution to another may remain part of your academic file for your tenure on campus.

Equally important are those letters requesting references from friends, former professors, and employers. Your tone and helpful information in those requests will increase your chances that these individuals will, in turn, write you an effective reference letter, one that is specific and sincere.

On those occasions when you yourself are asked to supply a reference for a friend or employee returning to academia, consider the request a compliment to your achievements and position in life. An effective referral may shape someone's future.

MAKING APPLICATION

Guidelines

State your interest in attending the school, being specific about which semester you plan to attend.

Ask what the entrance requirements are, particularly any necessary paperwork that you must initiate.

Ask for any necessary information on tuition costs, housing, scholarships, payment plans, work-study programs, and so forth.

❖ ❖ ❖

Dear Registrar:

I am interested in attending your university as a full-time student for the spring semester, 19—. My major field of study will be business administration.

Would you please let me know what the entrance requirements are with regard to test scores, transcripts, medical records, and other various forms to be completed. I plan to transfer approximately 60 hours of previous work from a nearby junior college. If there are any special considerations other than requesting a transcript for this transfer, please let me know immediately.

Also, please send me information on tuition costs and payment plans, housing, available scholarships, and work-study programs. After I've had an opportunity to review the materials, complete the applications, and transfer all the appropriate records, I'll look forward to studying at your university.

Sincerely,

❖ ❖ ❖

REQUESTING REFERENCES

Guidelines and Alternate Phrasing

Request the reference and state your reason. If you wish, you may want to mention any specific plans for a field of study or special interests.

⇨ Would you consider writing a letter of reference for me to include as part of my admission package to Louisiana State University?

⇨ I need your help in the admission process at LSU. Would you agree to write a letter of reference for me?

⇨ I'm applying for law school at LSU next year and need letters for reference for admission. Would you please take the time to provide such a character reference?

Remind the individual of your association, giving the dates and length of your acquaintance, if necessary.

Express your gratitude for the time involved, and make response as easy as possible. Be sure to state whether the reference should go to you or directly to the university.

⇨ Thank you so much for taking the time to write this reference. I know the university will respect your opinion, and I appreciate your reference so much.

⇨ I appreciate your helping me in this way.

⇨ Thank you very much for your time and effort in helping me.

⇨ I'll appreciate the reference very much. Admission requirements are stringent and your letter will matter a great deal.

❖ ❖ ❖

Dear Ms. Sanders:

I'm applying for admission to Ardmore in the fall, and the university requires that we submit three letters of reference with our application. Would you please write such a letter for me and send it directly to the school in the attached, stamped envelope?

As you recall, I've worked for your company for the past two summers as a data processor in the accounting department and would appreciate your comments about character, dependability, attitude, and chances for future success at the university.

Thank you for taking the time to help me in this way.

Sincerely,

❖ ❖ ❖

SUPPLYING REFERENCES

Guidelines and Alternate Phrasing

State your general recommendation that the specific student be admitted to the school.

⇨ Jake Jacobitz comes highly recommended as a successful high school student ready to embark on a challenging college career.

⇨ Jake Jacobitz has been a student at our high school for the past three years, and as his football coach, I can attest to his academic achievements, his winning attitude, and his ability to get along well with his peers.

Elaborate on your opinion of the student and his or her abilities and character: the length of time you've known the student, school grades or work performance and attitudes, and personal attitudes and attributes.

⇨ Jake is respectful to his teachers and those in authority while not being afraid to voice new ideas about improvements in the educational system.

⇨ Jake has proved to be a motivating leader of his peers in several arenas: captain of the basketball team, student council representative, and class treasurer. Jake works well alone and with his peer group.

⇨ Jake's grades have been exceptional.

⇨ During his summer employment with us, Jake managed to maintain an excellent attendance record while still participating in his extracurricular school activities. I think this speaks highly of his ability to organize his time and set priorities.

⇨ Jake shows talent in several areas: music, drama, and debate.

⇨ I've known Jake and his family for approximately ten years, and during this time I've observed his dependability, his pleasing personality, and his knack for juggling school, work, and fun. To my knowledge, he's never been in serious trouble at school or with the law and indeed displays evidence of a lasting, sound value system instilled in his home.

Summarize again your opinion of the student's chances for success at the school.

⇨ In my opinion as his former counselor, Jake will make a very successful college student.

⇨ Jake will be a welcome addition to any student body.

⇨ Jake's values, his academic background, and his penchant for accomplishing his goals will make him an excellent student.

⇨ You will be most pleased at Jake's success at your school.

⇨ Your university will give Jake an excellent forum to prove his mettle academically.

⇨ Jake will be most successful in his university studies.

⇨ I predict that Jake will achieve many awards at your university.

⇨ Based on his past record, Jake will make an excellent student at any university.

⇨ I have the highest regard for Jake and think any university will be lucky to have him among the student body.

❖ ❖ ❖

Ladies and Gentlemen:

I am pleased to recommend that Jake Jacobitz be admitted to your university for future study toward a music degree.

Jake became my student for private piano lessons in the seventh grade and has continued to study with me for the past five years. He has willingly devoted the extra time necessary for practice to master the wide variety of arrangements I've given him. Additionally, he's been an active member of the high school choir, serving as their accompanist during his senior year.

In addition to his music talents, Jake has always been a dependable student of the highest integrity. He was punctual to his lessons, responsible in phoning when he had schedule conflicts, and amenable to difficult tasks with which I've challenged him. To my knowledge, he has been equally successful with his other academic studies.

Jake should be a welcome addition to your student body.

Sincerely,

❖ ❖ ❖

COMPLAINTS/REQUESTS FOR ADJUSTMENTS

On first thought, complaint letters seem easy to write. Certainly, the motivation to write is strong, particularly if the situation involves a great sum of money or embarrassment. The adrenalin flows freely, and the cause seems just.

But before you begin, consider the definition of an effective complaint. An effective letter not only points out a problem but asks for a specific resolution. The letters that follow will help in addressing those situations all too common for most of us: billing errors, car and home repairs inadequately completed, defective products, misleading ads, personal service fiascoes, rent disputes, poor restaurant and hotel services, and unpleasant and unsatisfactory dealings with governmental agencies and corporations.

Guidelines

Summarize the problem briefly, giving all pertinent information (names, dates, amounts) so the reader can investigate the situation before responding to you.

State what adjustment you expect.

Assume a firm and objective tone, expressing confidence that the reader will correct the matter appropriately.

Attach copies of all necessary paperwork such as receipts, canceled checks, past correspondence, guarantees, and so forth.

BILLING ERROR

❖ ❖ ❖

Dear Account Manager:

On my June credit card statement, I've discovered an error of $132.78 for two purchases made on May 27 and returned for credit on May 29: 1) transaction #2689 for a $78.82 sweater and 2) transaction #2690 for a $53.96 glass serving tray. I've enclosed copies of both credit receipts and have deducted $132.78 from the amount due.

When I returned the items, I do recall that the clerk who handled the returns was new to the job and had great difficulty in completing the paperwork. A more experienced clerk tried to "talk her through" the process while herself helping other customers. Possibly, that accounts for the mishandling or misplacement of your own credit receipts.

Thank you for correcting your records and removing the charges.

Sincerely,

❖ ❖ ❖

CAR

❖ ❖ ❖

Dear Mr. Grimes:

I've had my 19— Buick Regal in your shop for a general tune-up on three occasions (April 7, April 10, and May 2) and am still having the same problem: sluggishness during acceleration. As you can see from copies of the enclosed work orders, the problem summary and the diagnosis have been the same each time.

Because the car problem is still not corrected, I plan to take the car to another repair shop. However, I think Fairfax Auto Repair owes me a refund of $235 for labor charges on the second and third visits. The only reason I paid the bill for the third visit (before checking the car's performance) was that when I picked the car up after hours, the mechanic on duty would not open the gate and release the car until I had paid the invoice left on the windshield by your business office.

I ask that you refund the $235 amount immediately.

Sincerely,

❖ ❖ ❖

DEFECTIVE PRODUCT

❖ ❖ ❖

Dear Manager:

I purchased a defective garment bag from your mail order ad in *Sky* magazine on January 9. The bag arrived on Tuesday afternoon; I packed it for a business trip that evening and left for the airport early Wednesday morning. By the time I checked my bag at the ticket counter, the handle had come off the bag and one roller no longer rolled smoothly. All this happened *before* I even turned the bag over to the airline baggage handlers!

I'm returning the bag to you separately for a complete refund or replacement. Of course, there are now a few other nicks on the bag because the bag did make that Wednesday trip with me; these, however, are not the reason for the return.

Please let me know immediately whether you intend to replace the bag or refund the money so that I can make another purchasing decision before my next business trip February 1.

Sincerely,

❖ ❖ ❖

HOME REPAIR

❖ ❖ ❖

Dear Mr. Connors:

The carpentry work your staff did for me in building bookcases in my family room remains unsatisfactorily "completed." I am holding your invoice without payment until you can provide some resolution to the situation.

As I explained to Mr. Leidman during the project, the stain on the shelving is uneven; that is, the middle two rows of shelves are obviously darker than the others. The second problem involves the way the door of the cabinets under the shelves opens back against a nearby window sill, leaving it scratched.

In my opinion, Mr. Leidman's cutting a narrow indentation on the window sill would be all that's necessary to correct the problem. When he restains the mismatched shelving, he could also retouch the window sill. Mr. Leidman seemed to agree with the solution I discussed with him and promised to return to complete the job, but to date he has not done so.

Would you please send a carpenter to complete my shelving project immediately? We are having house guests within three weeks and are looking forward to using this room. I hope you can complete this job to your normally high standards so that we can continue to recommend your work to our friends and neighbors.

Sincerely,

❖ ❖ ❖

MISLEADING AD

❖ ❖ ❖

Dear Ms. Henderson:

Your tour-group ad in the October issue of *Tourists* magazine was highly misleading on several accounts. After two letters and three phone calls to the Forscom travel agency, we discovered that the "lake cottage" meant four miles from the water, that the "babysitting service" was limited only to bed babies, that the "free transport" to and from "planned activities" referred to free access through the gate by way of our rental car.

You can imagine our own disappointment in learning the realities of the situation and our embarrassment in sharing the "get-away" weekend idea with our friends. Additionally, we have already purchased two $48-nonrefundable airlines tickets to your city, spent approximately $25 on long-distance calls, and wasted four hours of false starts on weekend plans to visit your resort.

We hope you agree that you owe us some apology and explanation. Certainly, such misleading claims create more ill will among would-be customers and loss of business than a straight-forward ad describing the real situation. We have registered a complaint with our local travel agency and expect to see some change in your advertising program.

Yours truly,

❖　❖　❖

PERSONAL SERVICE

❖　❖　❖

Dear Ms. Blumquist:

My recent stay at your hotel in Dallas (North Central Expressway location) was most frustrating. My dry cleaning (a $455 suit) was lost, and the waiting time for other housekeeping services was inexplicably excessive.

I am asking that you make some adjustment toward the replacement cost of the suit. Although the receipt has long been destroyed, the suit was purchased two years ago and was still in excellent condition. I consider a check for $200 to be an acceptable adjustment. Of course, if my suit reappears, you can forward it to the address I left with the concierge, Mark Stevens.

Let me detail the situation I encountered during my stay: On the morning of November 2, I left extremely early for a business meeting and phoned the hotel's concierge desk to have housekeeping pick up my suit from my room. (I already had the suit in the hotel-provided bag with the completed laundry ticket inside.) The hotel did not return the suit the following day or the next day; no one seemed willing to take responsibility to investigate the matter. Because I again had early airline connections, I did not have time to go from person to person to investigate the matter. In addition to this major problem, I did call on Housekeeping for an iron and for extra towels on two occasions. Both times I waited in excess of two hours for delivery of the items.

I normally choose to stay in your hotels because my previous experience has been pleasant. Can you restore my confidence in the service at your hotel?

Sincerely,

❖ ❖ ❖

RENT ISSUES

❖ ❖ ❖

Dear Mr. Johns:

We have phoned you on two occasions to let you know that the lawn has not been mowed since June 1 at our 6733 Orange St. residence. As you know, weekly yard maintenance is part of our rental agreement. Because the yard has not been maintained, neighbors are complaining about the unsightly condition. We need the grass mowed immediately and are hoping you will make the necessary arrangements. If you prefer, we can withhold $50 from our rent check each month and hire someone ourselves to maintain the lawn.

If we don't hear from you this week about this ongoing problem, we will begin to look for another home in a well-kept neighborhood.

Sincerely,

❖ ❖ ❖

RESTAURANT/FOOD SERVICE

❖ ❖ ❖

Dear Ms. Scotsdale:

My family and I ate in your restaurant on August 6 and all three of us became suddenly ill about two hours after the meal. As a result, we had to go to the emergency room of Cypress Hospital, where we were treated for food poisoning. We are asking for reimbursement of the meal charges that amounted to $47.39 and of the emergency room charges of $182.04.

The meal we selected from your menu was the salmon cabaret and also, from your desert buffet, coconut pie. We suggest that you investigate your preparation and serving procedures of these menu items for the future. This was a most unpleasant experience for us, and I'm sure you will be concerned that other customers don't have the same problem.

We ask that you please forward the reimbursement check to the above address immediately.

Sincerely,

❖ ❖ ❖

GOVERNMENTAL AGENCY _____

❖ ❖ ❖

Dear Mr. Catz:

My wife and I are having great difficulty in getting a consistent answer from your office about a sales tax permit to sell handicraft items at weekend fairs and through direct mail. Each time we call your office (Joe Blue, May 11; Freda Smith, May 12; Kim White, May 13), the person who deals with the issue seems unsure about the requirements, promises "to check into the matter," and then never phones again.

I need answers to the following questions:

- Do we need to collect sales tax under the two conditions stated above—weekend trade fairs and direct mail outside the state?

- I understand that our local metropolitan area is divided into five zones and the tax rate varies within each zone. Do we compute any sales tax due based on the location of the weekend trade fair or based on the location of our home (our place of business)?

If your office cannot answer these two questions, would you please direct me to whoever can answer them?

Sincerely,

❖ ❖ ❖

BETTER BUSINESS BUREAU

❖ ❖ ❖

Dear Director:

I want to report my experience with Tiemtz Literary Agency, reportedly doing business at 1234 Jones Blvd., Suite 260, and ask that you investigate its operations immediately.

This agency ran an ad in the Sunday edition of the *Houston Chronicle*, advertising new offices in the city and inviting people interested in having a book published to phone for an appointment with regard to literary representation.

When I arrived for my appointment with manuscript in hand, I was greeted by a secretary who informed me that I must leave a $300 deposit for the manuscript to be read and evaluated before I could meet with an agent. Having driven across town for such an opinion, I did leave a deposit and the manuscript. After I phoned to arrange the follow-up appointment and had difficulty getting an "opening" before August, I became suspicious. Further questions to the agent about details, procedures, and plans convinced me that the operation is not a legitimate literacy agency.

Would you please send me any necessary paperwork to file a formal complaint and to help me recover my $300.

Yours truly,

❖ ❖ ❖

CONDOLENCES

Our circle of friends grows smaller and tighter in the time of sorrow. When a personal friend loses a loved one, he or she needs our loving support, affirmation, and encouragement more than ever.

The letters that follow will help you express your sentiments and friendship at the time of death of a parent, spouse, or child. And on other occasions, such as an extended illness or loss of a home or business, a warm letter can turn defeat into a defiant resolve to overcome.

Guidelines and Alternate Phrasing

Express your regret and sorrow at hearing of the death or other misfortune.

⇨ I was so upset to hear about John's death.

⇨ We were devastated by the news of Mary's accident.

⇨ My family is taking John's death very hard; we all thought so much of him.

⇨ We want you to know how sorry we are to learn of your mother's illness and death.

⇨ Bob and I are so sorry to hear about the tragic accident involving Jack.

⇨ We were terribly upset to hear about the fire that destroyed your home.

Help the individual praise a loved one by mentioning something you remember about the person or by recalling something you've heard others say. In the case of another misfortune, let the reader know you understand the extent of the loss.

⇨ I've heard so many who knew him well say that he was always ...

⇨ You yourself have commented so many times on his loving nature and support of everything you were involved in.

⇨ What I most appreciated about John was his ability to ...

⇨ One of the best times we ever had together as a couple was the day we ...

⇨ He always was ready to help. I remember when ...

⇨ My girls always thought so much of your mother because she used to .,.

⇨ Anyone who raised children as solid, honest, and successful as his are must have been an excellent parent.

⇨ I know that you lost so many things in the fire that are simply irreplaceable. The waiting and watching and hoping must have taken so much courage.

⇨ The suddenness and the senselessness of such happenings destroy our peace of mind and create confusion for all of us. My heart goes out to you.

State specifically how you'd like to help. Vague offers sound insincere.

Choose an informal, conversational tone. Avoid cliches.

Use personal stationery and write in longhand. If you purchase a greeting card, add your own personal note inside.

ACCIDENT

❖ ❖ ❖

Dear Weldon:

Hospitals are great places to be—when you're in desperate need. But you and I both know they're not like home. The familiar is gone. Your favorite snack is not in the refrigerator. And people you don't know tell you what you can and can't do.

But then it's not necessarily any better than that in the office. The cleaning people have again thrown out the familiar. People keep eating your favorite snack because it's "growing" in the refrig. And the powers-that-be are still telling us what to do.

Come to think of it, you could do worse than to have someone in white dash to your room whenever you push the little buzzer. So if you're inclined to rest a little, stay put. Otherwise, we're pretty anxious to see you back around here. Well and in one piece, of course.

Sincerely,

❖ ❖ ❖

DEATH OF A CHILD _____

❖ ❖ ❖

Dear Meg and Marvin:

I was so upset to hear about Bonnie's accident. On our last visit, she was just bubbling over with excitement about her acceptance to the University. I guess that's the way I'll remember her—bubbly, excited, smart, ready to try anything new.

Bob and I can only imagine the pain you're going through at the senseless-ness of it all. Someone has said that the deepest agony on earth is burying one's own child. I'm sure that now you're numbed by the suddenness, by the weight of the loss, and by the decisions facing you. But in a few weeks when you feel the need to get away and must have time to yourselves, we want you to consider coming to stay a few days at our lakehouse. I've made an extra key and have enclosed that and a map. Just phone us to let us know when, and we'll make sure things are ready for you.

Please know that our hearts are breaking for what you must be experiencing now. We pray God's comfort.

Sincerely,

❖ ❖ ❖

DEATH OF A PARENT _____

❖ ❖ ❖

Dear Barry,

Peggy and Jack announced at the club dinner last night that your father had passed away and that you had gone to Chicago to be with the family. We were sorry to hear that he had been ill so long and then to hear of his death.

Although, of course, we've never met your father, I recall your speaking of him so fondly on many occasions. You've told us stories of the old farm days when he taught you the "value of a dollar" and of your first attempts at driving his truck. I'm sure your father knew of your love for him because of your frequent visits back there and your concern during his recent illness.

No matter the circumstances or their ages, I know it's never easy to give up parents—they teach us so much just by living. And it's only as we grow older ourselves that we understand more of the lessons and value their wisdom and perspective on life. Please accept our sympathies in this time of sadness and loss.

Sincerely,

❖ ❖ ❖

DEATH OF A SPOUSE

❖ ❖ ❖

Dear Juanelle,

I heard about Jack's heart attack this morning when I stopped by the gym on the way to work. You must be shocked and feel overwhelmed.

Just last week, Jack drove by to show his new golf clubs to Robert and to tell us about the vacation you were planning in a few weeks. Although we didn't know him in his executive role, I know you were proud of his accomplishments and his leadership abilities at Texaco. But aside from work, we certainly appreciated his wit around the dinner table. And when my mother was so ill, he was always so kind to ask about her and show his concern.

May I help in chauffeuring the girls to and from gym for a few days until things are a little more settled? I'll plan on picking them up on Monday evening unless I hear from you otherwise.

I'll be in touch, of course, but I just wanted to take this chance to let you know how sorry I am and how much we will miss Jack. We will be thinking of you constantly as you go through the next few days and weeks.

Sincerely,

❖ ❖ ❖

DEATH OF ANOTHER RELATIVE _____

❖ ❖ ❖

Dear Holly:

I just learned of your aunt's death. I'm so sorry. You've spoken of her so often, and I know she has been like a mother to you since childhood.

When loved ones must live so far away, we always feel that we should have been able to do more. But you should feel reassurance that you did all you could. I know she must have enjoyed so much having you visit her so frequently during the last few months. The handiwork that you brought back with you from the last trip will, I'm sure, be a reminder of her loving gestures and thoughts for others rather than herself. I know she must have been a wonderful person because of her influence on your own life.

If I can watch your apartment or take care of pets or any such thing while you're away during the next few days, please call on me. I'd consider it a chance to deepen our friendship. My thoughts are with you.

Sincerely,

❖ ❖ ❖

ILLNESS _____

❖ ❖ ❖

Dear Marguerite:

Sickness brings with it all kinds of unusual reactions—fear, pain, vulnerability, isolation, frustration. I can help with only the last two—isolation and frustration. This note is to say that I've been thinking about you during this difficult period and that you're really not alone.

What can I do to lessen the frustration of your being off work and "out of whack"? Please let me know if I can run some work errands such as hand-holding with existing customer accounts? Delivering mail back and forth? Transporting kids or groceries?

I hope you are able to take some time during your convalescence just to rest and enjoy your family. You deserve it. You're in my prayers until we see you back with us.

Sincerely,

❖ ❖ ❖

LOSS OF BUSINESS/HOME

❖ ❖ ❖

Dear Scott and Esther:

We heard about the fire at your home when we returned from the Christmas holidays with our parents. I wish we'd been here at the time at least to offer you moral support. What a loss. Although we've never been through that tragedy, I'm sure you must feel overwhelmed at starting over and just sick at heart for the loss of your personal keepsakes that simply can't be replaced. We're just grateful that none of you were seriously injured.

Someone has said that your immediate needs have been met, that you're staying with family at the present time. But we want to help. We intend to look through our photos of the children and find group shots of all the school and sporting activities where both your Michael and our Jeff were involved and then have duplicates made for you. And if you can think of anything else we can help with, please let us know.

Sincerely,

❖ ❖ ❖

CONGRATULATIONS

A major part of any accomplishment, career milestone, or happy personal event is recognition from others. A letter from a colleague on such an occasion encourages, affirms, and rewards us for our labor, talent, or good fortune.

Be sensitive to times when a congratulatory note can cement a relationship, as well as allow you to recognize another's achievement or good sense. Such letters should be brief, specific, and genuine. Handwritten notes add that special warmth that wraps the sentiment with individual care.

Guidelines

Congratulate the reader on the occasion.

Elaborate on the details and offer your wishes for a happy future.

Avoid mentioning any negatives that would remind the reader of past difficulties and disappointments.

Use personal stationery. If you send a greeting card, write a personal note inside.

ANNIVERSARY

❖ ❖ ❖

Dear Tom and Lana:

My calendar says you two have a very special day coming up—14 years together. In these times, that's an impressive record of commitment, caring, and sharing. You are both such special people whose friendship means a great deal to me. Have a wonderful anniversary and a wonderful life together.

Cordially,

❖ ❖ ❖

❖ ❖ ❖

Dear Kay and Blair:

You two must have all the answers—at least to the most important questions. You've spent 20 years together under the same roof and still have the same sweet spirit, the same fun-loving attitude, the same concern for your friends—and *new* successes each year. That says a lot for what kind of people you are when no one else is looking. Have the very happiest anniversary.

Sincerely,

❖ ❖ ❖

Dear Mike and Susan:

Congratulations on your first anniversary. No doubt, you've both made some adjustments and compromises, right? I'm so thrilled you've found each other and can share the significant and the small things of life together. I hope you're still as happy as the day you exchanged wedding vows!

Sincerely,

❖ ❖ ❖

BIRTH

❖ ❖ ❖

Dear Paul and Janet:

Congratulations on the birth of Trish Ann. We hear she's a cuddly bundle of energy with long locks of dark hair already. You must be so proud of her, and probably want to buy her the moon—were it not so hard to transport and store for the next 18 years. Enjoy her and each other in this special family time. There will be time for work and other obligations much later.

Cordially,

❖ ❖ ❖

Dear Loo and Maitryee:

We heard the good news—a healthy baby boy. He doesn't yet know how lucky he is yet to have been born into a family with such love and special values that will mold him into a man with character and strength. But he'll learn soon enough, day by day, as you talk with him, share his pains, laugh at his pranks, and support him in his goals. Congratulations to both of you and the baby.

Cordially,

❖ ❖ ❖

Dear Cary and Rush:

No more late Saturday mornings in bed, quiet dinners for two around the fireplace, and weekends skiing at Taos. Instead, it will be 5:00 A.M. feedings, a half-sandwich over the kitchen counter, and weekends at soccer games.

Seriously, you two know what a change you're in store for. But from experience let me assure you that there are few things as motivating as that peanut-butter kiss in the evening and as fulfilling as teaching him to ride a bike. You have years of fun and love in store. Congratulations.

Our love to you and the baby,

❖ ❖ ❖

BIRTHDAY

❖ ❖ ❖

Dear Mona:

I didn't want to let your special day go by without a birthday wish from me. Your friendship warms me when I'm cold and depressed, pulls me down to earth when I'm outrageous, and sets me back on track when I stray from where I want to go.

So sorry I had to be out of town today. Have a special birthday anyway and know I'm thinking of you.

With love,

❖ ❖ ❖

Dear Jason:

At our age, do we still celebrate birthdays? You bet we do! I hope you're still happy to see every year the Good Lord gives you. Just think what you no longer have to do:

- beg your old man for the car
- show an ID
- relieve your wife for the 2:00 A.M. feedings
- let your boss beat you at golf

Congratulations on another year in which to excel where it really counts—eating and sleeping!

My best,

❖ ❖ ❖

❖ ❖ ❖

Dear Carol:

Make it your day. Fly a kite. Lunch at Tony's. Collect your profit on Wall Street. Find love. Sail off into the sunset. And if none of those things happen today, you can say you've had the typical birthday. Except for me and a few hundred other friends who wish you a happy birthday and many more years to brighten the planet!

Regards,

❖ ❖ ❖

ENGAGEMENT/WEDDING

❖ ❖ ❖

Dear Tammy and Carlton:

You two really did marry your best friend, didn't you? It has been so special to watch your friendship grow and then blossom into love—like a rose opening on a spring morning. I'm so happy for both of you in finding that one person who will give meaning to life and always be there when the rest of the world goes away.

I wish for you a lifetime of happiness and love together.

Sincerely,

❖ ❖ ❖

Dear Max and Sabrina:

You both have experienced love all your life—from your parents, your families, your friends. That makes it so right for you to discover a new love in each other, because only those who have been loved understand how to give love. In my humble opinion, you two have always focused on the most important things in life and certainly love is at the top of the list.

You both are such creative, giving, optimistic people that your marriage should always be vibrant and fulfilling. Congratulations on your decision to build a life together.

Sincerely,

❖ ❖ ❖

Dear Forrest:

I've heard from my parents that you are engaged. Congratulations! My dad mentioned that the woman you're marrying is from California, someone you met through your work there. Knowing you and your personal and career goals and accomplishments, I'm sure she must be a classy lady with many credits to her own name. When do I get to meet her?

My best to you on the marriage. I wish you years of happiness.

Sincerely,

❖ ❖ ❖

GRADUATION

❖ ❖ ❖

Dear Kelly:

Congratulations on your achievements. In this day and age when so many kids make headlines for all the wrong things, I'm proud to know a young person like you who, for 18 years, has been respectful of the law, loving to her family and friends, and successful at school and life. Your future should be a bright one.

Sincerely,

❖ ❖ ❖

❖ ❖ ❖

Dear Richard:

Are you tired of hearing the old cliches like . . . This is the threshold of a new beginning. Today is the first day of the rest of your life. Tomorrow is a blank page. Graduation is not an ending; it's a beginning. Well, never mind that they're all true.

The important thing is that you know you have family and friends who'll love and support you every step of the way to a successful future. We're proud of you. Congratulations!

Love,

❖ ❖ ❖

Dear Gary:

We're so proud of you. No more 8:00 A.M. exams. No more all-night cram sessions. No more endless debates about how many angels can dance on the head of a pin. You're ready for the real world. The question is, is the world ready for GARY S. PETERSON?

Well, as one interested observer, I'd answer a great big yes. We're ready for your fresh outlook, your creativity, your sensitivity, your talent. Welcome to the real world! Our best wishes as you make it better.

Sincerely,

❖ ❖ ❖

CREDIT

Handling family finances and the related correspondence is a thankless fact of life: letters to change your billing address, to add credit card users to your account, to request increases in your credit line.

Although fairly routine matters, these letters can be time-consuming. And if they are unclear, each change or request may take three or four reiterations to clarify details and get action.

In other less-than-desirable financial circumstances, you may find yourself asking for special repayment arrangements or responding to collection letters. Your effective correspondence about how you plan to resolve these financial matters can mean the difference between success or failure in retaining a good credit rating.

Guidelines

State the situation, change, or request immediately.

Give all pertinent historical details as to dates, names, and account numbers so that the reader can investigate the credit history.

Enclose any letters, forms, or other documentation that will verify past claims or changes in the current situation.

CHANGES IN ACCOUNT RESPONSIBILITY/ARRANGEMENTS

❖ ❖ ❖

Credit Department:

My husband and I recently divorced, and I need you to change our credit card account (#234-MT56-7895959) to a single, rather than joint, account in my name only. My address will remain the same at 1245 Mainturn Street. I will accept responsibility for all current charges on the card.

Also, I want to request an additional credit card for my son, who is moving away from home to attend college.

Enclosed is my ex-husband's cut-up card.

Sincerely,

❖ ❖ ❖

REQUEST FOR EXTENDED CREDIT

❖ ❖ ❖

Dear Credit Manager:

We are requesting an extension of our credit line on our credit card account #2389899090 to $____. Our current credit limit of $____ was established when we opened the account eight years ago. As you will see from our past prompt-payment record, that limit has been no problem until recently when we've both started to travel with our jobs. A month's business airfares, hotels, and meals put us at our limit rather quickly, without even considering our normal monthly retail purchases.

Our current combined income is now $____, which we hope will qualify us for a higher credit limit. Our salary check stubs are enclosed for verification.

Will you let us know your decision immediately so we can continue to use your card as we travel?

Sincerely,

❖ ❖ ❖

REQUEST FOR SPECIAL REPAYMENT ARRANGEMENTS

Guidelines and Alternate Phrasing

⇨ Assure the reader that you intend to pay the amount due.

⇨ We have received your notices about our overdue account and do intend to make full payment.

⇨ We are aware that our account is past due and have every intention of making it current over the next few months.

⇨ Your past-due notice arrived this week. We do want to assure you that we will pay the amount due in full.

Enclose some amount toward repayment, and suggest a new repayment plan.

⇨ We need to work out a plan that will allow us to reduce the minimum payment each month.

⇨ I'd like to work with you in designing a plan that will lower our monthly payments to $200 for the next few months and then return them to the higher level later.

⇨ We can pay $500 now against the balance, and then we need to reduce our payments to $200 each month until we completely repay the total due.

Explain, briefly, your current difficulties in making payments.

⇨ My wife has recently lost her job, and we will need some time to adjust to one salary again.

⇨ Our small business has experienced growing difficulties, and we have had to invest all our available personal funds to keep the business operating.

⇨ Because of extended illness and unexpected medical bills, we find that we just can't meet our obligations at the moment.

⇨ We're embarrassed, but for the first time we have simply overextended ourselves. Having gone to a financial counselor, we have worked out a plan whereby we can pay all bills, but on a lower per-monthly arrangement.

Reassure the reader that you do intend to pay the account in full and want to continue to do business with the company.

⇨ We like your products and want to continue to deal with you in better times.

⇨ We have appreciated your prompt service and intend to meet our full obligations so that we can restore our good credit rating with your organization.

⇨ We do want to make things right as soon as possible and to continue to do business with you.

⇨ We appreciate your patience and understanding during our present difficulty so that we can eventually pay the entire amount we owe you.

❖ ❖ ❖

Dear Credit Manager:

We have received your statement for the furniture purchased from you in November, but we regret to tell you that we will be unable to pay the full $3,500 within the 30-day terms.

Exactly two days after you delivered the furniture, my husband lost his job and has not yet found other employment. In our present uncertain circumstances, we need to make other arrangements for monthly payments over a longer period.

Enclosed is a check for $300 against the balance. We will await your further instructions about how we can make reduced payments and on what timetable.

Thank you for working with us on this new repayment schedule. We have enjoyed shopping in your store and look forward to making further purchases there when our economic situation improves.

Sincerely,

❖ ❖ ❖

RESPONSE TO COLLECTION LETTER

❖ ❖ ❖

Dear Mr. Snell:

I received your letter about the "overdue" subscription fees, which *ZIP ZAP* magazine turned over to you for collection. I do not owe any subscription fee; I canceled my trial subscription immediately upon receipt of the first issue by writing "cancel" across the invoice, just as the instructions specified.

I've received four computer-generated invoices from this magazine, asking for payment or for some explanation of nonpayment. Each time I wrote a explanatory note on the bottom of the invoice and returned it, only to be greeted by another invoice and request on the next billing cycle. As you may imagine, I finally grew weary of responding to their requests for explanations and discarded the notices. I've enclosed a copy of the last invoice with my explanatory note, which apparently went unread each time.

Please remove my account from your collection list immediately.

Yours truly,

❖ ❖ ❖

FRIENDSHIP NOTES/GREETINGS

In our modern, fast-paced life, friendships must hold together despite distance and long gaps in time between personal get togethers. What better way than periodic notes and letters to keep in touch across the miles and the years? The following brief sentiments are appropriate for jotting inside greeting cards sent on special occasions such as birthdays or anniversaries, or for copying onto your personal stationery.

Just a few words can turn someone's dark day to sunlight, cement a new friendship, or deepen a long-valued relationship.

Guidelines and Alternate Phrasing

Be yourself and try to put your personality in your writing as you customize these phrases.

Prefer simple words and short sentences.

Prefer the specific to the general. For example, rather than saying, "I appreciate your help," say instead, "I appreciate your running errands for me" or "I appreciate the times you babysit the children when I'm running late at the office."

Be conversational in tone. You shouldn't have both a "writing voice" and a "talking voice"; instead they should be one and the same. You should sound natural, as though you are talking to the other individual.

NOTE: The following are expressions on the meaning of friendship. These lines are appropriate for a brief handwritten note on your personal stationery or for jotting inside purchased cards.

* * *

Thank you so much for being that someone special in my life. You've been a true friend in every sense of the word. Life is what we make it and what is made of it by the friends we choose. I feel blessed that we have chosen each other as friends forever.

324

* * *

Robert Louis Stevenson said, "A friend is a present you give yourself." Let's continue to unwrap the new layers of our relationship every time we meet, on every occasion we share, with every heartache we bear, for every joy we celebrate. You are the best present I've ever received.

* * *

A Russian proverb says that a mere friend will agree with you, but a real friend will argue. After the words we had recently, I just wanted to drop you a note to say that I appreciate you more than ever. You always seem to know exactly what I need said and when I need it said. You infuriate me. You motivate me. You make me feel special. You make me feel lousy. You take the wind out of my sails. You give me confidence. All these things I need at varying times. It's no wonder I appreciate you more than ever.

* * *

When did our friendship start? It's difficult to say. Was it the time I phoned you to ask about . . .? Or, was it the time we met at ... and shared our thoughts on . . .? When we crossed over the line from acquaintances to friends is not so important as to know that we now have a special relationship growing between us. Time spent with you is special to me. Thanks for being my friend.

* * *

You know the worst about me—my inner thoughts, my sometimes rotten disposition, my selfishness, and my fears. Yet, you're still my friend. That speaks volumes about the kind of patience and blind faith you have in me. Thank you for playing, sharing, listening, and staying with me through the rough times.

* * *

All I feel about our special friendship can never be fully expressed in words. Please know that it's felt and understood even when my attempts at words are inadequate.

✳ ✳ ✳

Some friends are special because they help you out of big trouble. Others forgive you when you've done some thoughtless thing. Some friends know how to celebrate the good times with you; others know just the right words when you're feeling down. Some friends always make you laugh when they turn on their charming wit; others make you feel that you yourself are as entertaining as the movies. Some friends give you an extra push when you need it; others hold you back from doing things you shouldn't do. Some friends teach you a lot of things; others love to learn from you and make you feel special for your wisdom. Some friends make you laugh; some friends make you think. In my way of thinking and feeling, you're all these special qualities wrapped into one.

✳ ✳ ✳

When is the last time I told you how much I appreciate your believing in me? You push me when I need it. You caution me when I don't want it. You disregard my faults and play to my strengths. You overlook your own needs at times to help me meet my mine. When's the last time you thought about doing all these things for me? Probably not often, because that's the kind of person you are. But I've thought about them a lot lately and wanted to say a big thanks. You're not taken for granted!

✳ ✳ ✳

Sometimes friendships are only hopes and dreams—we believe what we want to believe and hope. We hope the other person will always help in our worst times of needs. But our friendship—yours and mine—is more than a dream; it's real. You've proven yourself time and time again. You're a true friend in every sense of the word. That's a comforting reality.

✳ ✳ ✳

Just a note to say how great I think our friendship really is. Why? Because you let me be me first. We go our own ways, chase our own rainbows, fine-tune our own hobbies and interests. But when I need someone with whom to talk deeply, to really share, to hear my hurts and my "great" ideas, you're always that special someone. Thank you for being you and letting me be me.

* * *

This is a very special day in your life, and I couldn't let it pass without throwing in my two cents worth: Treasure your memories of the past, enjoy the pleasure of today, and look forward to promising tomorrows.

* * *

Knowing you and spending time together has given me a renewed awareness of how much friendship means—yours particularly. With you, I can really be myself—warts and all. And I can trust you, who knows me best, to overlook the worst and enjoy the best. Thanks for your gifts of time and understanding.

* * *

You've heard it said that you can judge a person by the friends he keeps. If that's really true, I must be held in high regard by all. My friend, you are uniquely special.

* * *

Others have said that to have a friend, you must be one. That, you certainly have been. I remember the time you . . . And then there's the time you ... And so many times, you have . . . You have won my admiration, my respect, my love. You will have my friendship forever.

* * *

I don't know how you feel about the matter of our friendship. But I'd say we've cultivated an intellectual soil and an emotional climate that can grow a lifetime of friendship. I appreciate your thoughtful advice and supportive sharing.

* * *

Never before have a kind word, a warm hug and handshake, and a sympathetic prayer meant so much to me as in the recent few months while I've been struggling with . . . Thank you so much for offering the word, hug, and prayer when I have needed them. The light of your friendship continues to brighten my days.

* * *

You have contributed to my good health, my sanity, and my wealth. Yes, positively. You force me to exercise with all the running around we do. Your patience and advice reduce my stress level. And you charge much less than a psychiatrist! Thanks for being my friend.

* * *

To my friend: If I've been careless or insensitive in saying the wrong thing or not saying the right thing, . . . if I've been unkind or selfish in not being there for you when you needed me, . . . if I've been self-absorbed in my own world when I should have been helping you build yours, . . . if I've been glib when you needed sympathy or sympathetic when you needed a push, ... if I've been the wrong things on the wrong days, please forgive me. Your friendship means a great deal to me; it's much too valuable to lose.

* * *

I miss you. You always seem to know me so well and love me despite . . . Some of the most important times of our lives we've shared, laughed about, cried over. Those memories are forever in my mind and they bind us together with loyalty and love. I respect your values and you respect mine.

We respect what each of us has become without diminishing what friendship we have built together. I miss you over the miles.

* * *

Friends are mirrors where we see ourselves more clearly. As a friend, you are very important in helping me form my views of the world, determine my values, and grow in kindness and commitment. I sure do like what I see in you.

* * *

My husband appreciates you—because you are the friend that helps me be me. You give me laughter, logic, and loyalty—all qualities that I can, in turn, contribute to my marriage. Because of our friendship—yours and mine—I am a better person, a better partner to my mate. Thank you for the qualities you add to my life.

* * *

As my friend, you've never tried to tell me what to do. But you've patiently been around to pick up the slack. You've supplied energy, hope, know-how, and emotional strength when mine has failed. Thanks for standing in the gap.

* * *

Friendship is the gift that becomes a present to both people involved. The relationship doesn't really work unless both people are willing to accept kindnesses and gifts as well as to give them. Thank you for letting me be your friend and offer help when I can. That means a lot to me.

* * *

Friendship—in my way of thinking—is a big underdeveloped resource in our country. What do you say to you and I doing our part to set the model? I appreciate your integrity, your sensitivity, and your support. Your friendship makes a difference in my career and personal life.

* * *

There are friends you'd rather laugh with than cry with. There are friends you'd rather cry with than laugh with. Some friends you're proud to show off to other acquaintances. And some friends might embarrass you from time to time. But I've learned which is which, and you fit into every positive category there is! Thanks for being an all-around great friend.

* * *

When you don't expect anything from a friendship, you often receive a lot. I've made a habit of trying not to "wear out my welcome" with friends—emotionally and otherwise. But with you, I feel that I'm taking more than I'm giving. Although I didn't intend to depend on our friendship so much, I hope you realize how much our relationship has meant to me. Thanks for giving so much.

INQUIRIES

When you have questions the TV ads, newspapers, fliers, and brochures don't answer, you often have to take the lead in communication. The following letters will help you gather the appropriate details on important events or new products and services of interest.

Guidelines and Alternate Phrasing

Request the information you need immediately, without going into lengthy background behind the request.

Be specific about names, dates, amounts, approvals, or questions related to the request. In other words, anticipate every possible detail that the reader will need to supply the information.

Mention any deadlines you have.

⇨ August 1 is our deadline; we hope you can help us.

⇨ We must make our decision by August 1. Would you, therefore, send the information by express mail in the enclosed postage-paid envelope.

⇨ Could you possibly forward the information by August 1?

Make it easy for the reader to respond; enclose a form, a checklist, a sample, or a self-addressed stamped envelope for easy reply.

Be courteous rather than demanding, particularly if the reader's response is voluntary.

⇨ I'll appreciate your help with this project.

⇨ Thank you so much for your time in providing this information.

⇨ This information will be critical to our decision. Thank you so much for your help.

⇨ Thank you for your efforts in gathering this data.

⇨ Your cooperation is invaluable in helping us make a truly informed decision.

⇨ The information will be so helpful in our research. Thank you.

⇨ This request certainly falls outside the call of duty, so I really appreciate your extra efforts.

INFORMATION ON EVENT

❖ ❖ ❖

Dear Meeting Planner:

I have received your enticing brochure about the women's conference to be held in Baltimore, June 24-28. But I do need the answer to a few questions before I make a final decision about registering.

Do you maintain a list of attendees who might wish to be matched with a hotel roommate for the week? Also, does attendance at this conference qualify for continuing education units? Finally, at the two evening galas, is the dress formal or business attire?

I've enclosed a self-addressed stamped envelope and notepaper for your convenience in giving me a quick answer. Thank you for taking the time to help with these details. Your conference topics sound both provocative and fun, and I'll be eager to hear from you.

Sincerely,

❖ ❖ ❖

INFORMATION ON PRODUCT/SERVICE

❖ ❖ ❖

Dear Sales Rep:

Here's a puzzle for you: I need information on a product you sell, but I don't know what the product is called.

Let me explain what I do know to help you identify and send me literature and pricing. At a recent seminar, the instructor used an overhead projector and wrote on dark blue foils with a highlight pen and, after a few seconds' delay, the lettering turned bright yellow. Although the instructor kept referring to it as his "magic pen," I'm sure you have a more technical name!

Do you carry such a product? If so, would you please send me information and pricing on the special foils and pen.

Thank you,

❖ ❖ ❖

ISSUES

Clear writing reflects clear thinking. And that's exactly the impression you want to convey when expressing your opinions to the editor of your favorite newspaper or magazine, to legislators, and to others you hope to influence on important issues. The following letters will help you express your ideas on complex social, religious, moral, or political issues, and demand attention for specific actions or resolutions.

The future of our world depends on the expressed attitudes and actions of forward-thinking people committed to the axiom: "Speak up and be counted."

Guidelines and Alternate Phrasing

Express agreement or disagreement with a particular opinion, issue, or bill. Stay focused on this one subject.

⇨ I appreciate your stance on ...

⇨ We agree wholeheartedly with your statement to ...

⇨ I couldn't disagree more with your conclusions to ...

⇨ Your statement that ... totally goes against all my experience with ...

⇨ We are totally against the current ... bill before the House to ...

Support your position with further detail or other evidence.

Add credibility and weight to your position by mentioning your association with, and avenues of influence over, others.

⇨ As chairman of Benton, Inc., I am in a position to share views with several heads of organizations within the industry and find complete agreement that ...

⇨ As a writer for various publications, I've stated in numerous articles that ... and will continue to air my views about officials who ...

⇨ As a president of my homeowner's association, I plan to share with our members your position as to ...

⇨ As taxpayers and frequent campaign contributors, my wife and I ...

⇨ As a very vocal member of several professional and civic organizations, I hear the views of others who ...

Thank the media or legislator for giving this matter the attention it deserves.

⇨ We will appreciate your careful review of this issue.

⇨ Thank you for your past record; we hope we can count on you for a similar stance in the future, however unpopular that may be.

⇨ Thank you for this vital service in informing the public of the true dangers of ...

⇨ Thank you for bringing to light the advantages of ...

⇨ We will be grateful for your considering each of your readers as you offer solutions on ...

⇨ We thank you for keeping this issue in the forefront of our minds and hearts. You carry a heavy responsibility.

Ask for a response or state that you will be watching the individual's voting record on stand on this issue.

⇨ We will be hoping to see your yes vote.

⇨ We will be eager to see where you stand on this issue.

⇨ We will be expecting a further explanation in an upcoming issue.

⇨ Please let us know if you intend to print information supporting the other side of this issue.

⇨ Please write us about how you intend to vote when this matter comes before the Senate. Please issue a statement to the press about your position on this vital issue.

⇨ I will be expecting to hear from you in a letter or through the media about your alternatives for ...

LETTER TO THE EDITOR

❖ ❖ ❖

Dear Editor:

I heartily commend you for your extensive coverage of the airline industry's record on treatment of customers, pricing policies, and safety regulations.

As the owner of a national travel agency, we hear at least ten such customer stories daily as those you cited in your article. In fact, six months ago we did an informal telephone survey of over 200 clients to ask them about their satisfaction with the travel plans we'd arranged for them. In 183 of the 200 responses, the client mentioned the "air travel" as the only unpleasant experience of their travel—with complaints ranging from canceled flights to two-hour routine maintenance checks made while passengers sat on a runway.

Thank you for bringing the behind-the-scenes "reasons" for unreasonable policies to the forefront. We certainly will be watching such "fancy footwork" as we advise travelers on which airlines and flight schedules to avoid. With this article, you have done all business and pleasure travelers a great service.

Sincerely,

❖ ❖ ❖

LETTER TO LEGISLATORS

❖ ❖ ❖

Dear Senator Russell:

I encourage you to support the "Fair Education" bill #_____ to give our children access to an equal education by ensuring that the property-tax base is statewide. Children should not be denied qualified teachers, excellent facilities, and character-building extra-curricular opportunities simply because they are born into a poor community with a restrictive property-tax base.

Historical statistics tell us that poor education costs us dearly in later years—in the form of welfare, crime, and workforce illiteracy.

As a taxpayer and the editor of a local suburban newspaper, I want to bring your views on this important issue to our readers. Would you please let me know how you plan to vote on this upcoming bill? Our community will long remember your leadership in educating our children.

Respectfully,

❖ ❖ ❖

LETTER TO MEET POLITICAL CANDIDATE _____

Guidelines and Alternate Phrasing

Extend the invitation to meet the candidate.

Give the details about the political race and the issues involved.

Overview the agenda.

Encourage attendance. You may or may not want to ask for an RSVP.

❖ ❖ ❖

Dear Mr. and Mrs. Brannon:

You are invited to meet Truett Nadir at our home (36783 Echo Lane) on Tuesday evening, April 28, from 6:00 to 8:00 P.M. As you know, Truett has agreed to run for election to the Boyton School Board, May 16.

Having lived in the community for eight years, Truett and Yvonne have four children currently in our school system and know intimately the needs of our schools and the values of our community. Truett's background as a mathematics professor and his current position as an engineer with Amoco certainly give him perspective from both the educational and the business arenas on the issues now facing us as a district: textbook selection, voluntary enrollments at satellite schools, and redistribution of our student population.

After an informal cocktail hour during which you can meet Truett, Yvonne, and your other neighbors, we'll ask Truett to share his views briefly on the above issues, and then he'll answer questions from the group. Feel free to drop by for a few minutes on your way home from the office or stay for the entire session. Either way, you'll be closer to understanding the vital issues that will affect our children's education.

If your schedule is rather predictable, we'd appreciate a call to let us know you're coming (467-6887). But if you have a last-minute change of plans, don't worry about the RSVP; come ahead and join us for an informative get-together.

Sincerely,

❖ ❖ ❖

LOVE NOTES/GREETINGS

Just because love runs deep, words do not necessarily flow smoothly. That's not to say, however, that all relationships, new or old, could not grow from words of love and appreciation. Expressing your love in writing is often difficult and awkward, but so appreciated by the loved one.

The following expressions are common, down-to-earth sentiments that might be spoken lightly in late night pillow talks or felt deeply as couples pray over a seriously ill child or elderly parent. Love, like life, is made of the little things as well as the big.

Guidelines and Alternate Phrasing

Be sincere. You don't have to be a novelist or poet to express words of love; you just have to write from your own heart and experience.

Prefer short sentences and simple words.

Choose specific words and ideas rather than abstract ones. Instead of saying, "You are considerate," say, "You always remember to ask how I feel when I've been sick."

Prefer a conversational tone. Write as you would speak the thoughts.

NOTE: The following are expressions of love. These lines are appropriate for a brief handwritten note on your personal stationery or for jotting inside purchased cards. More than the message by the author of the card, the loved one wants to read what *you* have to say personally about the meaning of your relationship. Take these thoughts as a start and customize them for your own loved one.

* * *

Two things about people are always true—they are all alike and they are all different. The same, of course, is true for you and me. We are alike in so many ways—
    stubbornness
    a sense of humor

a belief that the world should be fair
a craving for salted nuts and late-night bull sessions
sensitivity.
And we are different—
You're emotional; I'm calm.
You're always ready to go; I'm always wanting to stay.
You're open; I'm locked up inside.
You're into neatness; I prefer sloppy.
You're always giving; I'm always asking.
You're beautiful; I'm appreciative.
Let's keep it this way.

✳ ✳ ✳

They say people are a sum of their commitments. In other words, I am what I've chosen to become and the people I've chosen to live my life with. You're that primary, most important person that defines me.

Do you know what trust that implies? I trust you with my mental health, my possessions, my future. That adds up to a lot of love from me to you!

✳ ✳ ✳

I don't know whoever came up with the idea that if we are committed to another person that it will be our loss, not our gain. Committed to you—as lives meshed in all the right ways—I have grown so much in becoming the kind of person I want to be. Thank you for making me feel like a whole person with value in everything I do. My commitment to you has been nothing but gain.

✳ ✳ ✳

Time brings many good things. You are the best of them all. When I need someone to listen to the day's triumphs, you love to celebrate with me. On the other hand, when it has been a down day, you know how to make it all go away.

When I need advice, you ask some very relevant questions and help me come to some weighty conclusions. On the other hand, when I want approval rather than advice, you heap that on in loving spoonfuls.

When I need a playmate, you know how to laugh and enjoy the trivial and the classy. On the other hand, when I need someone to cry with, you feel my pain as if it were your own; I can see it in your eyes.

Stand by me and I'll do the same for you.

* * *

I like to celebrate often. Today I'm celebrating your smile—it's gift enough for me on almost any occasion.

* * *

I love you because you are willing to risk. You are willing to love me and still let me be me without trying to mold me into an extension of yourself. For that reason, we have a mature love and will belong to each other forever.

* * *

All my life, I have looked for someone who was strong enough to stay separate from me, open enough to be herself with me, sensitive enough not to say unkind things to me, caring enough to tell me kind truths, brave enough to risk being hurt by love. I've found all of these in you.

* * *

Love leads to completeness. I feel totally complete with you—my thoughts, my dreams, my work, my time. They're all wrapped up in you.

* * *

✳ ✳ ✳

Maybe it's time I tell you I love you again. I love all the things we do together. Like when we laugh on the street corner, watching weird people go by. Like when we try a new menu item and hate it. Like when we watch movies in bed and never see the ending. Like when we roam around on our hiking trail and lose the way. Have I told you lately what these little things mean to me? Well, consider yourself told! I love you.

✳ ✳ ✳

I don't really know why, but last weekend I felt so close to you. It felt like love would actually ooze out of the pores of my skin every time I saw you walk into the room. Even on an ordinary weekend, my love for you will always be extraordinary.

✳ ✳ ✳

I hear from all my friends that we have a truly unique marriage. Our relationship involves kindness, understanding, excitement. We haven't allowed jealousy, selfishness, or pretense to ruin things for us. I appreciate what we have together, especially knowing how rare such a "find" is. With all my love ...

✳ ✳ ✳

It may be difficult to define love—but I certainly know it when I feel it. You mean life to me.

✳ ✳ ✳

Loving you is my motivation to be the best I can be in life. You are my reason to wake up in the morning, to earn a living in the daytime, and to make love and rest in complete contentment in the nighttime. You're the greatest thing that's ever happened to me.

* * *

You have been a long road leading to real happiness. Although we've had hardships and disappointments along the way, I can say with all sincerity that I've never once wanted to turn around and travel in an opposite direction. As far as I'm concerned, you and I are traveling together for good.

* * *

People say that there's no guarantee in life. No guarantee that life will go on, that we will be successful and prosperous, that people will love you back, that people will treat you right. And I agree. But here's one guarantee you can count on: As long as there's breath within me, I will love you.

* * *

Many people spend their life looking for an elusive something—some contentment, some success, some fulfillment, some person. I've found everything in you.

* * *

It's obvious that some people have a sight problem. That is, some can't see what's right in front of their nose. Others have eyes in the back of their head. We all have better hindsight than foresight. But one vision problem I don't have. Without a doubt, I can see that you're the best thing that's ever happened to me.

* * *

They say that new love fades fast, that the intensity and the preoccupation with the other person goes away eventually. But "they" don't know me. I can't look in a store window without reflecting on how the jewelry would look on you. I can't eat lunch without thinking what you'd order—fries or onion rings? I can't grab a cab without seeing you wave your arm timidly in the air. I can't walk down the street without seeing a smile or a color or a gesture that reminds me of you. Even though the "new" has worn off, I'm still madly in love with you.

* * *

As long as we've been together, I thought I had already seen all the best of you—until today. Sometimes your sweet attitude and caring love overwhelm me all over again.

* * *

I miss you more than you can imagine. I close my eyes and think of you continually—your smile, your touch, your voice, your laughter. I can't think of much else because I'm hurting without you beside me. I love you.

* * *

On every business trip I made—on the plane, in the restaurants, in the corridors—I looked for her. My hopes would rise every time I saw a pretty woman step off the elevator. My dreams would go wild every time I stood to speak before a business group of faces. My expectations grew every time the telephone rang. I was always, always looking. Then one day I found you. You were worth all the hoping, waiting, dreaming.

* * *

Everything beautiful... everything wonderful . . . everything fresh . . . everything fun . . . everything provocative . . . everything compassionate . . . reminds me of you. I love you.

* * *

* * *

I like the way you walk. I like the way you think. I like the way you look. I like the way you hold my hand. I like the way you glance at me. I like the way you laugh. I like the way you share. I like everything about you. And that adds up to a pile of love.

* * *

Thank you for the happiness you have given me. I feel complete when I'm with you. Never go away.

* * *

You are my greatest contentment. What I've been looking for all my life, I've found in you.

* * *

You are everything I respect and admire. You're as thoughtful and kind and sincere under the surface as you are on the side that shows to the world. That's hard to find these days. And it makes me feel all over again how lucky I am to have you.

* * *

I'm so proud of you. When I walk into a room with you beside me, my face lights up. When I introduce you to my friends, their faces light up. You're everything I admire. Thank you.

* * *

Do you know how much I love you? Sometimes I feel as though love is spraying out of me like water from a fountain. I feel sorry all the people in the world who don't get to wake up beside you each morning.

* * *

You are a masterpiece, designed with heaven in mind. And while on this earth, I plan to capture every moment of heaven I can in being with you.

You excite me. After all these years, I see you across a room and I'm hypnotized by your beauty, your spell, your warmth. Too many dull things make business boring; when I come to you, it's like a child released from school for summer vacation. Life begins.

* * *

Life is fragile. Accidents happen every day. Buildings collapse and planes crash. Business deals fall through. Friends move away. Children take up their own lives. Only one thing is strong, solid, and forever—my love for you.

* * *

The first ingredient in a happy marriage is to find the right person to respect, to enjoy, to love. With you, I've found the recipe for happiness.

* * *

Being in love means truly being honest with each other about dreams, feelings, goals, responsibilities. We have an open, honest relationship that I don't want us ever to undermine by holding back ourselves and our inner thoughts. For the first time in my life, you have given me the confidence to be vulnerable and trusting.

* * *

* * *

I see each day we have together as a special gift from God. I don't take for granted that you put my preferences above yours. I don't take for granted that your moods are always upbeat and positive. I don't take for granted that you always ask my opinion on things. I don't take for granted that you listen to my advice. I don't take for granted that you can make your own decisions and make your own way in the world. And I promise that I'll never take for granted that you're with me each morning when we wake. I love you.

* * *

The more I learn about you, the more I love you.

* * *

You know what I really enjoy? Talking out the day's problems with you and having you help me sort them out. Sharing the other relationships in my life and having you help me to figure them out. Holding your hand when we're out shopping. Going for a long drive with you beside me. I couldn't enjoy life without you.

* * *

I took a risk on you. I risked letting myself feel again. I risked sharing who I really am inside. I risked letting you know my limitations. I risked feeling rejected. But never has a risk paid off so rewardingly. I love you with all my heart, my mind, and my soul.

* * *

I've been too busy lately. My job, my hobbies, other demands on my life have seemed to crowd out what's most important—you. When I have a moment to stop and think, I become as frightened as a little child. I wonder what would happen if I woke up one morning and you weren't there. You are the center of my life, and I want to stop feeling flung away to the outside like a tetherball. I want to fall limply back to your side—to share more time together as we used to. Forgive me for being too busy lately to spend time doing what I love best—being with you.

$$* * *$$

For years, I thought love was possible only in the movies and in storybooks. Never did I dream such a relationship could be for real—at least not for me. But now that I've found you, I've discovered that love can be even better than in my dreams. Forever I will love you.

$$* * *$$

I remember a lot of people from my past. Some were sensitive. Some were ready for a good time. Some were super intelligent. Some made me feel like a sage. Some were beautiful. Some were honest. Some were creative. Some were talented. Some were ambitious. Some were spiritual. The trouble was that I never found all the qualities in the same person. Until I met you.

$$* * *$$

THANK YOUS (PERSONAL)

Thank-you letters open many doors of opportunity and friendship. We often have to guard against the tendency to think that kindnesses done by close friends don't require formal, written thank-you's. Formal, no. Written, yes.

To both casual friends or acquaintances and to close friends, take a moment to say thanks: to that someone who wrote you a comforting note at the death of a loved one...to that one who prepared an elegant dinner party in your honor...to that one who extended weekend hospitality...to that one who did any special favor to make your life easier.

Guidelines

Thank the reader immediately for the kindness.

Tell why the note, occasion, or kindness was particularly meaningful to you.

Be sincere and avoid cliches.

COMFORTING NOTE

❖ ❖ ❖

Dear C.J.,

Your note came just after I returned from Alabama, where I buried my father. The solitude here and the recent loss weighed heavily on my mind, and your caring comments made things seem brighter. Thank you for writing.

Sincerely,

❖ ❖ ❖

❖ ❖ ❖

Dear Sylvia:

I enjoyed the card you sent while I was recovering from my surgery. At such times, the minutes drag and words from the outside are so welcome! Thank you for your thoughtfulness.

Sincerely,

❖ ❖ ❖

DINNER

❖ ❖ ❖

Dear Todd and Mariam:

Thank you so much for including us in your luau last Friday evening. Your lavish decorations and Hawaiian music made the occasion so festive that it was about as close to a weekend on Maui as we could hope for! We enjoyed so much the food and the opportunity to meet new friends, many of whom by the end of the evening we felt as though we'd known a lifetime.

I'll be looking forward to having you as my guests before too long.

Sincerely,

❖ ❖ ❖

HOSPITALITY

❖ ❖ ❖

Dear Cher and Nelson:

We appreciate so much your hospitality last week in showing us around the city and taking us to dinner. Even with my travel schedule, I believe the shrimp tempura at Andover's is the best I've ever eaten. Their address now appears in my little black travel book.

Additionally, you were so kind to meet us at the airport—no whimsical feat with the unpredictable schedules airlines fly these days. From finding a place for Sheila to buy her medication to driving us to watch the sunrise on the beach, you were such gracious hosts.

We hope to plan an equally interesting agenda for you when you give us the pleasure of returning the hospitality.

Sincerely,

❖ ❖ ❖

PERSONAL FAVOR

❖ ❖ ❖

Dear Bernie:

Thank you so much for your help in sponsoring the scouting activities this past year. After such events, those of us with children see the fun and gratitude in the eyes of our own sons and daughters. But you, with grown children of your own, must have a special place in heaven for continuing to volunteer year after year!

The cookies, the van rides, the "corralling"—I appreciate all your help. You're terrific.

Sincerely,

❖ ❖ ❖

INDEX

A

Accident, condolences, 307
Advertisements, misleading ad, 301-302
Agenda of meeting, announcement of, 194-197
Anniversaries
  congratulations, 312-313
  employees service to firm, 1-4
  of firm, 4-6
Announcements
  of acquisition/mergers/restructuring, 7-10
  of new hours/location/name/logo, 10-13
  of new policy/procedure, 13-19
  for new rates/prices/terms, 24-27
  for new service/product, 19-24
Appointments
  declining appointment, 33-36
  postponing or canceling, 31-33
  request for appointment, 28-30
Attendance
  meetings
    confirming attendance, 198-199
    declining attendance, 199-200
Audience, meetings, soliciting details about, 208-209
Awards, thank you for, 265-267

B

Benefits, explanation of, 163-165
Better business bureau, complaints, 305
Bids
  acceptance of, 41-43
  rejection of, 43-45
  soliciting, 37-41
Billing
  discrepancies, 119-122
  errors, 298-299
Birth, congratulations, 84-86, 313-314
Birthday, congratulations, 86-88, 315-316
Business, condolences on loss of, 311
Buying, thank you for, 272-274

C

Cancellation
  of appointment, 31-33
  of meeting, 201-202
Cars, complaints related to, 299
Charitable contributions, making contribution, 291-292
Civic achievement, congratulations, 89-90
Collection letters
  response to, 143-145, 322-323
  series of, 132-143
College
  application to, 293-294
  requesting references, 294-295
  supplying references, 295-297
Comforting note, 348-349
Commendations
  for outstanding service, 53-56
  response to commendation, 56-58
  to speaker, 46-49
  to staff, 49-53
Community service, thank you for, 274-276
Company event, invitations, 191-193
Complaints
  better business bureau, 305
  billing errors, 298-299
  car related, 299
  defective product, 300
  food service, 303-304
  governmental agency, 304-305
  home repair, 300-301
  misleading ad, 301-302
  personal service, 302-303
  poor service/delivery/performance/product/advertising/communication, 59-63
  rent issues, 303
  responding to when admitting fault, 64-69
  responding to without admitting fault, 69-74
  restaurant, 303-304
Condolences
  accident, 307
  to business associate, 75-77
  death of child, 308
  death of parent, 308-309
  death of relative, 310

Condolences (cont.)
  death of spouse, 309
  to family upon death of business
    associate, 78-81
  illness, 310-311
  loss of business/home, 311
Congratulations
  anniversary, 312-313
  awards/honors/distinction, 82-84
  birth, 84-86, 313-314
  birthday, 86-88, 315-316
  civic achievement, 89-90
  engagement/wedding, 90-92, 316-317
  graduation, 317-318
  new job, 93-95
  opening new business, 96-97
  promotion, 93-95
  publication, 98-100
  response to congratulatory note,
    105-106
  retirement, 100-102
  service award, 102-104
Copyrighted materials, permission to
  use, 223-225
Cover letters
  for invoices/explanation of fees,
    107-112
  for proposals/price quotes, 110-113
  for reports, 113-116
  for resumes, 116-118
Credit
  changes in account, 319-320
  request for extended credit, 320
  request for special repayment
    arrangements, 320-322
  response to collection letter, 322-323
Credit/collection
  billing discrepancies/errors, 119-122
  canceling credit, 130-132
  collection letters, 132-143
  offering of credit, 125-128
  refusing credit, 128-129
  response to collection letters, 143-145
  verification of credit records, 122-125
Crisis, response to, 213-215

D

Declining to do business, 146-149
Defective product, complaints, 300
Death
  condolences, 75-81
    of child, 308

Death (cont.)
  of parent, 308-309
  of relative, 310
  of spouse, 309
Dinner, thank you, 349
Donation, thank you for, 267-268

E

Editor, letter to, 216-217, 335-336
Employees
  anniversaries, 1-4
  commendation to, 49-53
  unsuitable employees, termination,
    261-262
Employment
  acknowledging receipt of resume, 150
  announcement of
    promotions/transfers, 151-152
  employment offers, 153-155
  nonselection of applicants
    no opening, 155-158
    otherwise unsuitable, 161-163
    salary requirements, 158-160
  policy/benefit
    statements/explanations, 163-165
  raise/promotion, request for, 169-171
  raise/promotion/transfer
    disapproval of, 173-176
    offer of, 172-17
  recruitment letters, 165-167
  reprimand, 167-169
  thank you, for interview, 176-178
Engagement, congratulations, 90-92,
  316-317
Events, inquiry for information, 332

F

Farewells
  from employee leaving, 179-181
  to employee leaving, 181-184
Fees, explanation of, cover letters for,
  107-112
Food service, complaints, 303-304
Friendship notes, 324-330

G

Gift, thank you for, 269-270
Governmental agency, complaints,
  304-305
Graduation, congratulations, 317-318

H

Holiday greetings, 185-188
Home, condolences on loss of, 311
Home repair, complaints, 300-301
Hospitality, thank you, 349-350
Hours, new, announcement of, 10-13

I

Illness, condolences, 310-311
Inquiries
  information on event, 332
  information on product/service,
    332-333
Interview
  suggestion for, 220-221
  thank you for, 176-178, 222-223
Invitations
  open house, 189-190
  special company event, 191-193
Invoices, cover letters for, 107-112
Issues
  letter to editor, 335-336
  letter to legislators, 336
  letter to meet political candidate, 337

L

Layoffs, 258-261
Legislators, letter to, 218-219, 336
Location, new, announcement of, 10-13
Logo, new, announcement of, 10-13
Love notes, 338-347

M

Meetings
  announcing agenda, 194-197
  canceling/postponing, 201-202
  confirming speaker, 206-208
  confirming attendance, 198-199
  declining attendance, 199-200
  inviting speaker, 202-205
  soliciting details about audience,
    208-209
  thank you for arranging, 263-265
  thank you for hospitality, 270-272
  thank you for opportunity to speak,
    209-212

Meetings (cont.)
  thank you to speaker, 212
Mergers/acquisitions, announcement
  of, 7-10

N

Name of business, new, announcement
  of, 10-13
New job, congratulations, 93-95

O

Open house, invitations, 189-190
Opening new business, congratulations,
  96-97
Outstanding service, commendation
  for, 53-56

P

Performance, complaints about, 59-63
Personal favor, thank you, 350
Personal service, complaints, 302-303
Policies
  explanation of, 163-165
  new, announcement of, 13-19
Political candidate, letter to, 337
Postponement
  of appointment, 28-30
  of meeting, 201-202
Price quotes, cover letter for, 110-113
Prices, new, announcement of, 24-27
Product
  inquiry for information, 332-333
  new, announcement of, 19-24
Promotion
  announcement of, 151-152
  congratulations, 93-95
  disapproval of, 173-176
  offer of, 172-173
  request for, 169-171
Proposals, cover letter for, 110-113
Publication, congratulations, 98-100
Public relations
  letter to editor, 216-217
  letter to legislators, 218-219
  permission to use quoted/copyrighted
    materials, 223-225
  response to crisis, 213-215
  suggestion for interview, 220-221
  thank you for interview, 222-223

Q

Quoted materials, permission to use,
223-225

R

Raise
  disapproval of, 173-176
  offer of, 172-173
  request for, 169-171
Recruitment letters, 165-167
References
  college
    requesting references, 295-297
    supplying references, 295-297
  requesting from supervisor/colleague,
    226-228
  supplying from suitable employee,
    229-231
  supplying for unsuitable employee,
    231-232
Referrals
  offering, 235-236
  requesting, 233-234
  thank you for, 280-282
Rent issues, complaints, 303
Reports, cover letter for, 113-116
Reprimand, 167-169
Rates, new, announcement of, 24-27
Resignation
  accepting, 241-243
  offering, 237-241
Restaurant, complaints, 303-304
Resumes, cover letter for, 116-118
Retirement, congratulations, 100-102

S

Salary requirements, 158-160
Service
  complaints about, 59-63
  inquiry for information, 332-333
  new, announcement of, 19-24
Service award, congratulations, 102-104
Solicitations
  negative response, 251-253
  positive response, 253-255
  seeking, 244-250
  thank you for successful campaign,
    255-257

Speakers
  commendation to, 46-49
  meetings
    confirming speaker, 206-208
    inviting speaker, 202-205
  thank you for, 276-279
Supervisor, requesting references from,
  226-228

T

Terminations
  layoffs, 258-261
  unsuitable employees, 261-262
Terms, new, announcement of, 24-27
Thank you
  for arranging meeting/conference,
    263-265
  for award/bonus, 265-267
  for buying, 272-274
  comforting note, 348-349
  dinner, 349
  for donation, 267-268
  for gift, 269-270
  hospitality, 349-350
  for hospitality at meeting/conference,
    270-272
  for interview, 176-178
  for opportunity to speak, 209-212
  personal favor, 350
  for referral/reference, 280-282
  for service to community, 274-276
  to speaker, 212
  for speaking, 276-279
  for successful campaign, 255-257
Transfer
  announcement of, 151-152
  disapproval of, 173-176
  offer of, 172-173

W

Wedding, congratulations, 90-92,
  316-317
Welcomes
  to new staff, 283-285
  to potential clients in new to
    community, 286-287